The Life and Journeys of

PAUL

Charles Ferguson Ball

moody press
chicago

© 1951 by
THE MOODY BIBLE INSTITUTE
OF CHICAGO

Revised Edition, 1971

Fourth Printing, 1976

All scripture quotations set in block form have been
paraphrased by the author from the King James Version.

ISBN: 0-8024-4720-1

Printed in the United States of America

0873

Contents

1

The Gates of the West

THE PROVINCE of Cilicia stretched like a narrow ribbon along
the northeastern coast of the Mediterranean Sea. From north
to south it was only about seventy miles wide, but from west
to east it extended from Pamphylia to the mountains of Syria.
The blue waters of the Mediterranean Sea bathed its southern
shores, from which the land stretched out in fertile plains and
rolling hills until it reached the dark Taurus Mountains.

These rocks on three sides of Cilicia were a barrier and a
protection. They made the land secure, isolating it completely from its neighbors except for two famous mountain passes.
The passes were easy to guard, being only wide enough in
some places for one wagon to squeeze through. Their fame
was known in all the East because they were the guardians of
the only land route between Syria and the West.

On the road to Antioch and the south stood the pass known
as the Syrian Gate. All traffic out of Asia and the south had
to go either by sea or by the mountain roads into Cilicia. At
the western end of Cilicia, crossing the steep rocks toward
distant Greece and Europe, was another narrow pass called
the Cilician Gate. The trade and the travel of the centuries
entered and left by these gates, and Cilicia profited immensely
by its strategic location. But through these gates also marched
the armies of empires; and in the event of war, the battle
would be won by the commander who seized the mountain
roads first. Cilicia had been conquered and reconquered many
times. It had been fought over by the Greeks and the Ro-

mans, and now it belonged to Rome. However, the language spoken in the streets of the cities remained Greek.

If these gates could tell their story, what a tale it would be of conquerors and crusaders, soldiers and beggars, rascals and pilgrims on their journeys between Europe and Asia. Here, indeed, was the gateway to the West.

From a deep valley in the rocks, the river Cydnus gushed forth, leaping from ledge to ledge until it reached the low country to the south. Along the way it was joined by other smaller streams, each filled with the melted snows of the high Taurus range, until it became a river. Slowly it widened and wandered sluggishly to the sea.

Small villages, farms, and dark, mud huts dotted the plain. To the west, the land was rolling and less fertile. Not suitable for growing crops, it was used by shepherds to pasture their flocks. But to the east, the soil was rich and crops were good. Nestled between the forbidding, snowcapped peaks and the warm blue sea, Cilicia was a pleasant home for its people.

TARSUS, SAUL'S BIRTHPLACE

The chief city and capital of Cilicia was Tarsus, where Paul was born and raised. Today it is just a little Turkish town, but once it was one of the great cities of the Roman Empire. Some of its thick, fortifying walls are still there but have crumbled, and grass and flowers sprout from their crevices. Outside the present town of Tarsus stands a bridge under whose arches the Cydnus River once flowed. If only these ancient stones could speak! But now we can only look at the ruins and historical records of the city that nurtured Paul as a youth and imagine what influence its schools and athletic arenas had on his life.

Tarsus won distinction among the great cities of its day, but not because it was the most ancient. Indeed, it was older than either Athens or Rome; but compared with Damascus or Jerusalem, it was only a child. It was first recognized in the days of Alexander the Great, when many wealthy Greeks made it their favorite residence and built palaces there. But it won its fame chiefly because so great was the enthusiasm of its inhabitants for learning that they fostered schools and attracted philosophers and teachers of worldwide reputation. The claim that Tarsus outshone any city in the world as a center for great schools was well justified.

A FAMOUS CITY

Long before Paul's time, the philosophers and great scholars of Tarsus were teaching rhetoric, mathematics, ethics, grammar, and music. Long before Paul played in the city's streets, great poets, doctors, orators, and philosophers had been trained in its colleges and had carried its fame to other lands. This reputation was so well accepted that Caesar Augustus, himself educated by Athenodorus of Tarsus, chose Nestor, another Tarsus educator, when looking for a teacher to educate his son.

Mark Antony, the great Roman general, lived in Tarsus and liked it so well that he made it a free city; that is, he allowed its citizens to make their own laws for governing the city without any interference from Rome and without any taxation. Emperor Augustus was so impressed with the city's culture that he permitted it to have its own courts and to choose its own magistrates. Thus Tarsus became a favored city and enjoyed the envy of neighboring towns.

But its fame was not only for learning. It was a city of commerce and trade. The trade routes gave it prominence, and in Paul's day the river Cydnus was so large that ocean-going vessels sailed twelve miles up the river and unloaded their cargoes at the city wharves. The docks were a colorful sight. There were men from Egypt, with faces red as copper, and men from Africa, black and strong. Ships from Crete, Cyprus, Rhodes, and Jaffa brought their strange mixture of hearty seamen, who spoke of the greatness of Tarsus as an international port.

Down the Cydnus River, men were guiding rafts and crude

boats with poles and ropes, carrying bales of goods from their farms or from workshops. These were hauled up, loaded into the ships, and exchanged for sacks and bundles of grain, skins, and wool, and casks of oil and wine. The wharves were a confusion of men and long strings of donkeys, mules, and horses. And when at last the ship was laden, the shouts of sailors and dock hands rent the air as the ropes were cast off and the vessel made for the glittering sea. This was a daily picture of the port of Tarsus.

CLEOPATRA'S GOLDEN BOAT

The most wonderful ship that had ever sailed into Tarsus was now only a memory, but it had created a great sensation. It was the golden boat of Cleopatra, the dusky queen of Egypt. She had come to meet Mark Antony and conquer him with her charms. Her lips were painted red and her fingernails, a bright crocus yellow. Her beauty was famous everywhere.

On that bygone day, the banks of the river were lined with anxious people, seeking to get a glimpse of the beautiful queen. The day was sunny and bright, and the skies were blue. On the tall mast a great purple sail of silk fluttered in the breeze; and streamers of yellow, crimson, blue, and white flew from the mast top. The city was in carnival spirit as the ship moved up the river. People could see the high stern plated with shining gold and shaded by a golden-hued canopy. There on a couch of soft cushions lay the beautiful Cleopatra, splendid with sparkling jewels.

The broad oars on either side of the ship were overlaid with silver that glittered as they rose and fell. It was a day never to be forgotten, and no doubt the story of its splendor was told over and over as the years went by.

Tarsus had many public buildings besides its palaces and humble homes. There was a great open-air theater, built to accommodate thousands of people. It was built in a large hollow at the foot of a slope, and row upon row of marble seats stretched out in a great semicircle. Greek plays were acted out on the central stage, and these always attracted throngs of people. Here the music of the day was presented and poetry was read. The theater held a large place in the lives of rich and poor alike.

THE GAMES

Both the Greeks and the Romans were fond of athletic contests, and they made as much of the young man who excelled in races as they did of a man who conquered in battle. They even set up statues of such men in the streets. The race course was a huge, open place like the theater. On one side were row upon row of seats, built up in stadium fashion for the crowds of spectators who came to see the games and races. Thousands of the young men of the city trained for these games and made it their greatest ambition to win the prizes.

To the east of the city, on the slope of a hill, a magnificent building rose in its splendor. It was the gymnasium—a place where the boys were taught to be graceful and strong. From the ages of sixteen to eighteen, boys were taught nothing but athletics. Other parts of their education came later, but the most important thing to the Greeks and Romans was the development of the body. Boys were taught to run, jump, wrestle, and swim. Hot and cold baths were there, and after the games the boys bathed and rubbed their bodies with olive oil.

The gymnasium was a lively spot, resounding with the shouts and laughter of hundreds of boys. The building itself was stately with huge pillars and sculptured marble statuary representing great teachers, philosophers, and men of grace and strength. Thus the boys were surrounded with illustrations of learned and strong men who were the leaders of their day.

THE GREATNESS OF SAUL

Of all the illustrious men of Tarsus, products of its gymnasium and famous schools, not one of its scholars has ever been as great as Paul. He rose to a height far beyond them all. They are forgotten, and in all their greatness they made only a small mark on history. But Paul, the great apostle of Christ, has so captured the hearts of millions in all ages and has risen to such prominence that Tarsus itself is remembered, not for its schools or its commerce, but because Paul lived there.

SAUL'S WORLD

In that day the entire life of the world centered around the Mediterranean. All the great civilizations grew up near the sea that was named to signify the center of the earth. *Mediterranean* comes from two words which together mean "the middle of the earth." All the interests of human life were concentrated in a narrow rim of land extending around the southern coast of Europe, the northern coast of Africa, and the western coasts of Syria and Palestine. Beyond this narrow border there were unexplored regions inhabited by barbaric people who did not enter into the full stream of civilization until later years.

Only three nations were strong and great enough to leave their marks forever on other nations. They were Rome, Greece, and Israel.

ROME

The Romans ruled the world. They had won that right by the strength of their armies. They had a genius for colonization and government. Because their power was feared and their legions of soldiers were stationed in every colony, they were the masters of the world. Their empire was great because they did not take advantage of the conquered people; rather they sought to build them into the empire and give them a place of honor.

Rome sent out great builders and architects, who laid down magnificent roads and erected public buildings and temples everywhere. Roman laws and political institutions were famous for their fairness to all, offering the right of trial by Roman courts to all citizens. It was this law to which Paul appealed when it became obvious that the local courts of Judea were prejudiced against him.

But the picture was not entirely bright. With the increase of power and wealth, Rome became corrupt and frivolous, a nation devoted to luxury, sin, and ease. After years of this, its people became soft and weak; and their boasted empire crumbled before the attacks of the barbarians who plundered and invaded from the north. Even in the days of their greatest strength they had no spiritual strength, but they delighted in coarse and brutal pleasures like gladiatorial fights. The gladiators were trained fighters who grappled to their death in the arenas to make a Roman holiday. In the reign of Trajan, ten thousand gladiators fought in a half year. They fought each other like lions and tigers, and thousands of spectators cheered to see these men kill each other. Multitudes would gather in the Colosseum at Rome to see Christians clawed to death by lions.

But with all their greatness and their weakness, the Romans left a mark upon history that can never be blotted out; and it must be said for them that they built the greatest empire the world has ever seen.

GREECE

Truly the Romans led the world in law and government, but the Greeks led it in culture and learning. Art, science, and literature had their greatest development in Greece; and even though the empire was Roman, the Greek language was recognized as the language for people of culture.

Scholars of every eastern nation spoke and wrote in Greek. That is why the Old Testament was translated into Greek long before the time of Christ; and the oldest copies that exist of the New Testament are in Greek. The Greeks were the people of genius. Led by Alexander the Great, they had once taken possession of the world and sought to make it Greek. They did their work so thoroughly that, even after Alexander died and the empire was torn asunder by strife, a measure of Greek art and literature remained in every nation. The city of Alexandria in Egypt was a Greek city, so influenced by Greek culture that it took the name of the great emperor. Greek teachers and philosophers were the acknowledged scholars of the day; and they carried the literature, architecture, and scientific thought of their country to every land.

Many of the Jews of Paul's time read their sacred scripture from the Greek translation, called the Septuagint, because the Hebrew tongue was fast becoming a dead language.

When Christianity came into the world, every marketplace had its share of Greek scholars who enjoyed nothing more than to dispute over words and phrases, and whose genuis in thought had degenerated into confusion. Often the confusion was so great that thousands of people, both conquerors and conquered, gave up belief in their gods or in their systems of philosophy. Actually, heathen religions were in a state of utter collapse, decay, and corruption. This was the world of culture when Jesus and Paul were born.

ISRAEL

But there is a third nation that has left its mark upon civilization—a mark that can never be erased. The Jews, though not mighty in military strength, were distinguished for their religion. Scattered through all the lands, they had built synagogues for the worship of God. Strabo, one of the great historians of the time of Christ, wrote: "It is hard to find a place in the habitable earth that hath not admitted this tribe of men and is not possessed by it."

This of course was because Assyria, Babylon, and Rome had invaded Palestine and had taken thousands of Jews captive. Wherever they went, they took their sacred Scriptures and their prophecies of a coming Messiah.

They were proud and exclusive and wrapped their righteous robes around themselves as they turned their backs on the great purpose for which they had been called—the purpose of representing God among the people of the world. Paul, in writing to the Romans, summed up their place in the world and pointed out their failure in biting words:

> Now if you call yourself a Jew and rely upon the law, and boast about God, and understand His will, and by being instructed in the law can know the things that excel; and if you are sure that you are a guide to the blind, a light to those in darkness, a tutor of the foolish, a teacher of the young; since you have a knowledge of the truth as formulated in the law, you who teach others, do you not teach yourself, too? You who preach that men should not steal, do you steal, yourself?
>
> For, as the Scripture says, the name of God is abused among the heathen because of you (Ro 2:17-21, 24).

Although the Jews' failure to carry out God's plans was painfully obvious, they did establish synagogues from far-away Babylon to the great city of Rome itself. In the story of Pentecost, the Jews who returned to Jerusalem included countrymen from all the provinces of the Roman Empire: "Parthians, and Medes, and Elamites, and the dwellers in Mesopotamia, and in Judaea, and Cappadocia, in Pontus, and Asia, Phrygia, and Pamphylia, in Egypt, and in the parts of Libya about Cyrene, and strangers of Rome, Jews and proselytes, Cretes and Arabians (Ac 2:9-11). Luke summed it up by saying the Jews were from "every nation under heaven" (v. 5).

Wherever the Jews built their synagogues and carried on their ritual, they established a center for the worship of the one true God.

Their presence in the empire was a great help and served as an open door to the future program of the church. When

Paul traveled to a new place, he always sought out the synagogue and preached there. This was usually the beginning of a new church.

PAUL'S WORLD

This is a glimpse of the world into which Paul was born. It is a picture of confusion, strife, and dissatisfaction. It is a picture of need—need that could not be met by Roman law, Grecian learning, or Jewish religion.

But it was at this time that God chose a man who by natural gifts was able to appeal to all classes of people. Through his background and training he was fitted to speak with authority to the Roman, the Greek, or the Hebrew. God put His hand upon this man, changed the whole course of his life, and used him to strengthen the church in a wonderful way. Saul of Tarsus, God's choice, became one of the greatest thinkers and certainly the greatest leader and theologian of the church.

2

The Home in Tarsus

A complete biography of Paul has never been written. It is an impossible task because the beginning and the end of the story are missing. Our records of his activities begin at the time when he, a young man, entered upon his ministry for Christ. It was then that Luke met him and included him in his story of the growth of the early church. Beyond that we have only a few personal notes in Paul's thirteen epistles or letters that he wrote to churches and individuals in different parts of the Roman Empire. There are many gaps in the record, but enough is known to make this one of the really thrilling stories of history.

It is plain there were no dull moments in Paul's life. Graphically he touched on some incidents as he summarized the years. "Of the Jews five times received I forty stripes save one. Thrice was I beaten with rods, once was I stoned, thrice I suffered shipwreck, a night and a day I have been in the deep; in journeyings often, in perils of waters, in perils of robbers, in perils by mine own countrymen, in perils by the heathen, in perils in the city, in perils in the wilderness, in perils in the sea, in perils among false brethren; in weariness and painfulness, in watchings often, in hunger and thirst, in fasting often, in cold and nakedness" (2 Co 11:24-27).

But nowhere is this story completely told. Beyond a brief account of one, the shipwrecks are not described. There is no word of that terrible night and day spent in the deep, clinging perhaps to some floating wreckage. Neither is there a description of those robber attacks in the mountain passes, where highwaymen had become such a menace that travelers went in caravans. Then there were the swollen rivers and the floods, with no bridges to cross over. For one who has a vivid imagination, here is exciting true adventure!

Although there is no record of Paul's early life, a very interesting story can be surmised by gathering together information from history, tradition, and the few personal notes in Paul's writings.

SAUL'S BIRTH

About A.D. 3, Paul, the great apostle, was born into the home of a devout couple who lived in the Jewish quarters of Tarsus. The streets were narrow and the houses poor, but it was a happy day for that family. Since their first child had been a girl, they had prayed that God might now give them a boy. The days of waiting had been long, but finally their prayers had been answered. They gazed down into the face of a son, and they were proud and contented.

From the very day of his birth, his father and mother resolved to dedicate him to the service of God and to do all they could, even in Gentile surroundings, to bring him up to be a good Jew.

Father belonged to the tribe of Benjamin and made much of that fact whenever the neighbors boasted of their family trees. Everyone knew that Saul, the first king of Israel, was of that tribe.

Although the family lived in Tarsus, it was not the intention to dwell there permanently. Like many devout Jews, they looked beyond the eastern mountains to Palestine as their real home. To them, Jerusalem was the most beautiful city in the world, and the great temple of God was there. They sent offerings to keep the temple in repair; each year they planned to visit the holy city at Passover. After they had made enough money, they expected to return there to live. What Jew wanted to die in a Gentile land? Father was in the tent business and was laying aside money for the future. Like many of his countrymen who had to live in a foreign land, he considered the residence in Cilicia only temporary.

Eight days after the child was born, his parents gave him two names, and the ceremony was followed by a supper at which all the friends and relatives gathered and brought gifts. He was given the good Hebrew name of Saul. This was a name close to the hearts of all the descendants of Benjamin, because it was the name of Israel's first king. But, after all, they lived in a Roman world, so they also used the Latin form of the name and called him Paul. In business he was Paul because it made a better impression on the Gentiles, and Tarsus was a Gentile city! But Mother always called him Saul, because it suited her heart's desire for her son.

EARLY TRAINING AT HOME

Saul's father was very strict. Being a Pharisee, he believed that the commands of Moses, as interpreted by the rabbis and scribes, should be kept to the very letter. That same strictness which was in the home in Tarsus appeared in Saul when he became a man.

A shiny metal box about three or four inches long was fastened to their house on the door jamb. When visitors came or went, they touched the box and kissed their fingers, mumbling a few words of Scripture to themselves. Inside that box, written on a piece of parchment, were verses of the law of Moses, beginning with the familiar words, "Hear, O Israel: The LORD our God is one LORD: and thou shalt love the LORD thy God with all thine heart, and with all thy soul, and with all thy might" (Deu 6:4-5). This box was called a mezuzah. Before little Saul was old enough to talk, he would imitate what others did. From his mother's arms he would reach out a chubby hand to touch the shining box, kissing his hand as he had seen others do; and Mother smiled and patted his little head.

As Saul grew, he was taught to kneel with his face turned toward distant Jerusalem and with his hands clasped before him to say a morning and an evening prayer. When he asked why he must turn toward Jerusalem, he was told that the

golden temple was there and that in the holy place, behind
the great purple curtain, God dwelt in the midst of His people. He didn't quite understand it, but he was greatly impressed because Mother's voice grew solemn, and she bowed
her head as she spoke of God.

And then she would tell him how the prophet Daniel, when
he was a prisoner in a strange Gentile land, never forgot to
open his windows toward the Holy City and pray. When
Daniel was ordered to stop praying, he refused; and as a
result he was cast into the den of lions. But the beasts did
not hurt him, for God stopped their mouths and they could
do Daniel no harm.

Saul's mother taught her son Bible stories until he was four
years of age. She told him about the oppression in Egypt
and how God delivered His people from the hand of Pharaoh
and brought them in triumph through the Red Sea. She never
tired of telling about Saul, the king for whom her son was
named, and of how he was the tallest, most handsome, and
most kingly of all the men of Israel. She emphasized over
and over the failure of the judges and how Saul, the first
king, was a man of great humility. Because of this, she said,
he was honored of God. The final picture of King Saul's
pride was emblazoned on his young namesake's mind forever
as a warning of how God rejects the man who gets his eyes
off the Lord and seeks his own honor. Saul's mother used to
conclude her teaching by quoting the Scripture: "Them that
honour me I will honour, and they that despise me shall be
lightly esteemed" (1 Sa 2:30). She told Saul of Abraham,
the father of their race; of Moses, the great lawgiver; of
Gideon; of Samson; and of Queen Esther, the daughter of a
poor Jew. The heroes of the Jewish nation became a part of
his thinking and his daily conversation. Of all the stories, he
liked the tales of adventure and fighting best.

As the great hot sun sank behind the hills of Pamphylia
and the stars appeared in the purple sky, bedtime came for
every little boy in the city. Saul and his sister sat by his

mother's knee and listened as she told of David, the shepherd boy who killed a bear and a lion that had come to steal his father's sheep. And then she told of the great King Solomon, whose glory was so famed that all the world marveled and the queen of Sheba came, as Cleopatra had come to Tarsus, to see if all these stories of his wisdom and wealth were true.

One of Saul's favorite stories was about the prophet Elijah, who hid himself in a cave and was fed by the ravens. On a great day at Mount Carmel, with all the prophets of Baal against him, he called down fire from heaven and showed the people of Israel who was the God of power.

Gradually, but surely, there was developing in the heart of this boy a consciousness that be belonged to a great people, and a pride that although he was outnumbered in Tarsus, God was the God of the Jews and had always blessed His people whenever they acknowledged Him.

As the long winter nights came to Tarsus and the shutters and doors were closed tightly to keep out the cold winds from the north, the family sat together around the brightly burning oil lamp. Mother was spinning cloth to make a little coat for Saul; and as her fingers guided the threads, she quietly told her children of the coat that Jacob made for Joseph and of how he became the object of jealousy and was sold into slavery in Egypt. But God was with Joseph, and he became prime minister in Pharaoh's government. He was the means of saving his people from the great famine that came over the land of Canaan.

No mother of any other nation had so great a fund of stories to tell, and no mother ever told them with greater pride and conviction.

THE SYNAGOGUE

As soon as Saul was old enough, he was taken by his mother to the synagogue. There they first washed the dust of the street from their feet and then sat down in the women's section, separated from the men by a stone lattice. Through the lattice he could see his father sitting on the stone floor with the men and listening as the rabbi read the law and addressed the congregation.

> Hear, O Israel, the Lord our God is one Lord; thou shalt love Him with all thy heart and soul and might. The words which I command thee shall be upon thy heart. Thou shalt teach them diligently to thy children and shalt talk of them when thou sittest in thy house and when thou walkest by the way, when thou liest down and when thou risest up. Thou shalt bind them for a sign upon thy hand. They shall be as frontlets upon thy brow. And thou shalt write them upon the doorposts of thine house and upon thy gate (Deu 6:4-9).

Little Saul did not understand much that went on in the synagogue then; but his mother thought he should be introduced to it early so that when he grew older, he would be encouraged to continue going to the synagogue. She could imagine him in a few years, sitting with the other men, discussing the ways of God, and in a few more years, a rabbi, explaining the Scriptures and teaching others. Her heart thrilled at the privilege of raising a son of Israel who had attended the synagogue of Tarsus all his life.

So, during these tender years, his mother was Saul's only teacher. Pure eyes looked into eyes of trust, and life for Saul took on the pattern which Mother had designed. She realized fully that it was the duty of every Jewish woman to make her child know and love the Scriptures, for Moses had said:

> When thy son shall ask thee in time to come, "What mean the commandments which God has commanded?" then thou shalt say to thy son, "We were slaves in Egypt and God brought us out" (Deu 6:20-21).

FATHER'S TEACHING

The old rabbis said that at five a child's home lessons should begin. The father was then to be the chief teacher and was bound to take a hand in his son's education. So school officially began for Saul at that early age. From then on it was not so much a matter of learning the stories as it was of memorizing the verses of the Old Testament and the songs of the synagogue. David's psalms were used as hymns for their worship, and these were taught to every boy along with the commandments of Moses and the traditions of the great rabbis.

Education was largely a task of learning by heart, and with Saul it began at five and continued until he was about thirty. With the Jews, no other textbooks were to be studied. The Scriptures alone contained all the wisdom of life. Bible stories were their only delight, and knowledge from any other source was discouraged and looked upon with suspicion.

Saul's first lesson was from a verse in the book of Deuteronomy and said to him in Greek. He repeated the lesson over and over again until he knew it by heart: What does the Lord require of me but to worship Him and walk in all His ways, to love and serve Him with all my heart and soul, and to keep His commandments which God commands me this day to keep for my good.

After that he learned verse after verse, and many of the promises of God, for his parents believed that if a Jew were good and worshiped God, God would bless his home, fields, and business. But if he did not love the Lord and worship Him, God would surely punish by withholding His blessing. And so from childhood's years Saul was taught to believe everything that the Scriptures said, and later on he was required also to accept everything the rabbi said.

When Saul was six, his parents led him by the hand to the rabbi's school. It was with wistful looks and a tear in his eye that he let go of his mother's hand and was given over to the schoolmaster. The surroundings were not as comfortable as those at home, and the teacher was a bearded stranger; but Father stayed awhile and watched him sitting cross-legged with about thirty other youngsters who gazed at the stern face of the teacher.

Father and Mother returned to their home with mixed feelings. They were proud that their boy was growing up but sad that the days of their teaching were nearly over. However, they were satisfied that their son was going to be raised as a true Hebrew should be, even if it was in a Greek city far away from the temple at Jerusalem.

In the synagogue school there was no drawing or painting such as the Greeks encouraged in their schools. To make a figure of a man, a bird, or a beast was forbidden in the law. That was what the heathen did, and it led to idolatry. The Greek games and athletics had no place in the schools of the rabbis. These were pagan customs despised by true Jewish scholars.

In home and in school Saul learned that the greatest thing in the world was to worship God with all his heart and keep the commandments of Moses.

There were no books to carry, for not even the teacher had books. In a loud, monotonous voice he would tell the children to repeat the lesson after him. It was repeat, repeat, repeat, until it was fastened upon the memory.

Like all boys, Saul asked many questions; and his parents encouraged him to ask them, especially about all the religious acts he saw them do. He would ask why Mother swept the house clean and lit a candle which she gave to Father to search in every corner of the room for crumbs. Why did they eat unleavened bread with their heads covered as if they were ready to run from an enemy? Why did Mother light a candle for each night until after eight nights the house was ablaze with candles? Why did they watch so carefully for the first sight of the new moon in the sky? All these things and many more he asked. So with great pride his father told him what they meant, how they were commemorating great days in their history, and how God had commanded them to remember these days. Thus the Jews were different from all the people of the world, and in this difference was their pride and joy.

All his education led the child to believe that the Jews were God's favorite people and that they were to live to themselves and not become contaminated with Gentiles. They shunned all strangers and had no dealings with any who were not of the synagogue. The lad grew to hate all idolators, despise all that were not Jews, and believe that all who did not worship God deserved to be destroyed just as the Canaanites were destroyed so many years earlier. Thus there was forming in his young life a hatred for all foreigners and a pride in his own people. If he played at all with Greek or Cilician children, he felt that they were different from him and very wicked, as his teachers had said.

Then came the learning of the alphabet, both in Hebrew and in Greek, for in the synagogue Hebrew was spoken and read, but in the home and on the street even the Jews spoke Greek. So Saul had to learn two languages. Father would often bring out the sacred scrolls which he kept hidden in a box and look with great pride upon his boy as he read in the beloved Hebrew language.

THE SABBATH DAY

Every Saturday was a holiday from school, and all the Jewish children looked forward to that day. The citizens of Tarsus did not have any Sabbath day, and they hated the Jews because they were so different. On Friday Father stopped work earlier than usual and looked pleased to see the house swept and tidied, the children dressed in their best, and the evening meal ready upon the table. The Sabbath began with the going down of the sun on Friday and lasted until sundown on Saturday.

As darkness stole over the city, the sound of a trumpet was heard from the roof of the synagogue. Father and Mother bowed together, and Father asked a blessing on the household. Then he washed his hands in a basin of water and poured out some wine in a cup. As they stood around the table, they all tasted the wine while Father said a few words about the Lord, and dipping a piece of bread in salt, he gave it to each member of the family. This was the beginning of the best day of the week. They sat down to a meal of fish, soup, bread, and fruit. It was the Sabbath day, and no cloud of smoke was seen from the fire of any Jew, for God had made the Sabbath a day of rest. No fire was lit in the house, no food was cooked, and Father said with gravity that anyone who did so deserved to be put to death. Did not Moses condemn to death the man found gathering sticks for a fire on the Sabbath?

On Saturday they all went to the synagogue, and behind the lattice separating the women and children from the main part of the building Saul could see his father in the big room where the seven-branched candlesticks burned. He had removed his shoes and tied phylacteries on both arm and brow, and with a blue prayer shawl over his head he turned with the other men in the synagogue to face Jerusalem and pray.

Then the doors were closed, and somewhere a voice chanted, "Blessed is the Lord, King of the world, who made light and darkness, who makes peace and creates all things, and who in mercy gives light to the earth, who in goodness day by day renews the works of creation." From the worshipers could be heard a low amen, and the heads of all in the synagogue were bowed.

As Saul watched, he saw one of the men take up a large parchment roll and heard him read in the Hebrew language. It was the Law of Moses. After a sentence was read, someone repeated it in Greek so all could understand. Then the chief men of the synagogue discussed these words and sometimes argued heatedly, quoting opinions of great rabbis of the past. They also asked hard questions and sought to answer these with great authority. After the questions, a short blessing sent the people home quietly. Sometimes they met in each other's homes on the Sabbath, but never did they go out walking, for it was a wicked thing to walk more than a half mile on that day. And when the sun went down on Saturday night, Father gathered his family around him and prayed for each one of them, asking God's blessing upon the departing day, for the Sabbath had ended.

THE STRICTNESS OF THE PHARISEES

All the rules Saul learned at school he saw his father carrying out with the greatest care at home. Father was even particular about how he washed his hands, being careful to wash them in a certain manner both before and after he had eaten food. Saul's home was even stricter than the homes of some of his friends, because his father was a Pharisee and had made up his mind to raise his son a Pharisee also. To be a Pharisee meant to belong to one of two important sects of the Jews. The Sadducees were the rich upper class who ruled the land. They were the aristocracy who held most of the high offices of the nation, but they were not too careful about what they believed or how they lived. They accepted the Scriptures in general but did not believe in a heaven or angels or any life after death. The Pharisees pitied them and thought that the desire to be fashionable and modern had turned their heads. A Pharisee accepted not only the Scriptures in their fulness but also the oral traditions of the rabbis. This, they said, was because these had come from the Word of God in the first place. The Pharisees were continually quarreling and arguing with the Sadducees because they felt they themselves had reached a higher position than any other class of men in the world. They were proud and intolerant, and they thanked God that they were not like other people.

Therefore, walking a mile, carrying a stick, and lighting a fire on the Sabbath were counted great offenses by Saul and his father. Even eating an egg which a hen had laid on the Sabbath was a wicked thing, to be punished severely. Saul thought, worked, and grew in the wisdom of his Pharisee

father and gradually prepared himself for leadership in that
narrow religion which one day he cast away as a heavy chain
from which Christ had set him free.

GENTILE INFLUENCES

Just a short distance to the north of the city was a race
course where foot races were run at certain seasons and
where the whole town went to enjoy the events of the day.
No boy could grow up in Tarsus and escape the influence of
this place. The young people of Greece and Rome were so
fond of running and gave it such an important place in their
lives that a winner was made a national hero, and a statue of
him was erected somewhere in the city.

Saul was so influenced by the memory of this race course
that he often used the idea of a race when he later wrote about
the Christian life. He considered that the life in Christ has
a starting point, a track, and a goal. The Christian is no
wanderer; he keeps the goal constantly before him, looking
for the prize. As Saul's own life drew to its end, his mind
went back to the race course again; and he wrote to Timothy:
"I have finished my course" (2 Ti 4:7).

But probably Saul was never allowed to see these games.
They were Gentile pastimes and unworthy of a good Jew,
much less a Pharisee. Nevertheless, he saw young Greeks
training for the races and could not help but be interested
in who the winner was.

The theater, too, attracted thousands of the educated people; and the best in music, poetry, and drama was presented
there. But the Jews did not like such shallowness, and Saul's
father thought that this frivolity was unfit for the son of a
Pharisee.

When his father did allow him to see the boys in the gymnasium, leaping, jumping, running, and playing athletic games
of all descriptions, he would tell Saul that this sort of thing
was fine for making strong soldiers, but the boy who studied
the Law of Moses would grow up a better man.

A SON OF THE LAW

Saul passed into a new stage of life altogether when he reached the age of thirteen. Gradually there was dawning upon him the fact that the responsibilities of life were now his. The rabbis said that, when a boy became thirteen, he was responsible for his own acts and was admitted to the men's section of the synagogue. To mark this change, he was taken to the synagogue for a ceremony which is now known as Bar Mitzvah. His father told him that until now he had been learning the law, but the time had come for him to obey it. He had arrived at the age of accountability. They had done all that parents could do to bring him up in the purity of the faith. Now he was on his own in the eyes of the Mosaic Law; and if he failed to obey it, he could be punished as a man by the synagogue court.

After a solemn examination, Saul was declared fit to have the phylactery bound to his arm as a sign of having reached manhood. In the dimly lit synagogue the friends of the family gathered while the father presented his son to the rabbi, who bound the little black box upon his upper arm and told him he must never enter the synagogue without wearing this little box. Then, for the first time in public, he demonstrated that he was educated as a true Hebrew should be—by reading from the Torah. After that, an address was given by his old friend and teacher, the rabbi, in which were summed up many of the lessons he had been taught in school. With words of good advice, the rabbi welcomed him to the fellowship of the synagogue.

Out in the audience, behind the lattice screen, his mother's eyes filled with tears as she heard her little boy, Saul, declared a son of the law. She sighed and wept, for she knew that he would never again sit with her in the synagogue. It seemed to her that he had become a full-grown man overnight, and no mother is quite ready to accept this change in her boy.

In that box bound to his arm were thirty verses of scripture, written on parchment, beginning with the admonition: "It shall be for a sign unto thee upon thine hand and between thine eyes, that the law of the Lord may be in thy mouth. Thou shalt diligently keep the commandments of the Lord, and His Law."

There followed the celebration at home—a party to which friends brought gifts and words of congratulation. This was their public acceptance of Saul as a man among them. And thus he passed from boyhood into manhood in the eyes of his people. No longer was he a mere schoolboy. He was now a student. He did not give up his studies; he only changed his way of studying.

TENTMAKING

The rabbis had a saying that the man who did not teach his son a trade wished him to be a thief, for whoever did not work for his bread ate the bread of someone else. Saul's father was well aware of this, and accordingly he was ambitious that his son should learn a trade. His own trade was tentmaking. He had decided to live in Tarsus because it was a city famed for its skilled weavers. This reputation was due to the fact that a special kind of cloth called cilicium was a product of the province. It was made from the long hair of the goat that grazed upon the Cilician hills to the west and north of the city. The cloth woven from this hair was so hard that it was almost waterproof. It was thought to be the best kind of material for tents. It was in demand for ship sails and rough outer garments for fishermen and sailors.

There was a little workshop at the back of Saul's home. It was only a long low shed, open at the end; but it housed a crude loom for weaving cloth, wheels for spinning thread, vats for dying the goat hair, and a bench for cutting the leather and sewing the tents together. Bundles of goat hair were heaped in a corner, just as they had come from the shepherd.

Several times a year Saul's father would take a trip to the

distant mountains to buy goat hair. He knew the shepherds who sold the longest, toughest hair to be found in all Cilicia; and when he had completed his buying, he would load up the donkeys that carried the hair back to the workshop. Then the hair had to be combed and made ready for spinning into thread. Some of it was dyed red, some yellow, some purple, and some green, to make it attractive to the merchants. Then the thread was wound on spindles and made ready for the weaver's shuttle and the big hand loom.

After weaving came the tentmaking. Saul watched his father cutting the cloth in lengths and sewing them together with tough thread and a large bronze needle. The secret was to sew it so well and so tightly that not a drop of rain could get through and no wind could tear it apart. It was no easy job to sew a good tent. It involved shaping, rope twisting, pole making, and the fastening of hooks and loops of leather to hang up pots and pans and harness. Then came the decorations. Some tents were colored with broad bands of yellow, red, or blue. But the common sort had no bands; they were plain black or gray.

And as time went by, Saul became an expert in every part of this trade and could make tents as strong and excellent as those of his father. He never forgot how to make tents; and in later years he turned to it in many of the cities he visited, for he would not take money from the churches for his support. A tentmaker from Tarsus was always in demand. His skill in tentmaking was recognized throughout the world.

However, it was not his parents' intention that their boy should be only a tentmaker. They were ambitious that he should be a teacher of the law of Moses—a rabbi. In that day every rabbi had a trade, for it was not the custom to take money for what he taught.

"Use not the law for a spade to dig with," said one of the famous ones.

"Do any kind of work," said another, "even to skinning

a horse by the roadside; and do not say as an excuse, 'I am a priest.' "

JEWISH HOLIDAYS

The biggest week of the year was the week of the Passover. It was to a Jew what the Fourth of July is to an American, only it had a great religious significance. It celebrated the deliverance of the Israelites from the slavery of Egypt. Of course there were other holidays, such as the Feast of Tabernacles, when the children went into the country with their parents to cut down branches and carry them home to build a little house on the flat rooftop. This was to keep in their memory the time long ago when, after leaving Egypt, the Jews camped in tents. With no permanent dwelling they had wandered among the rocks of the wilderness.

There was also the Feast of First Fruits, Purim, and Yom Kippur; and for each great day, a company of devout pilgrims would leave Tarsus to go back to Jerusalem. Saul was still too young to go; but since Tarsus was along the main road, he was familiar with the sight of hundreds of Jews resting there for the night on their journey south. In fact, many times uncles and cousins and other relatives stayed at his home. Saul remembered how at least once a year his father would join these traveling bands. He would gather his best clothing in a bundle to have it ready to put on when he neared Jerusalem; then he would saddle the donkey and in jubilation start out on the highway which led over the mountains to the golden temple.

After months of absence his father returned, filled with stories of high adventure and wonder to entertain the family in the weeks ahead. The boy who had never seen Jerusalem listened with rapt interest to the glowing accounts which Father brought, and he thought the great city must be next to heaven for glory and grandeur. Father told of the blowing of the trumpets of the priests as the day's worship began in the temple and of the choirs of Levites, robed in white, singing the great psalms from the marble steps.

The streets were filled with happy throngs of tourists from all over the world. Interesting costumes were everywhere, and strange languages were heard as groups gathered at meeting places. Young Saul listened to these stories until his mind was filled with visions and dreams. When would he be able to go to Jerusalem?

"Be patient, my son. It will not be long now until you shall go with Father," his mother told him.

In fact, on his latest trip his father had made some plans. It had always been his hope and ambition that sometime he could send Saul away from the Gentile city of Tarsus and give him the advantage of a school in Jerusalem. Every good rabbi had been trained there. To be a good teacher, it was necessary to associate with the great rabbis of the temple.

Since Mother agreed to this plan, there was no longer any doubt. Business in the tent factory had been good, and nothing but the highest and best would suffice for their son. While in Jerusalem, the talk had been of nothing but the great Gamaliel. Many had sought him out during the holiday and had proved his wisdom. It was no rumor. His addresses were powerful, and he spoke with authority. So it was determined that Saul should go to the Holy City, perhaps to return in later years as one of the great rabbis of Israel.

3

In the School of Gamaliel

THERE WAS GREAT PRIDE in the synagogue of Tarsus when the people learned that one of their own boys was to go to Jerusalem to study with the great rabbis. Many of the neighbors had friends or relatives there to whom they offered to write, telling of Saul's coming and asking that they befriend him in a strange city. Everybody wanted to be helpful, and at a supper given in honor of his going, they presented gifts and offered good advice and congratulations. They had always known him to be a fine student, and now they expected great things of him in Jerusalem. They all said that some day he would return to speak, and perhaps to teach, in their own synagogue.

For weeks before the departure, Saul's mother was busy making new clothing and fixing things for him to wear in the great city, for it was considered a sign of wealth and good breeding to have several changes of clothing, and she wanted her son to have a good start. Fear and joy pursued each other up and down the corridors of her soul as she thought of her boy leaving home and of the great emptiness this would leave in her life; but at the same time, she thought of the honor and privilege of sacrificing, as every mother must do, to have her son stand among the mighty in Israel. Father was silent and looked afar off, but in his eye was a glow of pride when he thought of his boy in the school of Gamaliel.

Saul had often watched the caravans, laden with all manner of baggage, starting in the early morning to take advantage of as much daylight as possible. Once Saul had looked upon

34

these caravans with great envy; now he was to go with them
perhaps not to return for many years. A sense of fear and
loneliness took hold of him. It was his first time away from
home, and the world seemed so big. And yet he was not sad,
for they were counted fortunate who could afford to take
such a journey. Not every boy had such advantages or such
promise for the future.

Eastward, like a narrow white ribbon, the road could be
seen stretching over the broad plain and disappearing in the
distant hills. From the caravan of pilgrims a shout of joy
went up as they waved green branches to those who had come
to bid them farewell.

THE FAREWELL

Saul joined the strange company of old and young, rich
and poor, and slowly they left Tarsus behind them. His eyes
were filled with tears as he turned back again and again to
wave good-bye to Mother and Father until a turn in the road
blotted them and the city out of sight. The little company
plodded on slowly, laughing, talking, and exchanging stories,
but Saul's heart was heavy, and he said scarcely a word all
day. He was thinking of his home and of his father and
mother. How good they had been, and how carefully they
had guarded his life against anything that was wrong! But
now he was on his own for the first time, and it would be his
ambition to make his parents proud of him. He could never
forget his mother's tears when she bade him farewell.

As the sun sank, they neared the town of Adana, some
twenty miles away from home. There they set up their tents
to camp for the night. Some of the wealthier ones went into
Adana to the inn, but most of the group camped outside the
city wall. The inn was simply an open space surrounded with
a thick wall for shelter and protection. In the middle of the
enclosure was a well, and under little arched porches which
lined the wall the travelers lay down for the night. There
was no furniture of any kind. They made their own beds

by unrolling sleeping mats, and they brought their own pots and pans for cooking. At least they were safe from thieves.

They were an interesting band of travelers. There was an aged beggar with his staff and ragged clothing. He had made the journey many times, and thought nothing of it. There was the bright-eyed boy with his father. They rode on horses and were aloof from the rest, for they were rich. The father was taking his son to see the greatest sight in the world. There was the fat, turbaned merchant who walked alongside his well-laden donkeys with a long knife sticking through his belt. He seemed not to trust people and did not speak much. But for the most part the travelers were talkative and happy, and the days went by quickly. Many were full of anticipation as they thought of the journey's end.

Through Historic Lands

Day after day they journeyed, pitching their tents and striking camp. The road was paved with smooth worn stones, for the armies of many nations had marched over it. Merchants with their camels had trudged its length. Gangs of weary slaves, chained each to the other, had been driven along it like cattle till their feet were sore and bleeding. On the fourth day they would be close to the seashore, for the road ran near a large bay of blue water at the eastern end of the Mediterranean. Soon they would be able to turn their faces southward, for they had come to the borders of Cilicia.

In front of them loomed the high mountains of Syria, and the road wound over the hills, climbing from ledge to ledge until it brought them to a narrow and difficult pass which marked the border of their province and Syria. It was the great Syrian Gate. After they had come out of the pass, Saul would be on the other side of the mountains which had been the boundary of his world. The ancient city of Antioch lay ahead, strange and different. It had massive walls, and it looked like a fortress high on a hill. Antioch was the capital of Syria. Its theaters and temples were more splendid than any in Tarsus. Herod the Great of Jerusalem had paved the principal street, and adorned it with marble pillars. It was a beautiful city indeed and was even richer than Tarsus.

From Antioch they went over the high road to Damascus and on through the mountains until they neared the promised land. Away in the distance the snows of Mount Hermon gleamed white in the sun, and the forests of Lebanon, with their beautiful, tall cedar trees, reminded him of cne of the Psalms that he knew and loved so well.

They came to Nazareth, a town of inns, where travelers always rested for the night. It was just a little town and did not have a good reputation, so they hastened on to the Jordan River. Here at last Saul was coming into land made famous in Hebrew history. He thought of Joshua who, many years earlier, had led the children of Israel across into a land flowing with milk and honey. Mount Tabor, with its thick forests, was the place where Deborah and Barak had gathered ten thousand men and defeated Sisera with his iron chariots.

To the south of Tabor were the plains of Esdraelon, dotted with little villages and verdant fields. Many great battles had been fought there. Off in the distance was Mount Gilboa, where King Saul fell upon his own sword after losing the hard-fought battle.

The people of Samaria were unfriendly to all Jews, so travelers to the holy city thought it best to cross to the east side of Jordan into Decapolis and Peraea to avoid insult and attack. However, Samaria was quickly passed, and they arrived at the place where the Israelites had crossed the Jordan a thousand years before. Saul and all the company plunged into the cool waters with deep joy, even as Jewish travelers do today. They crossed to the other side, where he stood for the first time in the land which was dear to every member of the tribe of Benjamin. Here was the once impregnable Jericho, where the walls fell at the blast of Joshua's trumpets. Here, too, was Gilgal, where the people gathered to make David king. Every stone, stream, valley, and hill had some story dear to the heart of a devout Jew, and Saul saw for the first time the land where his people had been made great. The hills and the towns on every side took on a greatness in his mind which they did not really possess, and the land became peopled with the tall but imaginary figures of heroes and heroines.

Beyond Jericho the land became rougher, and the plain narrowed down into a valley with steep enclosing hills. The road twisted and turned like a serpent, and danger from robber bands faced them. Even though the climb was steep and the travelers weary, they were glad in the anticipation that just over the hill they would come to the Mount of Olives—and the fairest city on earth.

THE CITY OF GOD

At last, on the crest of the road, they could see the city of God built upon a hill, lower than the Mount of Olives. Across a deep glen, its walls, towers, and domed buildings looked magnificent in the golden light of the setting sun. With glowing eyes the pilgrims turned toward each other, and some eyes were filled with tears. Each felt a surge of joy and pride in the greatness of his native home. Some of the domes and towers were plated with pure gold. From the mountain, Saul could see across the Kedron Valley into the temple court, and upon the highest point of all, he could see the building in which the Lord dwelt beneath the outstretched wings of the golden cherubim.

As they gazed in rapt interest and reverence, the pilgrim band began to sing one of the psalms which travelers for centuries have chanted as they neared the walls of Jerusalem:

Beautiful for situation, the joy of the whole earth, is mount
  Zion,
On the sides of the north, the city of the great King.
Walk about Zion, and go round about her:
Tell the towers thereof.
Mark ye well her bulwarks, consider her palaces;

That ye may tell it to the generation following.
For this God is our God forever and ever (Ps 48:2, 12-14).

That night Saul slept in the home of his sister who had married and gone to Jerusalem to live. It had been arranged that this should be his home while he was in the school of Gamaliel. Tired and lonely he went to his bed and dreamed of the coming day.

THE TEMPLE

The streets were crowded as the sun rose in the eastern sky. Three blasts of the trumpet sounded from within the temple walls, proclaiming that a new day of worship had dawned. It took twenty men to open the temple gates, and as these massive doors swung upon their hinges, the crowd surged into the outer courts. The morning sacrifice was burning upon the great white altar, and Saul stood for the first time in the temple of Jehovah. With his eyes raised to the golden roof of the Holy Place, he said his morning prayers with a feeling of strength and nearness that he had never experienced in Tarsus.

Standing in this place, the hymns of Israel seemed to have a new meaning:

> My soul longeth, yea, even fainteth for the courts of the Lord: my heart . . . crieth out for the living God. Yea, the sparrow hath found an house, and the swallow a nest for herself, where she may lay her young, even thine altars, O Lord of hosts, my King, and my God. Blessed are they that dwell in thy house: they will be still praising thee.
>
> I would rather be a doorkeeper in the house of my God, than to dwell in the tents of wickedness (84:1-4, 10).
>
> I was glad when they said unto me, Let us go into the house of the Lord (122:1).

The great outer court was paved with colored stones, and many worshipers were there from foreign countries. Over against the wall were stalls, where sheep were offered for sale, and willow cages, where pigeons were kept. These were all used in the daily sacrifices. Then there was the money exchange, where Roman and Greek coins were given for the currency of Israel, for only Hebrew money was acceptable as an offering in the temple. There was buying and selling, bargaining and cheating, for the sellers of animals did not seem to feel the same reverence as did the visitors.

Saul had never seen such beautiful pillars, such a magnificent pavement, such throngs of white-robed priests, or such heaps of money. At the far end of the court, a long row of steps led up to a higher terrace. As Saul approached the steps, he read in both Greek and Latin these words, "A foreigner must not ascend these steps under penalty of death."

He went up to the inner court and did not dream that one day his life would be threatened at that very spot. Beyond this second court the women could not go, but Saul crossed it quickly, ascended a second low tier of steps, and passed through the Nicanor Gate, made of pure silver and gold, into the court of the men and the priests.

There in the center of the pavement stood the great altar where the fire never went out. Its stones were rough, for they had never been touched with hammer or chisel. He saw the tables on which the sheep were killed, and he saw long lines of worshipers, carrying sheep or doves, waiting their turn as the priests offered the sacrifices one by one.

Then on another terrace, higher still, stood the magnificent Holy Place. Its stones were overlaid with gold. Great white pillars held up the roof. Inside was a door of pure gold, but covering the door was an outer curtain woven of blue and scarlet, purple and white. Behind that curtain and golden door, where no one could go except the high priest, annually, were things so sacred that Saul was afraid even to raise his eyes. He knelt, and with his eyes closed and his face to the ground prayed to the Lord God who dwelt within the veil. He was deeply moved.

Saul learned that this temple had already taken forty years

to build but it was not finished yet. There were houses for the priests and the temple guards, making it like a city within a city. There were twenty thousand priests and many more Levites and temple guards. Each man had to serve for only two weeks in the year, so they were not overworked except at the great festivals when all had to be there. The Levites were singers, musicians, or gatekeepers.

This was no mere synagogue; it was the center of worship for a great nation. The treasury was the safest place in the world to keep gold and jewels. Rich gifts from wealthy Jews, golden dishes from foreign princes, and heaps of treasures from every land on earth were stored in it. The daily offerings of the worshipers, collected in the boxes at the gates, were also kept in this treasury.

In the outer court were many pillared porches where crowds congregated to listen to the rabbis. They would listen to one for a while and then move on to hear another. Sometimes a rabbi would speak with a voice clear and strong, sometimes old and weak. Some were orators attracting great crowds; some had only their little groups, drawn by the wisdom of the rabbi rather than by the loud voice. As Saul went from one to another, he heard nothing new. It was much the same as he had heard in Tarsus. He had no questions to ask, for he never doubted the learning of these great men. He had come to worship at their feet. Not until the sun was setting and the evening sacrifice was burning low did he leave these pillared courts. This was to him the house of God. He had come at last to the golden Temple.

Day after day he spent in the courts of the Lord, learning all about the worship of God. Day after day he was more impressed with its beauty and splendor. The time would come when he could say he knew and loved every stone in the temple. As Saul worshiped before the altar, he became more and more confirmed in his ambition to teach the law of God. He often pictured himself as a well-known rabbi, sitting in one of the cloistered porches, interpreting the Word of God to the throngs of people, and showing himself master of the learning of all the ages.

THE SCHOOL OF GAMALIEL

Of the many rabbis in Jerusalem, Saul's father had selected Gamaliel; first, because he was a Pharisee, and he would warn Saul against the Sadducees; second, because he had a reputation beyond many others for wisdom and kindness; and last, because he was the son of Rabbi Simeon and the grandson of the most learned rabbi the Jews had ever had. Hillel was long dead, but all the modern opinions were still based on what he had said or written. To be the grandson of so illustrious a teacher gave Gamaliel a prestige beyond all others.

Gamaliel was a man of middle age, vigorous and strong, and thought of so highly among his people that he was called a "rabban." Although he was a strict Pharisee, he was fair and more tolerant than many. Years after this, when Peter, the great apostle, was tried before the Sanhedrin for speaking about Jesus, Gamaliel counseled his fellow members to let Peter alone. "For," said he,

> if this man's message is not of God, it will fail to move the people and will be forgotten. But if it is, fighting against it will only mean defeat for you because you will be fighting against God (Ac 5:38-39).

It is evident that Gamaliel followed his father and grandfather in their broad-mindedness, but there were many rabbis who were more severe and unbending. Rabbi Shammai was so narrow in his views that he was called "The Binder." He bound his followers by so many petty rules that religion became a great burden. Hillel, on the other hand, had been called "The Looser," for he was always kind, generous, and broad-minded. He had once been a porter, carrying heavy burdens on his back, and had been so poor that, when he became a student, he could not afford warm clothing.

And so Gamaliel looked down at the young lad, Saul, and with a kindly word he welcomed him into his school. Gamaliel soon discovered in Saul a zealous and obedient student, and as the months passed he grew to like Saul and to expect great things from him. He felt that in him were real possibilities of leadership. He was so sincere in all his learning that he captured the heart of his teacher. More than that, Saul's parents had seen to it that the deepest thing in him was his religion. With some students there was no real love for the world of learning and worship, but with Saul there was an almost fanatical love that made him devout, not only on festival days, but all the time.

Little by little Saul was strengthened in his zeal. He found that life in Jerusalem was different from that of Tarsus, because here nobody laughed at the Jews or persecuted them. Here there was nothing to hinder his development. There was no Gentile influence but only encouragement to go deeper into the mysteries of Judaism. During the months which followed, the boy became a young man, independent of other men and of Mother and Father; and Gamaliel rejoiced to see the progress he had made. After a year had passed, his parents made the journey to Jerusalem for the Passover, but the greatest reason of all was to see their boy. It was a great day! They looked on with pride as Saul discussed various features of the Passover with them. They thought they could detect a note of authority as he quoted many of the things he had heard from Gamaliel and proved them with verses from the Scriptures. He could even marshal his arguments against the Sadducees. Saul, they thought to themselves, had always been good in argument and logical in his thought, but now it was being brought to the surface, and they were satisfied with him.

PREDICTIONS OF THE COMING MESSIAH

But when all the religion of the Jews was analyzed, it was only a religion of promises and hopes. At the very heart of it there was sadness mingled with its splendor. Every Jew felt very keenly the yoke of Rome, and every Jew longed and prayed for the day when the nation would be set free and the armies of Rome driven away. Thousands of pilgrims, who gloried in the temple, wept bitterly in their homes and cried to the Lord for deliverance. All of the sacrifices and all of the ceremony of the temple seemed meaningless if they were to go on forever under a foreign king. Surely God would one day free His people and bless them as He had in former years.

There was a well-organized group of patriotic Jews known as the Zealots, who held secret meetings and made plans to stir up revolt against Rome. The Roman authorities were kept busy seeking them out and punishing them. But the society worked under cover, like spies, and kept alive the hope that some day God would raise up a mighty deliverer like Moses, who would lead his people out of this bondage and back to a place of greatness.

One of the things that Gamaliel taught with great certainty was like a ray of hope through a cloud of gloom. It had the strength of the Scripture behind it, too, and was evidently the expectation of all the great prophets of Israel. It was the teaching that there was a day coming when a Leader would appear, anointed of God and seen by all His prophets, to gather the people from all parts of the world, to drive out the Romans, and to reign as king in Jerusalem forever. This was the promise which God made to King David, that his throne would never come to an end, no matter how black the sky appeared. This great Redeemer, who was to bring salvation to the nation, was called the Messiah.

Saul knew that His coming had been spoken of by the prophets a thousand years earlier, but Gamaliel said more about it than did any of the rabbis in Tarsus, for he was daily expecting Him to come. He would read passage after passage about Him in the prophets, and he could even find promises of His coming in the Torah. He would tell what kind of

Messiah He would be and how He would judge all nations, stamp out all evil, and rule in righteousness.

Every Jew knew that the Messiah would belong to the royal tribe of Judah and that He would be born in Bethlehem, for Micah the prophet had clearly predicted it. Saul's teacher told him that when He came, He would be hidden for a time until the ancient prophet Elijah appeared again to anoint Him King. Then He would gather the people and march on to Jerusalem to scatter the Romans and reign forever by the power of God.

TWO OPINIONS

But the thing Saul had not learned until now was that the rabbis were divided in their views of the Messiah. Some read that He would be a mighty Prince, delivering His nation by warfare, and that the mountains would be dyed red by the blood of His enemies. Some of the rabbis even said that flames would come out of His mouth to destroy all who opposed Him. There was a smaller group, however, that was much confused about passages like the fifty-third chapter of Isaiah and the twenty-second Psalm. It was plain from these verses that the Messiah would suffer. At the same time no one could deny that He would come in power to reign. Therefore, the idea grew that there would be two Messiahs—one a suffering Messiah and the other a triumphant King. In the synagogues and in the cloistered porches of the temple, this difference was discussed and argued with great eloquence by learned men. Some did not believe it, but others did.

Saul began to see very clearly that the hopes of his nation depended upon this coming Saviour, and he zealously looked for a leader and warrior who would marshal great armies to fight against Rome. There were many stories told by rabbis about the coming Messiah. Some of them were wild and silly dreams. Some of them were fantastic and unreal and not founded on God's promises at all. The latter came out of the imaginations of an oppressed people who did not understand

the ways of God. Some of the rabbis hated the Romans so
thoroughly that they pictured the Messiah doing all manner
of cruel things to retaliate for the oppression that His people
had suffered.

The years spent by Saul in study were not only filled with
wonder but to some extent with drudgery and monotony.
There was no encouragement to develop anything original
but only to increase the powers of memory. Under such
training it is not surprising that day by day Saul's life grew
narrower. Pharisees were his only companions, and little by
little he found himself deeper in the jungles of men's rules.
He grew in his hatred of all things Gentile and became quite
a follower of the zealous bands who sought to stir up trouble
for Rome. His love of debate made him the center of many a
dispute, and whenever the occasion arose to defend the priests
or the rabbis or the system of temple worship against the foreigners, Saul would enter the battlefield with sharp tongue
and fiery spirit.

SAUL'S RETURN TO TARSUS

Teachers were required to study for ten years before they
were considered ready to begin their own work, but even
then it took years to build up a reputation and speak with
the voice of authority. Before Saul was in his mid-twenties
he went home to Tarsus. His days of study and learning
never ended, but he had been a long time with Gamaliel, and
the opinions of the great rabbis on all religious subjects were
known to him. He felt that he could now stand on his own
feet. He had learned and seen much. He had met people
from all over the world and had become quite a student of
its history, especially as it related to the Roman Empire.
The time had come to leave Jerusalem and the great rabbis
and, with the knowledge and experience he had gained, return
to Tarsus. There he would take up tentmaking with his
father, in the hope that his instruction would make him well-
known and sought after as a rabbi in Tarsus.

Of one thing he was sure—the only hope for his nation was the coming of the Messiah. Among devout Jews this was the topic of conversation. In every heart there were deep yearnings. Some even thought that He was already on earth, awaiting the time God had appointed for his appearing.

4

The Beginnings of the Church

YEARS OF WAITING IN TARSUS

IT WAS PROBABLY in the year A.D. 26 that Saul left Jerusalem
and went back to Tarsus to live. He was not yet a rabbi, for
he was too young to occupy that high position. But he took
his place with the men of the synagogue, sitting in the chief
seats facing the congregation. He was recognized by all as a
learned young Jew who had newly come from the very foun-
tainhead of knowledge. As he grew older in years and experience, he might be acceptable to the people as their rabbi, but
in the meantime he resumed his trade of weaving cloth, sewing tents, and selling the finished products to people in the
marketplace.

For nine or ten years he lived in Tarsus, growing in zeal
for Israel and gaining the respect of all his friends, who were
sure that one day he would be their leader. Even now his
arguments in the synagogue were listened to with more interest than those of the rabbi. His was a new voice, and his
contact with the great Gamaliel gave him a degree of fame
that few of the other men could reach. All he needed now
was the authority of age; after a few more years he would be
outstanding as a leader in Tarsus.

DAWN OF THE CHRISTIAN ERA

While Saul waited patiently in Tarsus, an event of deepest
importance took place in Palestine. Jesus Christ, from the
little town of Nazareth, had gathered a group of friends
around Him, made up, for the most part, of the followers of
John the Baptist. John had so preached that thousands of

people accepted him as another prophet of God, perhaps to be compared with Isaiah or Jeremiah. He had many disciples, and his ministry was the talk of the countryside. But when Jesus appeared, John faded out of the picture and pointed his many followers to Jesus, saying that He was the long-expected Messiah. For a time there was great excitement, and many wondered if He would lead them in revolt against Rome. But instead, He gathered together a few disciples and appeared to withdraw to the countryside to teach them about a kingdom of heaven.

But within three months Jesus had gone to the temple in Jerusalem and, looking about on all its marvelous beauty, had dared to contradict much that its rabbis taught. He had spoken so positively that He had given offense to the priests. In fact, He had made them so angry that every synagogue had orders to keep Him out. The priests and rabbis were desperately trying to catch Him in some inconsistency with respect to the Sabbath in order to condemn Him to death.

When Saul met the rabbis of the temple, he had nothing but the greatest of reverence for them, and their interpretations of Scripture were to him divine. It was not so with Jesus. At every turn He found Himself in conflict with the traditions of men, and when He spoke, it was with the authority of God. The religious leaders were aroused because He claimed to be God and was able to strengthen His claim with many miraculous works. Some said that He deserved death when He brazenly challenged them to destroy the golden temple which had now taken forty-nine years to build. They distinctly heard Him say that He would build it again in three days!

It was easy for some to dismiss Him as a madman, but the difficulty was that many of the common people had heard Him preach and had declared that He fed more than five thousand of them out on the hillside with only five loaves of bread and two small fish. Multitudes of people believed that He was the promised Messiah and were willing to fight against

Rome under His leadership. Some said He attracted only the commonest people—publicans and sinners and people of questionable reputation; but it was known that many rulers and rabbis came to Him, too, and many were changed and went about preaching that He was the Messiah. Rabbi Nicodemus was one who taught that this Jesus fulfilled many of the Scriptures in the Torah and in the prophets. Everybody knew that he accepted the claims of Jesus, and for that reason the temple authorities were suspicious of him.

THE TEACHINGS OF JESUS

Then came the time when Jesus gave a great address in which He spoke of the principles of His kingdom. The sermon was revolutionary, for it placed the word of Jesus above the words of Moses. To a Jew, that was unthinkable and as wicked as blasphemy. There was no doubt about it, He deserved to die! He had broken the Sabbath, had claimed to forgive sins, and had admitted to the Pharisees that He was the Messiah, the Son of God!

Over and over again He rebuked the Pharisees and Sadducees alike, using language that stabbed like a knife. On one occasion He called them "whited sepulchers," (Mt 23:27) and a "generation of vipers" (v. 33). He told them that they were not of God, but of their father, the devil (Jn 8:44). No wonder the rabbis hated Him, for they could not be comfortable in His presence. But when they tried to arrest Him, He somehow managed to disappear from their sight. He became the greatest mystery of the age. When they encountered Him, their rage mounted because they could not stand in the light of His wisdom. In their own counsels they had already condemned Him to death.

The rabbis said that no man should teach until he had spent many years in the temple school at Jerusalem. That was the way Saul had been educated, but here was a Man from Galilee, who spoke with greater authority than all the rabbis and was able to heal sicknesses. Some had seen

Lazarus after he had been raised from the dead, and they could not deny it. But Jesus had never attended their school. They denounced Him as having no authority. The priests gave orders that the people should not listen to His teaching.

But when lame people are made to walk and blind are made to see, no rules, even if they had been made by the high priest himself, could keep the needy ones away from Jesus. They came by the thousands and went away healed of their diseases, and they proclaimed to everyone that they had found the Messiah and He had healed them.

For three marvelous years Jesus went through the countryside, preaching in Judea, Samaria, the Decapolis, Galilee, and Perea. His fame had spread over the whole land, and the leaders in Israel were at their wits' end to know what to do. Then came the day when Jesus rode into Jerusalem to the acclaim of the people. They were shouting to everyone that their king had come. Perhaps this was the spark that would call the people of the land to revolt!

But Jesus went directly to the temple and deliberately offended the priests by making a lash out of twisted cords and laying it upon the backs of those who sold doves and sheep in the temple courts. With a shout of indignation He upset the tables of the money-changers, and their coins rolled all over the many-colored pavement. Crowds stood amazed and a little frightened, for no one had ever dared to upset the temple in this manner. The priests and rabbis were horrified and embarrassed. The worshipers had seen a display of authority that they would never forget. Many an Israelite had wondered why his temple should be profaned by sheep pens and dove cages, and why his own priests had not set this right long ago, but no one had dared to speak against it.

The rage of the priests knew no bounds, but when they tried to lay hands on Him, they feared the multitude, for most of the common people took Him to be a prophet. In all their history no one had ever spoken such cutting words. Jesus told the multitudes that their leaders bound heavy burdens upon them which they themselves would not lift a finger to bear; that they did their works to be seen of men; that they loved the chief seats in the synagogue; and that they loved to be called rabbis. With the fire of heaven flashing in His eye, He called down woes upon the scribes and Pharisees, branding them hypocrites who shut up the kingdom of heaven against men, not wishing to enter themselves and acting as a barrier to others who might want to enter. He called them blind guides who made the outside of the cup clean while the inside was filthy and who were so small in their view of things that they would strain at a gnat and swallow a camel.

THE CRUCIFIXION

Little wonder the priests and rabbis held a meeting at Caiaphas' palace for the purpose of laying plans to arrest Jesus and do away with Him quietly before the people were aroused. It was at that time that Judas Iscariot made a bargain with them to deliver Jesus into their hands for thirty pieces of silver.

In Gethsemane's garden the Messiah knelt to pray while His disciples slept. As He was in prayer, His enemies advanced. They came into the garden with swords and staves, led by Judas, who evidently knew that Jesus often went to Gethesmane to pray. A great multitude had come, and they were determined to seize Him and take Him back to the chief priest.

At the palace of the high priest an illegal meeting of the Sanhedrin was called. They were afraid to hold the meeting on the following day, because the people might hear of it and release Him. Now that He was in the hands of the temple authorities, they would see to it that nothing could stop them. So the court met at night and in almost no time read their sentence: "Guilty of death."

But according to Roman law, no Jewish court could impose the death sentence. It was necessary to take Christ to

Pilate, the Roman governor. Pilate tried to shift the responsibility by sending Him to Herod, who represented Caesar in all of Galilee, and Pilate had heard that Jesus was from Galilee. Herod soon returned Him to Pilate, however, who sought to please the Jews by turning Him over to them again. Since they clamored for His death, Pilate permitted it, and the execution was carried out on a hill called "Calvary," just outside the city wall.

The priests and the rabbis breathed a sigh of relief when they saw Jesus die. At last the trouble was over. No longer would the people be disturbed by their false Messiah. This should end forever the little group who followed Him as disciples. It was a blow that almost did scatter the followers of Christ, for they were discouraged and defeated. They went back to their regular ways of life more mystified than they had ever been and with a sadness in their hearts that it was all over.

THE RESURRECTION

On the first day of the new week, after the Sabbath had ended, the discouraged little group was electrified by the greatest miracle that had ever been known. Jesus had come forth from the grave and had appeared to many of His disciples! By His resurrection from the grave every word they had ever heard Him say was proved to be the truth. They were now experiencing a feeling of victory which never left them and which made them willing to suffer death rather than deny what they had seen with their own eyes.

THE ASCENSION

Out of this great miracle came the little group of Christ's disciples who, a few days later, were formed into a church by the power of the Holy Spirit. For forty days the Saviour met with His followers, proving the reality of His resurrection and strengthening them in their stand for Him. And then one day He left them. As they watched Him, He ascended to heaven, and a cloud received Him out of their sight.

But before He left them, He called them together and promised them that they would soon receive the gift of the Holy Spirit and would be made strong by the Spirit's power to preach the gospel to the whole world.

PENTECOST

As the days went by, the little group of believers gathered in Jerusalem to pray for the promised gift. One day, when the Jewish festival of Pentecost had come, they had met again to pray; suddenly the power of God shook the place, and the Holy Spirit descended upon them. It was such a tremendous experience that the disciples shouted for joy, and the power of God so came upon them that they began to praise God in foreign languages, which they had never spoken before. It was another miracle and an evidence that the Lord was still with them, keeping His promise.

As soon as the report of this miracle spread through the city, a great crowd gathered about the disciples. Some said that the followers of Jesus were so happy that they must be drunk. In order to account for the strange events, Peter preached a sermon to the vast multitude. He explained that the coming of the Holy Spirit was in fulfillment of a prophecy. He accused them of killing their own Messiah but told how God had raised Him up in fulfillment of the words of David, their king. He ended his sermon by saying that all these followers of Christ were witnesses of this resurrection and that they now possessed a gospel to preach which had the stamp of heaven upon it.

When Peter finished his sermon, many who were deeply moved by the words they heard asked what they must do if this were so.

"Repent, and be baptized . . . in the name of Jesus Christ," was the swift answer (Ac 2:38). They repented, and the Spirit of God fell in power upon three thousand of them. It was a great day for the followers of Jesus. It was the birthday of the Christian church. Luke, in a few brief sentences in Acts, has given a beautiful picture of the joy and gladness that filled the early Christians. Their lives were radiant.

But the first miracle was not the only one to strengthen the faith of the Christians. Peter and all the disciples went forth to preach, and many mighty things were done in the name of Christ. Enemies did their best to end the testimony of the newly-formed church. The priests and rabbis were violently opposed to it. The new sect which they called the Nazarenes (because Jesus was from Nazareth) had dropped the Sabbath restrictions and was meeting on the first day of the week. This the Nazarenes called the "Lord's Day," because Jesus had come forth from the tomb on a Sunday. Not only did they meet for worship, they also made plans to win other Jews away from the temple to their mystic fellowship.

LIFE OF THE EARLY CHRISTIANS

The life of these early Christians was marked by simplicity and goodness. They sought to live among men as Jesus had lived. There was a bond that drew them together into a brotherhood and filled their hearts with gladness. At home and in their place of worship their lives were a perpetual prayer, and a zeal, which was greater than any Jew had ever had for his temple, took hold of them and made them witnesses and evangelists whereever they went. So the church grew daily, as more people heard the gospel of Christ from the mouths of His disciples. In the temple they told about Christ, the Messiah of Israel. In the home they talked of His saving grace. At their work they continued to be witnesses, and the miraculous power of God accompanied their words, so that everywhere men and women who came in contact with them were won to Christ.

They now had a message to preach which transformed their lives and gave them not only hope for this life but also promise of resurrection beyond the grave.

Wherever these Christians went, they greeted each other with the word "Maranatha," which meant, "The Lord is at hand." The coming of the Lord was their daily expectation and hope, for Jesus had promised to come again. At the hour of His ascension, as they gazed after Him, there came a clear voice from heaven saying, "Ye men of Galilee, why stand ye gazing up into heaven? this same Jesus, which is taken up from you into heaven, shall so come in like manner as ye have seen him go into heaven" (Ac 1:11).

Therefore the early church lived each day as if their Saviour would return that day, and the promise of His coming made a deep impression on their lives. It made them pure, and it detached them from many of the pleasures of this world, filling the entire horizon of their lives with a zeal for Christ.

But all was not well with the people in this newly formed church. They were regarded with suspicion and hatred by the Pharisees and Sadducees—in fact, by all the leaders in Israel. The enemies of Jesus were still the enemies of His church, and it became their task to stamp out those who were of this "Way," wherever they found them.

THE MINISTRIES OF PETER AND JOHN

One day when Peter and John went up to the temple at the hour of prayer, a beggar, who had been crippled since birth, sat at the gate asking for money. It had been his custom to beg each day, and all he expected was a gift to support him in his weakness. But Peter, by the power of God, healed the man of his infirmity, and immediately a great crowd gathered in amazement about the two disciples. Peter took advantage of this opportunity, and standing in one of the porches of the outer court, where the rabbis usually taught, he preached a sermon to the throng. The theme of his address was Jesus, the Messiah. Peter told the people that this power to heal was not any power which was in him; it was the Lord's power. He went on to say that the God of Abraham, Isaac, and Jacob had glorified His Son, Jesus, whom they had delivered to Pilate and condemned to death. He spoke of how God raised Him from the grave and took Him home to heaven, there to remain until the day that the prophecies of old would be fulfilled. When those prophecies are fulfilled, He will return to His people again and bring judgment on all his enemies. Peter called upon all the people to repent and be converted, so that their sins might be blotted out. God used that testimony just as He did the one on the day of Pentecost, for about five thousand men believed and opened their hearts to Jesus. The church was growing quickly.

The priests, the temple authorities, and the Sadducees, who did not believe in life after death, were enraged because these men who were not rabbis dared to teach, and especially because they taught the doctrine of the resurrection of Jesus. They sent the temple guard to break up the meeting and to seize Peter and John and put them into prison.

On the day after their arrest, the two disciples were brought before the seven-member council and asked by what authority they did these things. They replied that they taught and healed in the name of the Lord Jesus. Peter never lost an opportunity to preach the gospel of Christ, and he did it before the Sanhedrin that day. However, when the council heard his statement and perceived that they were not educated men, but yet spoke boldly, the members marveled and said this boldness must have come from being with Christ. The authority with which Jesus spoke was still in their memory. So they warned them not to do this again and set them free. They were aware that the lame man was known to all the people, and to sentence men who had worked such a miracle might have angered the crowd.

Day by day new believers were coming into the church. The Spirit's power working in the disciples and the Christlike example of all the believers brought multitudes of converts. Their faith was confirmed by many miracles. God gave these miracles as signs to a church which, as yet, had no New Testament for a guide and nothing to lean on except the experiences of the disciples and the daily outpourings of God's mighty power.

Having failed the first time, the Sadducees made a second attempt to put down the new faith, and after they had cast the apostles into prison, they were shaken to learn that an angel had miraculously freed them and they were back with their friends again.

Continued Growth of The Persecuted Church

Try as they would to stamp out Christianity, they seemed only to fan the flame. The great fact of the resurrection had given the people a hope and an assurance which they had never been able to find before. Until Christ arose, there was no proof of life after death, but now it was different. All the longings of Israel, all their prophecies, all their sacrifices, and all their hopes were fulfilled in Jesus the Messiah, but the nation missed its greatest opportunity and rejected him. This gospel, which is so evident to millions of Christians now, was just dawning upon the hearts of many Jews who were devout in their own religion but who found it to be an endless bondage of rules and promises with no freedom in sight. The wail of Judaism has come down the centuries. Its cry is always the same, but it is only a cry. Nowhere is there a sign of hope except in Jesus, and many fail to recognize Him as their Messiah.

But under the preaching of the gospel, many were seeing for the first time the fulfillment of all their hopes in Christ. At the third arrest of the disciples they were again brought before the Sanhedrin on the charge that they had not obeyed the order to cease preaching. Boldly, Peter stood before the group, and in his defense proclaimed again the resurrection of Christ, charging that the members of this very council had been responsible for His death. They were stung by the burning words and cried out for the death of the disciples. At last they would stamp out this sect by silencing its chief preachers and leaders. With great coolness and good sense,

Gamaliel, the famous rabbi who had taught Saul of Tarsus, cautioned the council, reminding them that in former times God had raised up prophets who had been rejected by the nation, but who bore the message of God. His advice was that they should let the disciples go, for if their message were of God, even the Sanhedrin could not stamp it out; if it were not of God, it would die, as so many other sects had died in the past. It was both a charitable and a wise conclusion, and after beating the disciples, the council dismissed them with a warning.

THE ORGANIZATION OF THE CHURCH

As the church grew and persecution increased, the number of needy people dependent on the common funds increased. Eventually, the apostles found they had little time for anything but the distributing of food and clothing. In order to have more time for preaching and teaching, the apostles appointed seven helpers, called deacons, to take charge of ministering to the poor. It was the beginning of organization in the church, and God blessed it and used it to the strengthening of His people.

THE HATRED OF THE WORLD

Never has it been popular to be a Christian, and the families of those who were known as followers of Jesus were hated and often made outcasts from society. Sometimes they were dismissed from their employment and found it hard to make a living. There was always the necessity of helping the poor. Christians banded together for their mutual protection and encouragement, and in those early days their love for each other was so voluntary and their detachment from the world so real that many sold all their belongings and put the money into the common fund so that the less fortunate might be helped.

Wave after wave of hatred and persecution rolled over the church. Some members were weak, and with an eye to their

personal safety and comfort, they deserted the company of believers. Others, however, stood like a rock against the storm.
Every time the armed hand of the enemy was raised, God
seemed to find others to carry on His work. When Herod
the king persecuted the church and had James, the brother of
John, killed with a sword, he thought he had ended that work
forever, but when Luke wrote the story of it all in the Acts
of the Apostles, he finished the account by saying: "But the
word of God grew and multiplied" (Ac 12:24).

The greater the persecution, the more rapidly the church
seemed to grow. Sometimes they had to worship in secret,
but they never wavered. When their preachers were put in
prison, they gathered for prayer. Somehow the Lord always
heard their prayer and blessed His people, and He even used
the hardships as an instrument to strengthen His church.

But Christianity was not to be found only in Jerusalem.
Those who had heard it preached by Peter on the day of
Pentecost were from all over the Roman Empire. One of
the great facts about the gospel is that once it is received in
the heart, the lips cannot be silent about it. Wherever these
people went, they carried the good news of salvation from
their sins through Christ and the promise of resurrection from
the dead. There were many small groups of Christians meeting together in upper rooms, giving no offense to the authorities of the synagogue. They quietly strengthened their fellowship as they met Sunday after Sunday to break bread in
memory of the death of their Lord and to pray. Each little
gathering was a center of power and peace. Here their souls
were strengthened; here the hand of God was seen in miraculous power; here they met with their invisible Lord. It was
like heaven on earth; it was so different from the austerity of
the synagogue with its burdening rules. They had all the
promise and hope of the synagogue, but they had more—they
had the fulfillment of it all. Down through the long years the
walls of their synagogues had reverberated with the disputings
of their worthiest rabbis. Some were of one mind and some

were of another. Even on the great question of the coming Messiah they were not in agreement. Some said that He would suffer, others said that He would reign in power and splendor, and the argument had no ending. But now in the new message of the church they had the real answer to all the rabbis' questions and disputes. They had within their hands the power to bless the whole world.

5

Fighting Against God

SAUL'S HATRED OF JESUS

UP IN TARSUS Saul heard stories from time to time about Jesus. Some of them were wild tales that bore no relationship to the truth, but stories have a way of growing as they pass from lip to lip. Many of the friends in the synagogue had attended the festivals at Jerusalem and were acquainted with what was taking place in the temple. Upon their return Saul and the leading men of the synagogue heard about the imposter from Nazareth, and they were angered that anyone would dare to defile the temple courts with such blasphemous teaching. And besides, He had no right to teach in the temple, for He was not educated according to the way of the rabbis. And yet everyone who heard Him said that no man ever spoke such words of wisdom—not even the great rabbis.

It was evident to Saul that Jesus could not be the Messiah, because He denounced the teachers of the law and seemed to be opposed to all their rules. He taught the people not to obey the rabbis and caused such a stir in the synagogues that every true Jew held Him to be an enemy of Israel.

When news came that He had been arrested, tried, and crucified, they all gave thanks to God that a blasphemer worthy of stoning to death had been stopped. He was just one more false Messiah who tried to upset the established religion of the land. Saul and every other Pharisee applauded when Jesus was crucified by Pilate, for they could not forgive anyone who called them vipers and hypocrites. Saul was no hypocrite. He had always been sincere, and his aim was to be a better Jew and to obey all the rules of the great rabbis.

That, in his view, was the only way to purity of life and the only path to heaven. Anyone who set himself against the old order deserved to die. It was with a sigh of relief and a sense of God's justice being done that the chief men of the Tarsus synagogue heard that Jesus had at last been put out of the way and His teaching ended.

But when they heard that the followers of the Nazarene had not been scattered, but instead had banded together in little groups to worship Jesus, declaring that He rose from the grave, their indignation burned to a white heat. They resolved to do all they could to fight this dangerous sect. Word came from Jerusalem that some of the Pharisees had turned from the truth and joined the Nazarenes. Members of the sect were openly preaching in the temple courts and in the synagogues that Jesus was the Messiah, and thousands had believed them. This had become quite a menace, for even some of the priests had forsaken the old order and were following the new Teacher. The Nazarenes went through the streets of the city, talking to the people in their houses and in little groups, persuading them to join the followers of Christ.

Saul was angry as he thought of them. He heard that a few of their leaders had been caught and brought before the Sanhedrin for speaking openly in the temple and that his old teacher Gamaliel had been lenient and had advised the council to let them go. Down in his young heart he was impatient with Gamaliel. How could they ever keep the religion of Israel pure if they allowed anybody to rise up and claim to be the Messiah? There could be no question that those who followed Jesus were worthy of death, and the council should have ended this threat against the temple forever.

His Persecution of the Nazarenes

With these thoughts in his mind, Saul decided to leave Tarsus and go back to Jerusalem. Perhaps he was so dissatisfied with the way the sect of Nazarenes was making headway that he decided to take a hand in fighting it himself. He immediately broke with Gamaliel and his school and offered his services to the high priest to stamp out any who opposed the way of the synagogue. He entered into his job of persecuting the church so fiercely that his name became the dread of every worshiping assembly. He was hot-tempered and merciless, and by his eloquence he fought them in the temple. He was swift to punish, and therefore he scattered many a weak congregation, dragging in men and women who were believers, casting them into prison, and sentencing them to death. He was blind in his rage and set about to crush the followers of Jesus so thoroughly that they would never be heard of again. In the inspired history of his people, had not the Lord blessed his nation when they separated themselves from all who were not truly of Israel? Did not He command His people to slay any priest who offered strange fire on the altar? Therefore, with the gleaming eye of a fanatic, Saul purposed to force a quick end to the sect of the Nazarenes.

SAUL CONFOUNDED BY STEPHEN

One of the seven men chosen by the church in Jerusalem to have charge of the poor was called Stephen. He was the most able and energetic of the seven. He was not a native of Jerusalem, but of one of the provinces of the Roman Empire, and had been given a Greek name. But he had seen and heard Jesus, and the light of His face and the sound of His voice had set his heart on fire. In the synagogues of the city he debated with the rabbis and proved to be too much for them in argument. His words were irresistible and winning, as were the words of Jesus, and his preaching was to the effect that salvation was through Christ Jesus, the Messiah, and not by the keeping of the law of Moses. Jerusalem had many synagogues where Jews from different nations often met together. Stephen went from one to the other, preaching the gospel and disputing wi   the leaders.

The Alexandrian synagogue had heard him. The Cyrenian

and Cilician congregations were acquainted with his arguments and fought bitterly against him, for he had persuaded some of their number to believe on Jesus.

Perhaps it was in the Cilician synagogue that Saul first met Stephen. He heard him with bitter scorn, and yet he could see how appealing and powerful were his words. This man was filled with a holy zeal far beyond anything he had seen in any rabbi. When he spoke of the resurrection, Saul had to admit to himself that this hope was the central doctrine of the Pharisees. He noted, too, that it was the Sadducees who bitterly opposed this belief, and Saul scorned the Sadducees and pitied them. Had it been only a question of the resurrection, Saul felt that he might hear this man gladly. But he spoke against the temple and against Moses and wished to change the old customs which had come down from the rabbis. It was therefore necessary to silence his voice.

Saul faced him in open debate and grew angry because he found that with all his learning he was not able to withstand the arguments of Stephen. It hurt his pride that he could not answer the Nazarene, and his only defense was a mounting rage and a determination to oppose him with all his might. He went from synagogue to synagogue and found that the followers of Jesus were everywhere. He told the people that those Nazarenes should be put down, even if it was by the sword. Their teachings were contrary to the law, and when they said Jesus was the Christ, they were speaking falsehood and blasphemy. He quoted from the Scriptures, but then he realized that even the unlearned men of the sect could quote the Scriptures, and they knew Jewish history as well as he did.

Stephen seemed to him to be the most powerful and learned of all the Nazarenes, so he determined to pursue and persecute him and drive him away. Whoever spoke against the law of Moses or said that the Carpenter of Nazareth was the Messiah deserved death, for he was a blasphemer! Wherever Saul went he was not afraid to say that. He was weary of deceivers who led the people astray, and since Stephen was one of the worst agitators troubling Judaism, Saul felt he was rendering a real service in getting rid of him. The strife grew in bitterness. It became clearer each day that if the people entertained those false ideas of the Nazarenes, the only thing to do was to punish them until they banished Jesus from their lives.

The more he thought of this sect and the advances it was making, the more agitated Saul became. Ultimately his rage became blind bigotry—no longer could he reason with these people from the Scriptures. His only desire was to exterminate them, just as King Saul was asked to exterminate Agag and all his nation (1 Sa 15).

STEPHEN BEFORE THE SANHEDRIN

When the news came that Stephen had been arrested and was to be brought before the Sanhedrin, Saul felt that the leader had been silenced, and it would be only a question of time until all of them had been rounded up and the menace ended.

He attended the Sanhedrin meeting that day. He wanted to be there when his opponent came to justice. He was not the only one, for it seemed that hundreds came to the hearing. Sadducees were there with a sneer on their faces. This was the day they had waited for. Pharisees were there in their white robes, along with priests, scribes, and a great crowd of people who had heard Stephen and were amazed at his boldness. Saul took his place among them and smiled as he waited.

It was the same Sanhedrin that had condemned Jesus. Annas was there, and Caiaphas, both retired from the office of high priest now. Jonathan, the high priest, was the president of the council. There sat Gamaliel, the wise and benevolent Pharisee. They were growing tired of this disturbance to their religion. Since the meeting in which Jesus was condemned, they had had trouble with Peter and John, His disciples. Each day brought others, for the new sect seemed tire-

less in its blasphemous preaching. Over and over they had
commanded them to keep silent about Jesus, but each time
their orders were disobeyed. The Nazarenes grew bolder,
even accusing the council of killing the Messiah. And now
it was Stephen, one of the boldest of them all.

As Stephen entered the court, all eyes were turned on him.
Some heads were bowed with fear, for his face looked serene
and calm, as if it had been the face of an angel. The witnesses were called, and they said they had heard him speaking
against the temple and the opinions of the rabbis and trying to
teach people that Jesus was the Messiah. When he was given
an opportunity to reply to the charges, he looked around on
the hushed crowd, searching for a friendly face. Finding
none, he cast himself on the mercy of the Lord, and with a
radiance upon his brow that came from heaven itself, he
began to speak.

Beginning with Abraham, Stephen spoke of Jewish history
to show that men might worship God apart from the temple.
He traced the ways of God with His people from Abraham
to Moses and showed that Moses prophesied of Christ, saying,
"A prophet shall the Lord your God raise up unto you of
your brethren, like unto me; him shall ye hear" (Ac 7:37).

He told how Moses was given the pattern of the tabernacle
and how Solomon built the temple, but he quoted the prophet
Isaiah to prove that the Most High dwells not in temples made
with hands, for did not the Lord say to Isaiah: "Heaven is
my throne, and earth is my footstool: what house will ye
build me? saith the Lord: or what is the place of my rest?
Hath not my hand made all these things?" (vv. 49-50).

They looked at him with hateful, gloomy eyes as he pro-
ceeded. At last, rising to the height of his speech, he boldly
told the Sanhedrin what he had been telling the people in
every synagogue:

> You stiff-necked hypocrites! You are resisting the power
> of the Holy Spirit as your fathers did before you. Which of
> the prophets have your fathers not persecuted? Have they

not slain the very men who told them of the coming of
Messiah? You are no different from them, for you have
killed your Messiah! You have received the law of Moses
as if it had been handed to you by the angels, but you do
not obey it! (vv. 51-53).

There was an uproar of angry voices in the hall, for these
words burned like fire and cut them to the heart. They were
insulting words! They were challenging words! Stephen's
voice had ceased, and in the awful silence that preceded the
storm, his head was raised to heaven, and a smile crept across
his face as if he had seen a vision in the skies. The people
heard him say, "I see the heavens opened, and the Son of
man standing on the right hand of God" (v. 56).

He was not allowed to say anything more. Some of the
Pharisees put their fingers in their ears so they could not
hear more of the blasphemous words. Others jumped to their
feet and sought to get their hands on the prisoner. Quickly
Stephen was led from the judgment hall before he could be
beaten by the enraged throng. Never had they heard such
bold words! Never had they been so cut to the heart!

The Stoning of Stephen

After the prisoner was taken away, the verdict was reached
quickly. In the opinion of all, he was guilty of death. The
law of Moses made it very plain:

> He that blasphemeth the name of God shall surely be put
> to death, and all the people shall stone him. A stranger as
> well as a local citizen shall be put to death when he blas-
> phemes God's name (Lev 24:16).

Saul had been moved greatly by this trial. He followed
every word of Stephen's address. He gloried in the history
of his people and thought how magnificently Stephen had
stated it. Never before had he come in contact with a man
who seemed so fearless, nor had he met anyone with such

knowledge of Scripture as Stephen seemed to have. He thought of the rabbis and their disputings; for a moment they seemed so petty. He considered his own views of the Messiah and what Gamaliel had taught him. He realized that the Pharisees believed in resurrection but had never been able to demonstrate it. Here was the only demonstration of it in the world—if it were only true. What a look of rapture on Stephen's face! It was as if he were living in another world. And his final words—what if he had actually seen Jesus at God's right hand?

No, this was the way it was with every fanatic. He was an imposter. Those last words about the hypocrisy of the rabbis were unforgivable. The man was an enemy of the law and of God. Death to the enemies of God! Let him be stoned! Saul was finally so convinced that the trial was just that he was ready to help in the carrying out of the sentence. Stephen's insulting words were still in his ears.

With the temple guards surrounding him, Stephen was led bound through the city streets and beyond the gate to a place near the wall. A cry of, "Death to the blasphemer! Death to the Nazarene!" rose from the crowd. It was the law of Moses that the first stone should be cast by those who had witnessed against him. This the witnesses prepared to do. They loosened their flowing robes and laid them in a heap at the feet of Saul. Saul's part was to watch them lest any thief make off with the elegant clothing.

Stephen knelt on the ground, and as if he were alone he prayed to God saying, "Lord Jesus, receive my spirit" (Ac 7:59). The rocks began to fall, and soon he was cut and bleeding. But before his soul left its earthly house for that home of many mansions, he was heard to cry out in a loud voice, "Lord, lay not this sin to their charge" (v. 60). In a moment it was all over. His kneeling body fell to the ground, but his soul went home to be with Jesus, who not long before had claimed it for His very own.

THE SPREAD OF CHRISTIANITY

Saul left the scene quietly and alone. He had witnessed something he had never seen before. He could not deny that he had been tremendously shaken. He had heard the prayer. Who ever heard of a man praying for his enemies? It was unbelievable. Saul's feeling of hatred was tempered with a feeling of pity. But that was only for a moment. A strong man could not let his emotions be ravaged this way. Stephen deserved to die! The stoning of this man would discourage others and perhaps end the Nazarene sect for good. And yet, the events of that day were burned so deeply into Saul's memory that they never left him.

After Stephen's death, Saul took up with vigor the persecution of the church. He soon found that the death of the leader had no effect on the Christians except that it seemed to make them bolder and stronger. Upon consultation with the Sanhedrin and the priests, it was decided that the best way to end this threat to Judaism was to visit each synagogue, find out those who were inclined toward belief in Jesus, and bring them to trial. Saul seemed to be the tool of the religious leaders in all of this. With his background as a Pharisee, he entered into the hateful job zealously, and soon he became known in all Judea as the most hated enemy of Christ. With whip and club, dagger and chains, he hunted for believers, throwing them into prison and putting them to death. His indignation against them burned like a fire, and his cry in every synagogue was, "Give up belief in Jesus or die!"

The persecution was so severe that believers were forced to leave their homes, and the Church members in Jerusalem were scattered throughout Judea and Samaria. But that certainly did not accomplish what Saul and the Sanhedrin wanted, for wherever disciples went, they told the story of Christ Jesus. Instead of one great church in Jerusalem, there grew up many small groups of believers meeting secretly in homes. All the efforts of Saul only scattered the fire and made it much harder to put out.

There were some, of course, for whom the love of ease and comfort proved too strong, and these deserted the church and went back to their miserable lives in the synagogue. At the point of the sword they were compelled to blaspheme the name of Jesus.

Terrible were the scenes resulting from the hatred of this fierce Pharisee. Saul literally dashed from synagogue to synagogue and from house to house, dragging forth men and women and compelling them to curse Jesus or die as traitors to Israel.

Many Christians went north in Samaria, where Saul had no power to follow. Among these was Philip, one of the seven deacons chosen in the Jerusalem Church. He had been a co-worker with Stephen and had fled for his life. The people of Samaria received him gladly at first, because they remembered Jesus and His ministry among them.

Samaria was north of Jerusalem. It was inhabited by a mixed people, partly eastern and partly Hebrew in origin. It had been the home of the ten northern tribes of Israel, but the Assyrians had taken these people captive, leaving only a few in the land. Thousands from Arabia intermarried with the Jews that remained, resulting in a mixed race. Upon these Samaritans every Jew looked with scorn. Philip preached Christ freely in Samaria and God blessed his testimony there, and as in Jerusalem, many became followers of the Nazarene.

When the apostles heard that a great work for Christ was being done in Samaria, they sent Peter and John to see if it were genuine, for they were not convinced that anybody could be a real follower of Jesus without being a Jew first. In Samaria, a land hated by the Jews, the apostles found that the Holy Spirit came upon believers, just as had happened in Jerusalem. Their visit to Samaria had great results, bringing many to Christ. Before the apostles left, they preached in village after village, and God gave a great increase. The church in Samaria grew almost without persecution.

BEGINNING OF SAUL'S CONVICTION

Saul was faced with a fresh difficulty. He had scattered the Nazarenes in Jerusalem and made it so uncomfortable for many that they fled, but as the weeks sped by he received reports that the Christians were not silent. They were spreading their teachings. The church, instead of diminishing, was growing. Saul was angry. He began to wonder if all his work would end in failure. Perhaps his wise old teacher, Gamaliel, was right when he said that if the Nazarene sect were of God, neither Sanhedrin nor mighty army could stop it. Was it really of God? Was Saul really fighting against God? Certainly he had been defeated in argument against these Nazarenes, for they had used his own Scriptures and silenced him in the synagogue. Stephen seemed to be victorious over his persecutors, and in the hour of his murder some strange power had possessed him which even Saul recognized and admired. Many a poor believer had gone to his death with a look of victory on his face that frightened Saul as he led the persecution. Thus far, Gamaliel had been right: persecution had only spread the new teaching.

The scenes of his life passed like a panorama before Saul's mind. He thought of his training as a strict Pharisee and of all the rules he had learned. He believed that in keeping these he would have eternal life. But he had to admit that his life was empty and that the infinite maze of rules which the rabbis bound on their people could not suffice for Israel without the hope of a coming Messiah. More and more, Saul found himself wondering about the Messiah and hoping that He would come to them soon.

The Nazarenes were preaching a false Messiah, he was sure, and yet all the reports he had heard of Jesus gave him the feeling that some great and mysterious power was in Him and had now come upon men like Stephen and others.

Saul asked himself why these men whom he condemned to death were willing to die for this new religion rather than deny it. He realized that men will stand by a thing that is false just as long as they are getting something out of it; but when the sword is put to their throats, they will give it up immediately. Why did the followers of Jesus hold on to their faith as if it were more precious than life itself?

He began to look at his own heart. How changed he was since the days in Tarsus when he made tents in his father's shop! Once he was Saul the student, then Saul the Pharisee, then Saul the teacher. But now, what had become of him? He was little better than a hangman! He was Saul the slayer, Saul the persecutor. He had flung away reason and had seized the scourge and the sword. He had filled the prisons with martyrs, and he was riding out for more. He was the most unhappy man in the world. His cause was a lost one. His quest was a failure. The very serenity of the martyrs was stabbing his own heart and raising questions in his soul that seemed as high as mountains. Was it possible that he could be wrong? Was it possible that Jesus was really the Christ?

6

The Turning Point

FROM THE TIME that these questions entered Saul's heart there was no more rest for him. Doubt and fear chased each other through his mind, and he found they were no easier to conquer than were the Nazarenes. But neither could he lay the questions aside and forget them. They had to be answered. Was he doing the right thing in persecuting the followers of Jesus, or was this a tremendous blunder? His brain was a whirlpool of confusion and agony when he thought of the possibility that he was fighting against the Messiah. Such a thing was unthinkable! Perhaps that was the very reason why his task had proven hopeless. And yet, with a growing fear in his heart and his conscience on fire, he pressed on. Was he right in trying to stamp out Christianity? His conscience whispered No, but his mind and his training as a Pharisee shouted *Yes!*

ON THE DAMASCUS ROAD

Saul was laying up bitter memories to think of in later days, but he was determined to carry on the fight. Angered at the spread of the church in spite of his efforts, he prepared an expedition to Damascus where he had heard many Nazarenes were hiding from the persecution in Jerusalem. Not only were they hiding, they were actively preaching Christ in the synagogues there. Saul thought it would deal the followers of Jesus a death blow to drive them out of this stronghold. So, accompanied by a troup of armed temple guards, he rode out of Jerusalem by the Damascus gate, breathing out threatenings and slaughter. It was more than one hundred and fifty miles to Damascus, and the road led through some of the most beautiful scenery in the world.

But Saul's purpose was not to see beautiful sights. The countryside was alive with historic memories. Two thousand years earlier Eleazar of Damascus had become Abraham's servant and had traveled that very road. Naaman, the leper, had been cured of his dreadful disease when he had traversed this highway in the centuries past. But Saul did not care to think of these things. He was both baffled and angry. He was hunting for Christians and planning to bring them back to Jerusalem in bonds, there to be tried and sentenced by the Sanhedrin. In his tunic was a piece of folded paper. It was a sealed letter, sent by the high priest to the rabbis at Damascus, commanding that Saul be given every assistance in his task, for he was the representative of the high priest in making these arrests.

The sun was hot as they neared the ancient city. Before them was a valley, well watered and heavily wooded with trees of every type. There were the feathery palm and the poplar, and the vineyards upon the hillsides were the richest in all Syria. Usually, travelers took advantage of these trees in the heat of the day as the sun rose to its height, but Saul was impatient and would not rest. Those whispering voices were following him, and long hours of silence were not good for him. They made him thoroughly miserable. In the city other things would fill his mind. He was a man of cities anyway. His chief interest was people and not the open spaces of the country. He saw the end of the journey and was eager to be there.

Already the people of the synagogue knew that Saul was on his way, and the Nazarenes, remembering the havoc he had made in Jerusalem, trembled at the thought that they would have to face the persecution all over again. It meant that families would be torn asunder and reduced to poverty or killed, but they made up their minds to be true to Christ whatever might be the consequences.

Noon found Saul near the edge of the city and hurrying on, despite the sun's glare. The roads were deserted in the heat of the day. Even the cattle had sought the shade of little clumps of trees and were lying down until the noonday sun had passed. The temple guards with him wondered why Saul did not rest, but when they saw the fierceness of his face, they asked no questions.

The little group reached the top of the hill from which could be seen the buildings of the city gleaming in the sun. No wonder the poet called it "a handful of pearls in a cup of emerald."

THE APPEARANCE OF CHRIST

As they started down the hill, a shaft of light brighter than the noonday sun fell upon the little company. Its radiance was so great that the sun seemed dim. They were dazzled by the sight and fell to the ground, some with their faces downward to protect them from the light and others with hands covering their eyes to shield them from the searing flash.

In bewilderment they looked from one to another for an explanation of what had happened, and then they beheld their leader. He was lying prone upon the ground, while the frightened animal upon which he had been riding stood near-by. He was speaking now, and it seemed as though there was a voice speaking to him, but they saw no man. And though it seemed like a voice, they did not understand its sound. Saul's lips were moving now and his hands were extended before him as if he were blind. He was trembling from head to foot. He realized that he was in the hands of an angry God.

There on the ground, with his sight taken away, he heard a voice speaking to him. It was the voice of God saying in Saul's beloved tongue: "Saul, Saul, Why persecutest thou me?" (Ac 9:4).

Troubled by all the thoughts which had been pursuing him

since the death of Stephen, he asked, fearfully, "Who art thou, Lord?" (v. 5).

"I am Jesus whom thou persecutest: it is hard for thee to kick against the pricks" (v. 5).

In the language of love beyond anything he had known he heard the words, "I am Jesus." Was this the same Jesus that he hated so bitterly? Was this the Jesus that he thought had been disgraced and forever silenced at Calvary? Was this the Jesus who had died? Abruptly there was dawning upon his soul the awful realization that he was wrong. In fact, his whole life had been wrong.

The turmoil that had been in his mind, the questions he had had, the growing conviction that he had been fighting against God—all these thoughts loomed before him now with a sudden clearness, and he could not withstand Him any longer.

All the pride of his pharisaical background, all the dignity of his office, and all the smugness of his position as the chief public prosecutor of Christianity collapsed as he lay on the road. His physical sight was taken away so that his soul might see. He was thinking of those words "I am Jesus whom thou persecutest: it is hard for thee to kick against the pricks" (v. 5).

How like the words of Jesus these were, taken from country life as were many of His illustrations! Saul had often seen an ox kicking against the goad, offering vain resistance. Instead of obeying the driver and being submissive to his leading, the ox was stubborn and kicked against the sharpened sticks which its owner used to prod him on. This was a good description of Saul's life. For months he had been doing just that, and he had found it very hard. He had gone out to hunt the followers of Jesus, but instead he found that he was being hunted by Jesus whom he persecuted.

This was the great crisis of Saul's life. He found himself face to face with the Messiah, and was forced to acknowledge that he was wrong and the Nazarenes were right: Jesus was the Christ.

At that moment all his struggling was over. A greater revolution took place within him than he had ever known. He lay broken and beaten, completely in the hands of the One whom he had thought was his enemy. The surrender was complete. Peace in his soul had been won at last.

"Lord, what wilt thou have me to do?" he asked, and a voice from heaven said, "Arise, and go into the city, and it shall be told thee what thou must do" (Ac 9:6).

THE TRANSFORMATION

It was all over in a few moments, but it was the greatest experience Saul ever had, and he thought of it until his dying day. In that moment Jesus had taken the mastery of him, and his life had been completely changed. Neither doubt nor question was possible to him from then on. It was no mere vision of Jesus that he had seen; it was, in fact, an appearance of the Christ, no longer with His glory veiled, as in the days of His earthly ministry, but with such fullness of glory that man could not bear the brightness.

Saul later spoke of this as the last of the appearances of Jesus to His followers after the resurrection. It was the kind of an experience that had been granted to Peter, James, and John at the transfiguration. It was what Moses saw on Mt. Sinai when the sight of the glory of the Lord was like devouring fire. It was what Isaiah saw when the Lord appeared to him. It was what John saw on Patmos, and after he had seen Him, he "fell at his feet as dead" (Rev 1:17). To Saul, the rabbi of Tarsus, was granted an interview with the risen Christ.

In later years there were those who doubted Saul's apostleship, saying that he had never seen the Lord, but to all his enemies he could say:

I saw Him and talked with Him, and received my commission to preach from Him. And He said to me, "Rise, and stand upon thy feet: for I have appeared unto thee for this purpose, to make thee a minister and a witness both of these things which thou hast seen, and of those things in the which I will appear unto thee; delivering thee from the people, and from the Gentiles, unto whom now I send thee, to open their eyes, and to turn them from darkness to light, and from the power of Satan unto God, that they may receive forgiveness of sins, and inheritance among those who are sanctified by faith in Me" (Ac 26:16-18).

When his companions recovered themselves and turned to help their leader to his feet, they discovered that he was blind, and they had to take him by the hand and lead him into the city. What a change had come over him! He had been a proud Pharisee, riding with pomp and authority, full of indignation and dignity. But in a moment he was changed to a trembling, groping servant, humbled and broken, clinging to the hand of a soldier who guided him to his destination. Being led to Damascus, he entered a room in the house of Judas on the street called Straight and asked to be left alone. He wanted time to think.

With all the world shut out by his blindness, he could gather his thoughts at last. He sat in the darkness, wondering how God could use a blind man.

For three days he neither ate nor drank. He was too absorbed in the thoughts which crowded each other through his mind. All of his past came before him. He thought of his father's zeal in bringing him up as a Pharisee. He remembered the rigor of his school in Tarsus and how the words of the rabbis were everything in his life. He thought of the golden temple and all its beautiful and pleasant scenes and of the throngs of worshipers bringing their sacrifices to the priests. Once it had meant everything, but it all seemed so unimportant now. The Messiah had appeared and had been crucified by the very people He had come to bless. Saul's whole former life seemed to be crumbling into fragments and

falling in ruin at his feet. He could see now how he had been
fighting against God. Blinded by his teaching and by his
position as a Pharisee, he had, in ignorance, persecuted the
Messiah. He had found it an uphill task, and at last he lay
broken in pieces at the Saviour's feet. By the force of this
one collision with Christ his whole life was changed. Stephen
had been right, and he and the Sanhedrin had been wrong.
The barren years were now ended, and the future must be
filled with telling others about these great discoveries.

When Saul arrested Nazarenes, it was in vengeance and
anger. He was their deadly enemy, but when Jesus of Nazareth arrested Saul, there was no vengeance and no wrath.
Never did He demand retribution for all the years of bitterness. As soon as the might of God threw him to the ground,
the love of God lifted him up and took possession of him.
He began to understand how Stephen could pray for his
enemies even when the stones were falling around him. In
Christ he discovered the peace which he had hoped could
come through strict keeping of the law.

While Saul, fasting in darkness, was thinking and praying
about the strange experience that had befallen him, he had
a vision in which a disciple named Ananias came to him and
restored his sight.

THE VISIONS OF SAUL AND ANANIAS

At the same time the Lord was preparing Ananias to visit
Saul. Ananias had once been honored in the synagogue as a
devout and good man who kept the law with the strictness
of a Pharisee, but since he had become a Christian, the Jews
were suspicious of him. Some said that it was Ananias whom
Saul came to arrest, for the Nazarenes recognized him as their
leader. In a vision, the Lord spoke to this man saying,

> Arise, Ananias, and go into a street which is called Straight,
> and inquire in the house of Judas for Saul of Tarsus; for
> I have prepared him by a vision, and he expects you (Ac
> 9:11-12).

Immediately, Ananias protested that this man was an enemy. The Nazarenes in Damascus had been in terror of him, for they knew of his cruelty in Jerusalem. In fact, word had reached them through a Christian brother just a few days earlier that Saul was on his way to Damascus in the name of the high priest to arrest some of them and bring them to trial in Jerusalem. Had not the believers prayed that God would prevent him? When the news came that he had been struck blind just outside the city wall, they thanked God and took hope. It was the answer to their prayer.

But now came the command from the Lord, "Go thy way: for he is a chosen vessel unto me, to bear my name before the Gentiles, and kings, and the children of Israel" (v. 15).

That was enough for Ananias. He started for the street called Straight, and at Judas' house he inquired for Saul, the rabbi from Jerusalem. He was taken into a back room where the terrible young Pharisee sat blind and shaken by the conflict in his soul. No longer was there any bitterness in him. He had been through deep waters during these three days; he had experienced a searching of his soul such as he had never dreamed possible. Ananias walked across the room to where Saul sat; and putting his hand upon the blind man's head, he said in a low voice, "Brother Saul, the Lord, even Jesus, that appeared unto thee in the way as thou camest, hath sent me, that thou mightest receive thy sight, and be filled with the Holy Ghost" (v. 17).

A Nazarene had called him "brother"! One whom he had come to arrest and imprison had reached out a hand of fellowship! In a moment the darkness turned to light and the Spirit of God filled his heart, and Saul saw the man who had come to him as an messenger of God.

He had just heard a confirmation of what he had heard on the Damascus road. How could he help but surrender? For a moment Saul doubted if he could ever be forgiven for the years of persecution and the havoc wrought on the early Christian Church, but the voice of Ananias brought assurance to him.

Saul knew that baptism was the Nazarene sign of repentance. It meant to the world that he had changed and had called on the name of the One whom he had hated.

Saul was ready. He had been in the hands of God; there was no doubt about it. He knelt with Ananias and prayed like a child, confessing his sin, asking the Lord to forgive for Jesus' sake, and calling upon His name for the first time in the Nazarene way. Then Ananias baptized him, thus marking his turning to the new life.

A LIFE FOR CHRIST

Saul had come from darkness into light. He was dead to the old life under the law and filled with the life of the Spirit, and he wanted to prove his repentance by a life of service for Christ. The prospect of it all gave him great joy, and after he had taken food to strengthen his weak body, he arose with a zeal for Christ which far exceeded his devotion to the temple.

Ananias went back to tell the Christians of Damascus that the danger was over. Not only was Saul giving up his persecution of them, he had been baptized and had called upon the name of Christ and was now a Nazarene. With great joy they received him and welcomed him as a brother.

Day by day the Damascus believers strengthened Saul in the warmth of their fellowship and talked with him concerning Jesus. Saul listened as he never had before. They told of their Saviour and of His life and work. They were surprised to see how well he knew the Scriptures and how quick he was now to discover that they pointed to Jesus. They were amazed at his ability as a scholar. He seemed to see strong arguments for Christ that had escaped them in their study of the Word of God. Their hearts glowed with joy to realize that he would become a teacher.

During the short time that Saul remained in Damascus—

a period of only a few days—he increased in spiritual strength and longed to be used by God in witnessing about the great experience he had on the Damascus road. Together with Ananias and other Nazarenes he visited the synagogue and preached Christ. He was skilled in all the arguments of the Pharisees, and being able in speech, he made a great impression on the people. Although he could not say much about the teachings of Jesus, he could appeal to the Jewish law and to the prophets and to the Psalms, for he was at home in that realm.

The first day he appeared in the crowded synagogue was a great day for the Nazarenes. Here was a young man, fearless and strong, who had the added dignity of being educated in the school of Gamaliel. Most of the Jews knew of his hatred for Christ, and some who were suspicious of the Nazarenes, felt that Saul's mission to Damascus was a good thing.

Saul told the story of his coming to Damascus and of what had happened to him on the road: how he had met Jesus of Nazareth and had seen with his own eyes the One he had been fighting and how his whole life had then been changed. He now believed that Jesus was the Christ, and with a rabbi's skill he repeated passage after passage to prove that this was so. As he ended his first speech, he confessed publicly his sin in persecuting the followers of Jesus and told of the new life that was in him through the indwelling Holy Spirit.

The people of the synagogue could not believe what they had heard.

> Is not this the man who in Jerusalem destroyed them which called on the name of Jesus, and didn't we hear that he came to Damascus with intention to do the same thing? Is he not going to take the Nazarenes bound before the high priest? (Ac 9:21).

And when they heard that he had broken publicly with his old religion and had taken up this new one, they were indignant. His first address as a Nazarene was answered by the

rabbis of the synagogue, who branded him a false teacher—
a traitor to his nation. They denied his use of the Scriptures
and disputed vigorously over their right meaning. But they
could not stand against the arguments which Saul presented
and against his experience on the Damascus road. When the
congregation went home that day, they were moved by the
story they had heard. Some believed, but most thought he
deserved to be put out of the synagogue and publicly scourged.

The determined, bigoted, hard enemy of Christ, in a remarkably brief period of time, had changed into an unshak-
able believer, just as determined to devote his whole life to
the service of the Saviour. As he fell before the blinding light
of the glory of the Lord, he became Christ's servant forever.
He had seen the risen Lord. He was absolutely certain of
that—so certain that he built all his hopes for eternity on it
and so certain that he preached with the authority of the other
disciples, telling everyone that he had seen the Lord (1 Co
9:1).

7

Saul's Gospel

SAUL'S PREPARATION FOR GOD'S WORK

WHEN A MAN is as suddenly converted and turned to Jesus Christ as Saul was, he is usually driven by a strong desire to tell about it immediately. Often those who hear the story are thrilled and impressed with the reality of a great experience. A soul is seeing for the first time the light of the unseen world, and the telling of it warms our hearts. But coming out of so rigid a background of Phariseeism, Saul had received quite a shock. His thinking was changed so suddenly that he needed time for rest and reflection. He wanted to think over the past, look logically and quietly at the future, and prepare himself for the great work to which God had called him. Had not the Lord said that he should bear the name of Christ before the Gentiles, before kings, and before the children of Israel?

Saul was a deep thinker. He did not make any moves without reasoning them through and knowing the consequences. It was not enough for him merely to experience anything; he had to know the reason why. Some people have the kind of mind that analyzes everything, and some are never concerned with those things. Saul had an analytic mind, so he needed time to fit all the new facts that had dawned upon him into the structure of his life.

Bidding farewell to the Christians of Damascus he disappeared into Arabia to be alone and to get his bearings in the new life.

In the letter which Saul wrote to the Galatians he told them that after his conversion he did not go to the apostles in Jerusalem or to any others to learn the gospel which he later preached. The gospel was revealed to him by God. Over and over he used to say, "I have received of the Lord that which I also delivered unto you" (1 Co 11:23).

IN ARABIA

Out in the desert, shut off from the noise and confusion of life, with the burning rocks and sands by day and the silent stars by night, Saul unwound the false bindings of a lifetime and freed himself from the prison of Jewish law and tradition. In the quiet of Arabia he walked with God, God revealed Himself to Saul, and the great truths which were the anchors of his preaching for the rest of his life dawned upon him in those solitary days. This is where he restudied the Scriptures and meditated upon the great doctrines which he would soon be able to teach in all the churches in the years to come. This is where he learned the blessedness of communion with God, and this is where he became sensitive to the will of the Lord.

Moses, the great leader of Israel, had wandered into a wilderness and had met God there. Elijah, in great despair, had sought the quietness of a desert to escape from his trouble. In a desert, manna fell to feed God's people so many years ago. What place could be better suited to Saul for another meeting with the Lord? Where could he be fed on the bread from heaven more appropriately than here?

The time spent in Arabia may have been a year or more. It is impossible to know the details of those hallowed days, but at last he emerged from the wilderness with great conviction, able to give a reason for the faith that was in him. He knew that as soon as he opened his lips in the synagogue, he would be bitterly opposed by the Pharisees, and he would be called a hypocrite and a traitor. Against all this he would have to defend himself and Jesus, the Saviour, with all his skill and might.

For the defense of the faith it was necessary that he have very clear ideas about the great salvation which Christ provided. To tell of an experience is a simple thing, but to be drawn into arguments with philosophers and champions of other religions requires very definite knowledge and some well-thought-out views which are not vague and unreasonable, but scientific and practical. One must know clearly more than the fact that Jesus died as the Scriptures predicted; he must know why it was necessary, what it accomplished, and why God demanded it.

Paul began to think of the purpose of life and its greatest happiness, and he concluded that what he learned as a child in the rabbi's school was a mighty truth: man's supreme purpose is to have the favor of God upon his life. The only way to have this favor is to have God's righteousness. God is at peace only with those who are righteous.

UNDERSTANDING THE GIFT OF GOD'S RIGHTEOUSNESS

The history of man from the beginning is the story of a departure from righteousness and a deliberate turning away from God. There are some who think they are righteous; these point the finger at all others and sit in judgment upon them, but their own hearts are not right with God. Others, like Saul's own Jewish people, are depending on their keeping the law to win them favor with God. That is how Saul had lived until he met Jesus. But Saul could see now the emptiness of this, and the fact that both Jew and Gentile are in the same sinful condition and stand in the same need.

In the great search for righteousness, the Gentiles failed. It was not because God didn't reveal Himself to them, for God gave even the heathen enough knowledge of Him to teach them that He required righteousness in them. But the Gentiles would not follow this light; they tried to extinguish it. They had come short of the favor of God and deserved His wrath. The Jews felt that they enjoyed great advantages over the rest of the world. They possessed the law and the prophets, but they did not benefit by them. It is the doing of the right, not the mere knowing of it, that counts. Saul had believed nearly all his life that the keeping of the law was the way to heaven, but not even he was satisfied with the way he kept it. Therefore it worried him that his sin against the law was worse in God's sight than that of the Gentiles who knew no law. He concluded, then, that Jews and Gentiles have both failed in the search for righteousness and that both have exposed themselves to the anger of God.

Saul argued that both Jews and Gentiles find it impossible to be good because they both inherited the sinful nature of Adam, and that nature makes a person too weak to be righteous. The law, with its clear description of sin, would have been a wonderful guide for a sound nature, but in a diseased nature the very command not to do a thing makes us feel that we want to do it. God gave the law for the very purpose of teaching man that he falls short of the divine standard of righteousness.

All these thoughts were forming in the mind of Saul as the Lord gradually gave him the message which he would later teach in all the churches.

But the greatest day for Saul was the day when he saw that God was offering him a plan of salvation that did not depend on keeping a law and showing him that he could never be righteous by his own efforts.

When man's attempts to be righteous had failed, God brought forth His plan. The salvation which Jesus brought to man was the gift of God's righteousness. When man has God's righteousness, all is well, and heaven's gate is open. Saul saw clearly that the way to receive God's righteousness is by faith alone—faith in Jesus Christ, the only righteous One who ever lived.

The righteousness of God is a free gift. A man receives it by acknowledging his need and accepting it from God. And when, in faith, he sees Christ dying upon the cross as his substitute and then accepts Him into his heart as Saviour and Master, he has peace with God and has reached his highest joy.

There were a hundred other thoughts that raced through Saul's mind as he thought of the righteousness of God, but they all required time to work out.

As the days went by, he began to grasp the complete picture of God's great salvation. This great revelation which God gave him in Arabia he referred to over and over as "my gospel." It was not arrived at by studying or reading. Saul said that he received it neither of man nor of any school, but that by a revelation from Jesus Christ he had come to a knowledge of these facts.

THE REAL MEANING OF CHURCH MEMBERSHIP

Out in the wilderness there appeared to Saul more vividly than to any other man the full picture of the church which was built on Jesus, the Son of God. He saw the real meaning of church membership. It was not just the joining of an organization, it was being baptized by the Holy Spirit into a great fellowship. Saul was the first one of all the disciples to realize that the church was not a small sect out of Israel, but a great, worldwide brotherhood extending far beyond the Jews to all nations and races of the world. Later on, he fought many a battle with narrow believers who were not willing to admit Gentiles into the church at all.

Saul thought of the church as a building with all the stones well fitted together and with Christ the chief cornerstone. Then he thought of it as a body with its many parts—arms, legs, toes, fingers, eyes and ears. These various parts were the believers, each related to the other and important to the other, and Jesus was the head of the body. This figure of speech helped him to see its unity and dependence on the Head.

Jesus had called upon Saul to give up rules and traditions, abandon all the past life in which he gloried, and follow Him. Others had done this before him and had faced opposition. The future would not be easier for Saul. He thought of Stephen and how mighty he had been in the gospel. If only

Saul's eyes had been opened to the truth earlier, what a host of believers might have been spared! But he would take Stephen's place and perhaps do a greater work for Christ than Stephen could have. Over and over he determined to be true to the heavenly vision and spend the rest of his life in preaching the liberty of the gospel to Jews and Gentiles alike.

THE WORLD, A MISSION FIELD

Saul began to think of the great world around him. He had seen only a small part, but the empire of Rome stretched beyond the Cilician Gates to the west and took in millions of people. What a world of darkness it was! Some worshiped strange gods of their own making. Their cities were full of idols, statues, altars, and temples, and the people were groping for something that was real. But their hearts were empty and their eyes were turned upon great blocks of stone. Even the hearts of the Jews were empty, despite their system of worship. If only they would see that Jesus Christ fulfilled every sacrifice that had ever been offered in their temple, for He was the Lamb of God from the foundation of the world! If only the Gentiles could see the emptiness of their temples, and the fact that only Christ could satisfy them! He thought it would be easier to convince the Gentiles than it would the Jews, and therefore he was happy that he had been chosen by the Lord to carry this great gospel of God's saving grace to the Gentiles.

Looking back at his former days, Saul thought he must have been mad and blind to imagine that the hatred and cruelty of his persecution would ever convert these Christian men to Judaism. God was dealing with him out in Arabia. He turned from his vicious methods and learned something of the great spirit that was in Stephen when he prayed for his enemies.

How long Saul stayed in Arabia is not known from the record we have of him. It may have been a whole year, however, or even a little longer. We do know that the best part of three years elapsed between his conversion on the Damascus road and his coming back to Jerusalem. After that time he was far from knowing all about Jesus, but at least he had come to the place where his thinking was settled and strong and where he was ready to preach the gospel with all that was in him, for he felt a sense of indebtedness to the Jew and to the Greek.

Not only did he want to preach to these people, he was better prepared to contend earnestly for the faith. In every synagogue the Pharisees would oppose him, sneer at his changed way of life, and call him a liar, and he would have to defend the gospel with all his might. He used to call it "my gospel," not because it was different from that of Peter or any of the other disciples but because God had given it to him directly.

Later he would learn from Peter and the early disciples many of the sayings of the Lord and many of His teachings, but he knew enough now to begin to preach Jesus as the Christ of the Scriptures, through whom a righteousness could be reached which was impossible by keeping the law. With the Lord's words in his heart, he felt he was able to go forth to establish churches and to strengthen them. He had killed others in his ignorance of Christ. Now with Christ in his heart he would offer his life in exchange. He would gladly face death itself without fear, for had not Jesus risen from the grave and conquered death? His mind was calmed, deepened, strengthened, and inspired of God as he left the desert of Arabia and returned to Damascus.

THE RETURN TO DAMASCUS

Among the believers in Damascus, Saul was warmly welcomed. They longed for his return, for not even Ananias was as able when it came to facing a crowd of Jews. They remembered how Saul silenced the rabbis before he left for Arabia, and they were glad to see him back to champion their cause among enemies. With increased power, Saul again took up his work in the synagogues. The Jewish opposition to him deepened into hatred, but his determination to preach Jesus Christ and His gospel did not slacken.

For a year or more he lived in Damascus with the Nazarenes, and each day men and women were coming to know Christ through his preaching. The synagogue council forbade him and did their best to turn Jewish ears away when he preached. But his message was from their own Scriptures and came with the authority of a rabbi and the irresistible power of a man with a keen mind empowered by Christ. Even the rabbis were afraid to bar from the synagogue any man who had so great a knowledge of the Torah.

Each discussion with the rabbis raised their anger and impelled them to summon Saul before the council of the synagogue. Time and time again he bettered them in his argument, but in their rage they thought to make him a public example and ordered him scourged before the synagogue door with thirty-nine stripes. As the lash fell on his bared back and the thongs cut into his quivering flesh, Saul experienced a strange sense of joy that he was counted worthy to suffer for Christ's sake. This was only what he had done to countless other Christians.

Throughout Saul's life his body was marked by these whips, and he wore the scars with a sense of pride, for they admitted him to a deeper fellowship with Christ and with his followers who were called upon to suffer for the faith.

In the end he was expelled from the synagogue, but somehow he managed to meet with Jews of Damascus and win them to Jesus. The rabbis were learning what Saul had learned so recently—that all their efforts to halt Christianity seemed to be spreading it. They ordered him to leave the city, but he turned his back on all their conmmands and preached Christ more vigorously than before. Then the council met in a secret session to decide what they would do. There was only one way to end this threat to the peace of their synagogue—seize him and kill him.

But even in their own group there were those who were inclined toward the Nazarenes, and the decision of the council was soon known to Saul. He hid himself in the city so that, search as they would, they did not find him. Every synagogue was watched, but he did not come. At length his enemies discovered that he knew of their plot, and since he was keeping out of sight, they argued that he would slip out of the city under the guise of a merchant or a traveler. They went to the governor of the city and made a formal charge against Saul saying that he was a disturber of the peace in their district and a teacher of such strange doctrines that the Jewish people were in an uproar. Promptly the governor sent out orders for Saul's arrest, and full descriptions of him were given to the soldiers who watched the gates. They searched every face as the caravans left Damascus, but Saul the criminal they could not find. As there were only four gates, the rabbis felt they would soon have him. The walls of the city were high and surrounded by a deep moat, and no man could escape by scaling the wall.

As the days passed, the Jews did not relax their vigil. This time they meant to put an end to the annoying sect by ridding themselves of its new leader. Saul's friends realized that if he were to be saved, he must get out of the city. The old walls were so broad in places that houses were built upon them, some with overhanging windows. One of these houses was the home of a Nazarene. As night came over the city, Saul was brought to this house. Several of his friends fastened a rope to a large basket, and with Saul in the basket, they lowered it over the wall until it came to rest below. Quickly its passenger swam across the moat and disappeared in the darkness as the basket was drawn back up to the window.

SAUL'S TRIP TO JERUSALEM

Saul was free. It was not until many days had passed that

the synagogue authorities got word that Saul was in Jerusalem troubling the people there as he had done in Damascus. It was exactly three years since he had left Jerusalem with an armed guard and a warrant for the arrest of the Nazarenes. Then he represented the temple and its priests and the Pharisees in all their opposition to Christ; now he represented Christ Jesus and was coming back to witness for the Saviour. He had found Christ, the way, the truth and the life, and he was satisfied.

His Friendship with Barnabas and Peter

But Saul's stay at Jerusalem was short. After two weeks the vigor of his message so angered the Jews that they sought to kill him. But when Saul entered the holy city, it was not as he had known it, friendly and magnificent. It was cold and unfriendly. He could not go to the school of Gamaliel or to the palace of the high priest. He was known and hated now in the synagogues; and the only thing for him to do was to seek out some of the Nazarenes. He knew that many of the disciples met at the house of Mary, the mother of Mark, so there he went, hoping to learn of the Christians in Jerusalem. At Mary's house he was recognized immediately and welcomed by Barnabas, Mark's uncle.

Barnabas was a foreign Jew who came from the island of Cyprus. He was a man of wealth, having large properties in Cyprus, and he also had been a temple Levite before he had become a Christian. Being well informed, he became a leader among the believers in the Jerusalem Church.

Barnabas listened to Saul's story and his heart was moved. He grasped him by the hand and welcomed him as a brother. But it was different with the other Nazarenes. They suspected some kind of treachery and could not believe Saul's story of his conversion on the Damascus road. What if this were another trick? This was the man who had persecuted the church so bitterly that believers were driven from the city and families broken. It was a cold reception for Saul, but he accepted it graciously and did not blame them in the least. This was what he deserved, and this was what he had to bear with God's help.

At least Barnabas was his friend. The respected leader took him to the apostles who, when they heard the story, believed and welcomed him as one of them. When Peter learned that Saul had come to Jerusalem especially to see him, he welcomed him into his home. For two weeks the young man who had sat at the feet of Gamaliel sat at the feet of a fisherman who told him more of the Words of Life in that short time than Gamaliel was able to do in many years.

Every time Peter told of Jesus, his eyes glowed with the rapture of it all. He told, without ever tiring, of the Christ who was without sin and who spoke as never man spoke before. The details of His life were fresh and vivid with Peter. It had been six years now since they had crucified Him on that hill called Calvary. Peter told of the great miracles and the gracious teachings. He spoke of the kingdom of God and how men everywhere failed to stand before the wisdom of the King. He told of how He was rejected and betrayed and crucified of men, and how the greatest miracle of all took place three days after the crucifixion—the miracle of Christ's resurrection. And Peter told with glowing words of the many times when the Saviour appeared to the disciples, and especially of the time when He called for Peter alone and spoke with him after His resurrection.

Each day Peter drew such a picture of the living Christ, as he had seen Him journeying through Galilee and teaching the multitudes, that Saul felt as sure of his knowledge of Jesus as if he had seen Him in those days, and his spirit was strong in him as he resolved to use all this knowledge in the preaching of the truth.

SAUL'S PERSECUTION IN JERUSALEM

While he stayed for two weeks in Jerusalem, he spent much time in proclaiming the gospel. Like Stephen, he went to the foreign synagogues and declared boldly to all that he was now a Nazarene. Many remembered him as the persecutor of that sect and were much amazed to hear him calling upon all the Jews to repent of their sin of rejecting Jesus and open their hearts to receive Him as their Lord. He told them that eternal life was not gained by keeping the law but by trusting in God's Son, who in grace bestowed the gift of salvation. Men of great zeal and rabbinical skill opposed him, and the debate grew hotter and hotter. Here in Jerusalem the rabbis, remembering Saul's former arguments against the Nazarenes, flung them back in his face. He himself had said that Jesus was an impostor deserving of death.

The battle was brief. He now had so many enemies that a movement sprang up to rid the Jewish religion of this curse. Why not do with him what they had done with Stephen? He deserved to die; he was an impostor, a blasphemer and a traitor! He was worse! He had been trained as a rabbi, yet he had come to hate the system that had nourished him.

THE CALL TO PREACH TO THE GENTILES

One day while Saul visited the temple, he knelt to pray, and as he besought the Lord for guidance and wisdom for his future and for an open door to preach to these Jews here at the center of their worship, he was granted an experience that determined the way he should take. He saw a vision of the Lord, who said to him, "Make haste, and get thee quickly out of Jerusalem: for they will not receive thy testimony concerning me." Immediately Saul replied, "Lord, they know that I imprisoned and beat in every synagogue them that believed on thee: and when the blood of thy martyr Stephen was shed, I also was standing by, and consented unto his death, and kept the raiment of them that slew him" (Ac 22:18-19).

Saul was conscious of his debt, and over and over again, in agony of soul, he confessed to the Lord his sin in persecuting the saints of the church. But Jesus spoke again in a vision, saying "Depart: for I will send thee far hence unto the Gentiles" (v. 21).

Just as suddenly as it had come, the vision of the Lord faded, and Saul came to himself again. His mind was filled with the mystery of it all, but of one thing he was certain, God was leading him on and had a great purpose for him— not among his own people but out in the lands beyond. He was more and more resigned to leave Jerusalem. He thought of the vast countries that lay west of the Cilician gates, and the last vestiges of reluctance vanished.

Hearing that plans were afoot to silence Saul, some of his friends warned him, and in a little group, disguised for their safety, they conducted him safely through the city walls and out on the road to Tarsus. The city of his dreams had proved to be a disappointment. Many of his old friends now hated him and would have stoned him in the name of the law of Moses. Even the Nazarenes, his new friends, were reserved in their approval, but Barnabas and Peter were open in their acceptance of him. They saw in Saul of Tarsus a strong champion of the faith and one who in coming years would be used of God in the defense of the gospel.

And so he left Jerusalem just fifteen days after he had entered it and began the familiar journey back home. He took the coastal road to the city of Caesarea, the Roman capital of Palestine.

SAUL'S RETURN TO TARSUS

In Caesarea Saul went to the docks and searched among the many ships for one that would take him home to Tarsus.

How different things were from the days when he was powerful and armed with the authority of the high priest! Now he was a fugitive, driven from city to city, hunted and hated, disguised, and with few friends; but in his heart was a lightness and a joy which he had never known before. It was the joy of Christ.

8

The First Missionary Journey

THE FURY OF THE SYNAGOGUE

BACK HOME there were those who wecomed Saul with open arms, but there were some who had heard the story of his change of heart and felt that his coming meant strife in the synagogue. They had listened to reports from friends who had visited Jerusalem and were disappointed to hear that Saul, from their own synagogue, was now a believer in the impostor, Jesus. Now that he was home, they heard it from his own lips, and they were angry. How could so learned a Pharisee, soon to become a rabbi, raised with such care by true Hebrew parents, fall into this place of scorn?

Just how his mother and father took the severe blow is not known. Perhaps they were prepared for it. Perhaps they felt a sense of shame among their neighbors that their son should turn out to be one who offered strange fire on the altar.

When he told of his experience in Damascus and his meeting and talking with the risen Christ, there were cries of wonder and annoyance. Many were the voices raised to oppose him, but none could silence his lips. Christ Jesus was so real to him that it did not matter if the world opposed his message, he would continue to preach it faithfully. In Tarsus he was beyond the shadow of the temple and the Sanhedrin, and since he was a remarkably able public speaker, crowds often gathered to hear his sermons. Some rejoiced in every word and openly became Nazarenes, declaring that the Jewish religion without Jesus was empty and barren.

The older rabbis, jealous of his ability, admonished him to cease speaking in a way that was contrary to the rules of the rabbis. When he refused, they determined to expel him from the synagogue. Perhaps in Tarsus, before the door of his own synagogue, he suffered one of the public whippings which he mentioned in a letter to the church of Corinth (2 Co 11:24). But in this he gloried, and the gospel had power to open blind eyes and bring hope into hearts that were hopeless. He was confident that nothing could stop him, for had not the Lord spoken to him, declaring that he was to become an apostle to the Gentiles?

OBSCURITY AND TENTMAKING

In spite of his confidence, so far as the divine call was concerned he entered into a period of inactivity. For seven or eight years scarcely anything was heard of him. These were years of waiting and of discipline in patience. Perhaps Saul needed those years to strengthen him and to show him the secret of patient waiting upon the Lord. He was a man with a commission but no opportunity to fulfill it. Perhaps in the plan of God, to whom time is nothing, a few years had to elapse until the bitterness of the rabbis subsided. Perhaps Saul was kept in Tarsus, facing opposition and sustaining himself in the tentmaker's shop, until God had completed a great step in the history of the church. During these years at Tarsus, Peter and the other apostles were learning that the church was not exclusively for the Jews but for the Gentiles as well. The Lord had given Simon Peter a vision of clean and unclean beasts and had prepared him for Cornelius, the Gentile of Caesarea, who was admitted to the church without first going through the rites of the Jewish synagogue. It was a far-reaching step, and it revolutionized the whole outlook of Christianity. Perhaps at the time Saul chafed and murmured at the delay in his ministry, but in later years he learned that God's delays were always for a purpose, and nothing could go wrong with His timetable.

But in the meanwhile, Saul lived in obscurity. He preached the new gospel not only in Tarsus but also out in the country-

side where he had gone as a boy to buy the long hair of the
Cilician goat. Wherever he journeyed, along the roads and
camel paths, through the woods and valleys, he sought out his
countrymen. He told them about Jesus who came as their
Messiah and called upon them to find their righteousness in
Him rather than in blind obedience to the law and the traditions.

Scattering of the Jerusalem Church

The fortunes of the Jerusalem church were not too smooth,
and at intervals, as the persecution increased, the Nazarenes
went into hiding. Some even forsook Palestine altogether,
and sought their abode in some foreign land. A great number
went to Damascus. Others continued until they reached
Antioch, the beautiful Roman capital of Syria, three hundred
miles north of Jerusalem. There in Antioch many foreign
Jews had become followers of Jesus. They were more liberal-
minded, and the spell of the high priest was not upon them.
Some had been born in Greece, some on the African coast in
Cyrene, and some in Cyprus. As the gospel was preached to
them, great numbers believed, and the Spirit of God so moved
in the preaching that many of the Antioch Gentiles were converted. Of course this gave offence to the strict Nazarenes,
who were very sure that Jesus Christ belonged only to the
Jews and that the only way to become a Nazarene was to be
first a proselyte to the synagogue.

Barnabas in Antioch

The Antioch movement grew to such proportions that a
word of alarm was sent back to the mother church. In Jerusalem, after deliberation, the broad-minded Barnabas, brother
of Mary, at whose house a church assembled, was sent to
investigate the genuineness of the so-called conversion of the
Gentiles.

Barnabas had heard the arguments of the narrowminded
Jews and also of the Grecian Jews from his own home in

Cyprus, and he had seen crowds of Gentiles who had given up their idols and were now very happy Christians. He could not deny the reality of their conviction. They, too, had suffered for Christ, for some of them were outcasts from their own people, even though they were now rejoicing in their new-found salvation.

Barnabas was much impressed with what he saw and rose up to speak. There was no criticism of the Gentiles in his sermon. He did not command that they be put from the church until they were first instructed in Judaism. He welcomed them gladly and marveled at the grace of God which was extended beyond the nation of Israel. His sermon was a joyous exhortation to them that they hold fast to Jesus even in the face of any persecution and never waver from the faith. His words delighted them, and there was a great unity of spirit in the church. The Lord added to the number daily.

THE CALL TO ANTIOCH

When Barnabas saw that a great work could be done in Antioch, he thought of only one man—a man he had met in Jerusalem, who had been brought up in a Gentile city, and who had many of the qualities needed for great leadership.

Besides all this, the Lord had laid on his heart a ministry to the Gentiles. It never occurred to Barnabas to go back to Jerusalem for any of the disciples, but the image of Saul of Tarsus immediately flashed into his mind, the man who so many years earlier had been on fire with the burden to preach Christ to foreigners. If only Saul were in Antioch with his burning zeal and his forceful words!

With no further delay Barnabas traveled the sixteen miles to the port of Seleucia. There he found a boat, and after a long day on the sea, he came to the Cydnus River, where the sail came rattling down, and the long oars brought them up the stream to the wharf at Tarsus.

Would he find Saul easily or not? Presently Barnabas did find him and they embraced in silence. They were friends who had not seen each other for eight years. Barnabas told the story and Saul listened to every word. Surely there was a great work to do in Antioch, and surely this was God's door opening! He agreed to leave at once.

As they boarded the boat together, Saul learned of the dispute in Jerusalem over Cornelius and the coming of the Gentiles into the Church. He heard that Peter's mind had been changed on that subject, but that James, the Lord's brother, was very much of a traditionalist and could not accept Gentiles or acknowledge their salvation.

SAUL IN ANTIOCH

Antioch in Syria was the third-largest city in the Roman Empire. It had a population of half a million people. The walls of Antioch were the most remarkable in the world. So strong were they that their ruins can still be seen. They were wide and fortified by many towers for additional protection. Mt. Silpius rose in the center of the city. It was crowned with a barracks which looked like a very strong castle. This housed the Roman soldiers who kept the city.

Many kings had spent large sums in making the city beautiful. Here were gardens, lily ponds, and magnificent palaces. Herod, the Jew, adorned one of its streets for two miles with marble pillars. Outside the city stood a great amphitheatre where the races were run and the games played.

The people of Antioch worshiped the stars and many idols, in whose honor they built large temples. Behind the city, the great sculptor, Licos, had fashioned a huge head with a crown upon it. He had carved it from a bold crag of rock that jutted from the ground. That figure became a symbol of Antioch, just as the Statue of Liberty has become a symbol of America. It can be seen on many of the coins of Antioch to this day.

The people were pleasure-mad and had a reputation in the empire for idleness and sin. Through the Daphne gate, a road stretched out for five miles into the country to the grove of Daphne and the temple of Apollo. It was lined with the homes and gardens of the rich. The grove, which was one of the most charming places in all the land, was a center of such wild, drunken and sinful feasts that even the citizens of Rome called them shameful. Visitors came to Antioch from everywhere in the world: black Africans and fair-skinned Greeks, Romans, Persians, coppery Egyptians, and Jews. People filled the streets, and in a spirit of perpetual holiday, they looked upon the grove of Daphne as the brightest and liveliest place in the world.

This was the city to which Saul was brought. The gospel of Jesus Christ had penetrated some hearts, and the power of the Holy Spirit was working in Jews and Gentiles alike. All their frivolity and all the grandeur of their lives in Antioch left them still hungry and needy. In Antioch, Barnabas led his friend to the place where the church met. It was a strong church, almost as strong as the one in Jerusalem. Saul met many of the leaders, among whom was Manaen, a relative of the Jewish prince, Herod Antipas. Evidently Manaen was a man of high position in Antioch and a firm believer. Then there were Simeon the black, from Africa, and Lucius, from Cyrene, and so many foreigners from strange places that Saul rejoiced to be among them. In Jerusalem and in every other place, the followers of Jesus were called Nazarenes, but here in Antioch the citizens had another name for them. They sneered as they labeled them "Christians." The name which we are proud of now was once a name spoken in contempt.

Saul, like any rabbi in Israel, established himself at his trade, for tentmakers could always find employment. In this way he earned his living, but his chief reason for being in Antioch was to help the Christian church and to strengthen its faith. Saul visited the synagogues and the bazaars daily and often stood by the roadside as the crowd thronged the race courses. He called upon men to repent and turn to God. He told them that Jesus of Nazareth, who had been crucified in Jerusalem some ten years before and had arisen from the grave, was the Christ of the Jewish Scriptures and the Son of God, who came into the world to save men from sin.

Saul called them from the emptiness of their idol worship to the fullness of the Christian life. Pleasure-seekers, merchants, tourists, women of society and of sin, and sober citizens—none could help but listen to the eloquence of Barnabas and the inescapable wisdom of Saul. Nor could they fail to admire their courage and zeal even in the face of the sneering, pleasure-mad crowd. At least there was no high priest here to raise his hand against them. The ministry of the gospel was unhampered, and the church grew rapidly, for each Christian was a tireless witness for Jesus.

For a year Saul labored for the gospel in this important city, speaking with great earnestness, and the Lord made his preaching and teaching fruitful. It was not long before Antioch became a stronger Christian center than Jerusalem, because the church in Antioch had peace.

OTHER PERSECUTIONS OF CHRISTIANS

In Judea it was not so. When Emperor Caligula was killed, Herod Agrippa happened to be in Rome, and because he aided the new emperor, Claudius, in his rise to power, he was given great honor and granted the authority to rule over the lands of his grandfather, Herod the Great. There was great rejoicing in Jerusalem when Agrippa came to rule, for it was known that he had been a Pharisee and understood the strictness of the Jewish religion. His first act as king was to put Annas the Sadducee from the high priesthood, and to make Gamaliel president of the Sanhedrin. This all looked hopeful to the Pharisees, and they were glad that a champion had arisen for them. However, when Agrippa went down to Caesarea to the palace, he put off the cloak of a Pharisee and openly lived the life of a wild and reckless Roman.

Herod Agrippa wanted to be on good terms with the rabbis, and knew he would please them if he persecuted the Christians. He therefore ordered the arrest of James, the "son of thunder," the brother of John, and beheaded him quickly. James was the first of Jesus' disciples to suffer death. The Sanhedrin was greatly pleased, and Herod's popularity as king in Israel grew. But he did not stop with James. He had Peter arrested and put in prison, intending after the Passover festival to have him slain as well. But an angel of God miraculousy opened the prison doors and set Peter free.

GIFTS TO THE JERUSALEM CHRISTIANS

While this persecution was at its height, a certain preacher named Agabus came to Antioch from Jerusalem. He stood up in the assembly, and by the Spirit of the Lord he proclaimed that God was going to bring a great dearth upon the empire. That meant hard times were ahead for everybody. When the hard times came upon Judea, the Christians at Antioch brought offerings according to their ability and determined to send them to their fellow Christians to help them in their extreme need. To carry the offering and the food, they chose Barnabas and Saul, who, after they had made preparations, said farewell to the church in Antioch and with Titus, a young convert to the church, set out for Jerusalem. Titus was gaining a rich experience with Saul, and in the years to come he would be a valued leader, entrusted with the work of founding churches throughout the island of Crete.

Boarding a ship at Seleucia, they sailed to Caesarea and quickly made the short journey inland to Jerusalem. What a touching scene it must have been as Barnabas and Saul unloaded the bales of provisions and emptied the sacks of money! All this was from Christians they had never seen before, some of whom were Gentiles!

THE GREAT CONTROVERSY

That question of Gentiles in the church was one of the things Saul wanted to settle on this trip; so, contrary to his usual habit, he did not go into the synagogues to preach. Instead he met with the leaders in an effort to have them see that Gentiles could come into the church without going through the rites and ceremonies of the synagogue.

But Saul found he still had enemies, for there were those who felt that Titus, being a Greek, was no Christian at all. In the mother church there were even some Pharisees who pretended to be followers of Jesus, but were traitors, whose presence in the church greatly hindered the growth of the gospel. They were enemy spies, and they did their utmost to turn the Nazarenes back to Judaism again.

Saul faced them, contended with them, and insisted that the grace of God extended to foreigners as well as to Jews. He was encouraged to see that Peter, John and some of the other disciples approved. He urged Peter and Barnabas to go and preach to foreigners, admitting them to the church without reference to the rites of the Jewish law.

But the question was still unsettled, for now some were teaching that the law was necessary and others, that it was not. With disturbed minds, Barnabas and Saul took leave of the church at Jerusalem and prepared for their long journey back to Antioch.

The house of Mary, the sister of Barnabas, was the place where the leading Christians met. They had enjoyed her hospitality during this visit, but they were especially attracted to her son Mark. He was just a lad, but he was an earnest follower of Jesus. As a child he had seen Jesus, and under the preaching of Peter and John at home he had developed into a zealous Nazarene. Barnabas was his uncle, and of course the older man felt that there were great possibilities in the lad. Saul was impressed with his devotion, and together they persuaded him to accompany them back to Antioch. It was his first long journey and the world was wide. The call of adventure was strong, and he went with real enthusiasm.

RETURN TO ANTIOCH

Back in Antioch the church welcomed the return of their leaders, rejoicing to hear how the Christians in Jerusalem were faring and how their gifts had encouraged and helped them in the time of distress.

Antioch was fast becoming the center of the church's activity. The hand of persecution was not as heavy in Antioch as it was under the shadow of the temple. Without the bitterness of the priests and the rulers of the synagogue, the church grew until other smaller Christian communities looked to Antioch for leadership rather than to Jerusalem.

Many of the believers in Antioch had been worshipers of idols and had come from Gentile homes. They naturally thought of their relatives scattered through the empire, and they believed that the same gospel of the Lord Jesus should be preached to them, too. Since Saul was called of the Lord to minister to the Gentiles, they felt that a missionary party should be formed and sent out to the neighboring countries to spread the good news of salvation.

THE FIRST MISSIONARY JOURNEY

After many meetings and much prayer the leaders of the church felt that it was God's will to send Barnabas and Saul on this mission. Who could be better fitted for it? Both were men of wide experience. Both were champions of the view that the Gentiles were to be partakers of the promises of God along with the Jews. Both had traveled extensively and seemed to be citizens of the world. Both were well able to represent Christ, and both had been called of God to do this great work.

At a meeting of the church, the leaders rose and, after the fashion of the priests of Israel, laid their hands in blessing upon the heads of Barnabas and Saul, solemnly charging them with the missionary task.

Before all the people, they accepted the challenge, and with their packs laden with provisions and gifts brought by members of the church, they set out on a journey that would not bring them home for more than two years. Behind them

The Life and Journeys of Paul

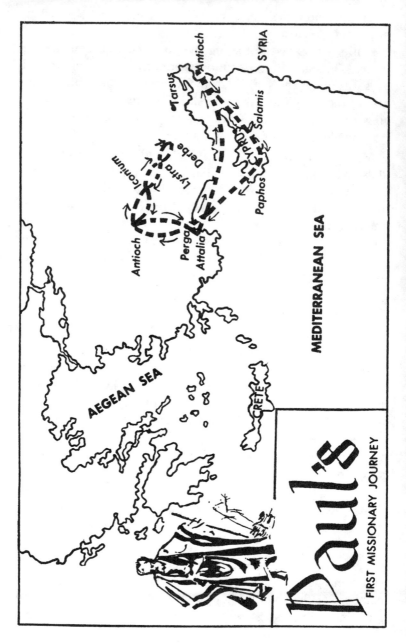

Paul's FIRST MISSIONARY JOURNEY

was a praying church which never failed to lift them up before God's throne.

For a traveling companion they took young Mark, and as springtime came to the hills of Syria the party of three set out, accompanied by many Christians who were there to see them off. Down the long paved road they walked to the port of Seleucia at the mouth of the river. The harbor was bustling with activity. There were merchant ships coming and going to ports all over the Mediterranean Sea. Many small boats carrying fruit from Cyprus some seventy miles away regularly sailed over the narrow stretch of blue water in about six hours, when the wind was fair. Cyprus was the home of Barnabas, and they could expect a welcome there. Besides, there were Christians on the island who had been driven out of Jerusalem when persecution came to the church there.

THE ISLAND OF CYPRUS

The little ship skirted the shore of the island and, sailing beneath its black rocky coast, came to the chief city, Salamis, at the mouth of the river. The harbor was a busy place. Two long stone seawalls extended like encircling arms into the beautiful blue of the water, beckoning ships from all over the world to its peaceful haven. The streets of the city were much like Tarsus. Everywhere could be seen the idol shrines and the temples erected to Grecian gods. The most popular building in the city was the temple of Venus, the goddess who represented beauty in womanhood and whose worship was carried on with shameful and sinful rites.

The priests of this temple used to tell how, long ago, the beautiful Venus rose out of the foam of the waves and, seeing the softness of the sandy beach, made her home forever on the isle of Cyprus. That, they said, was why the women of Cyprus were so tall and beautiful!

Each spring the birthday of Venus was celebrated with a gay festival. Life on the island was easy and carefree, and the chief pursuit of the people seemed to be pleasure. Certainly

Barnabas was well acquainted with these people and, after visiting his own friends and relatives, he spent much time in the synagogues. There Saul told the people of the new gospel and of the Christ who fulfilled Israel's promises and had come to be their Messiah. There were several synagogues in Salamis, and Barnabas and Saul told the story of Jesus in such a way that every Jew could hear it. No doubt Saul would tell them that he was brought up a rabbi and a Pharisee and that years were spent persecuting the Christians before he met the risen Lord on the Damascus road—the meeting had changed his life. Whether any were brought to Christ in Salamis, we do not know; but we do know that, after spending some time there, the three men journeyed on foot from one end of the island to the other.

Wherever they had an opportunity, they preached Christ. Perhaps it was at the copper mines or at the salt mines, in the orchards, in the factories, or wherever groups of people were found together. Certainly they visited the synagogues in the villages, and at last, after many weeks, they entered the valley which led down to the western sea and the city of Paphos. Here on the sun-kissed beach was the spot where Venus was said to have emerged from the waves. Her temple with its great marble pillars marked the place where she came ashore and was considered to be very holy. Paphos was the capital of Cyprus.

There was a Jewish quarter here, as in most towns, and Saul and Barnabas, accompanied by Mark, found their way there. Following his established custom, Saul preached Christ to the Jews, and some believed and some were offended.

Sergius Paulus had been sent by Rome to govern the island in Caesar's name. He was a man of education who interested himself in the science of his time. Science, however, was strangely mixed with sorcery and astrology, and often magicians were attached to the royal court. All his life, Paulus had been accustomed to the gods and goddesses of Rome, but he was still groping for something that would satisfy him.

When the governor heard that Saul and Barnabas had arrived, he sent for them, hoping to hear the new doctrine. This was Saul's great opportunity, and he seized upon it as an open door for the setting forth of the gospel. Humbly, but with his heart aglow with the excitement of it all, Saul went to the palace. Entering the throne room, he looked into the eyes of the great Roman governor and his wife. Other men of religion and of superstition were also there. They wanted to hear of the new belief. Saul, too, was a Roman citizen and a man of trained mind, so with all the skill he could command, he began to speak to this high Roman officer. He spoke of the Romans' love for truth and justice and of their open-mindedness and toleration of all religions. Then he told, one by one, the great facts of the gospel—the coming of Jesus the Christ, His rejection by His own people, His crucifixion, and finally, His resurrection. He recounted his own experience as an opponent of Christianity and how the Lord arrested him one day and changed his life completely.

Sergius Paulus was impressed. Saul's words pleased his ear. His heart was inclined toward God, and the battle for his soul was almost won. But a court magician named Bar-Jesus, also called Elymas, for he was a sorcerer, vigorously denied what Saul had been saying. Bar-Jesus, a Jew, lived in defiance of the law of Moses, for Moses condemned sorcery and banished it from among God's people. However, when this man listened to Saul speak, his Judaism revolted against the gospel, and he grew bolder and bolder in his arguments.

Saul disputed with him and, seeing that he had sold himself to Satan and was now obstructing the truth of God, he cried out against him, "O full of all subtilty and all mischief, thou child of the devil, thou enemy of all righteousness, wilt thou not cease to pervert the right ways of the Lord? And now, behold, the hand of the Lord is upon thee, and thou shalt be blind for a season" (Acts 13:10-11).

As Sergius Paulus watched, the eyes of Elymas grew misty, and the darkness of blindness fell upon him. He stretched out his hand in helplessness, groping to feel his way, but he had to be led from the room.

The Roman governor had seen the mighty hand of God in judgment upon a rebellious soul, and he was convinced. He rose from his couch, and his heart could hold out no longer against the gospel. He believed and was numbered with the Christians. It was a great step forward. God had honored Saul's ministry already and had given him the leading man of the island.

THE NEW MAN, PAUL

As Saul continued to move among the Gentiles, he was called Paul, for that was the Roman form of his name. During his earlier years, when he was in the synagogue, and even after he became a Christian, he was known by his friends as "Saul." But that was a Jewish name and somehow stood for all he had been as a Jew and a Pharisee. "Paul" stood for the new man and his new work, and increasingly as his lot was cast among the Gentile people of the provinces, he was known as Paul.

And as the years went by, to the very end of his life, he used his Roman name in signing all his letters.

ON TO PERGA

The circumstances in which Paul, Barnabas and Mark found themselves in Cyprus were pleasant; and before they realized it, several months had slipped away. But they did not plan to stay all winter. Summer had gone and the harvest had been gathered when the three said farewell to their friends and began the two-day voyage to the mainland province of Pamphylia. It was only one hundred miles west of Paul's home in Tarsus, but it was a gateway to the Gentile cities of Asia Minor.

The little boat hugged the rocky coast of Pamphylia, searching for the mouth of the Cestrus River. Eight miles up the river they came to the town of Perga. The sails were lowered, and the long oars brought the little ship at last to the wharf. There on the hillside stood the castle, the open-air amphitheater, the race course, and the temple of Diana.

The homes were like those of Tarsus—Grecian in style, and beautiful. At that time of the year many of the people of Perga went to the mountains to escape the unbearable heat.

But Perga was not a strategic city, and Paul and Barnabas decided to head for the mountain passes that led to the inland city of Antioch in Galatia. But Mark had had enough. He thought of his mother back in Jerusalem and of his comfortable home there. It had been a long time since he had seen his mother. The mountains of Pamphylia were dangerous, and the passes were infested by robber bands. Pliny had made a great speech against piracy on the high seas before the tribunal at Rome, and the result had been a campaign to drive pirate ships from the sea. These brigands took to the hills and became highway robbers, often molesting travelers who journeyed to distant cities. As Mark thought of these things and of the wild beasts in the ravines, fear took hold of him. He weighed it in his mind and decided to start for home.

Paul was very disappointed in him, and because Mark's uncle Barnabas defended him and took a more lenient view of the matter, there developed the first disagreement the two missionaries had ever had. However, it was not a serious one.

After Mark left, they pressed on through the mountain trails, following the course of the river. Sometimes the rocks were steep and the road narrow, and sometimes they journeyed through broad plains where pasture lands were burned brown by the hot sun. It took about a week to reach the cool highlands, where it was healthier to live and where, at the foot of the Sultan hills, the city of Antioch rose tier upon tier.

The Ministry in Antioch of Pisidia

Once Antioch had been a Greek city, but now a Roman garrison was there. It was the gateway to the inland of Asia

Minor. It was a place of great beauty, built largely of white marble which gleamed in the sunlight and made it look from the distance like a huge old castle.

Paul and Barnabas established themselves in Antioch, finding a place to live among their countrymen who were always hospitable to strangers of Israel. Tentmaking was Paul's trade, and he liked to earn his way in every city so that he would not be a burden to the church. Besides, his contacts with merchants and his trips to the bazaar to sell his wares gave him many an opportunity to tell of Jesus.

When the Sabbath day arrived they went together to the synagogue and were invited by the leaders there to have a part in the worship and to address the congregation. In the service there were always prayers and an opening ritual, followed by readings both from the law of Moses and from the Prophets. The meeting ended with an address or a discussion between the chief members of the synagogue over some part of the Scripture. When the leaders perceived that Paul and Barnabas were learned men and seemed to have something to say, they said, "Men and brethren, if ye have any word of exhortation for the people, say on" (Ac 13:15).

ONE OF PAUL'S GREAT SERMONS

There was a good-sized crowd present, both Jews and Gentile proselytes who had been won to Judaism. Barnabas recognized that Paul was better fitted by experience to bring the message, and he glanced at his friend with a smile that said, "This is your opportunity, make the most of it."

Paul was ready and getting to his feet, he raised his hand for the audience to be silent. There they sat as he used to sit, cross-legged upon the floor, with their prayer shawls over their shoulders. All eyes were turned toward him as he began to speak slowly:

> Here me, ye men of Israel, and ye that fear God! Our God chose our fathers and raised them up when they were slaves in Egypt, and with a high hand He brought them out of

their bondage, and for forty years He fed them in the wilderness as a nurse feedeth her child. He destroyed seven nations and gave their lands to Israel, and for about four hundred and fifty years He governed them by judges. Then they asked for a king and He gave them Saul; and when Saul was removed He anointed David, to whom God made the promise of a Saviour (13:16-22).

All this rehearsal of their history was familar to the Jews. Thus far they followed him with great interest and approval. But Paul only recounted these facts to introduce Jesus, and so he continued.

Of David's seed has God raised up, according to His promise, a Saviour, which is Jesus. This is the same one whom John the Baptist proclaimed. You remember that John said, "I am not that Christ, but there cometh one after me, the shoes of whose feet I am not worthy to make loose."

Brethren, this gospel of salvation is sent to you. Your brethren in Jerusalem and the rulers of the temple read the words of the prophets every day, but in spite of that they were so blind that they did not recognize Him. And although they found nothing deserving of death in Him, they asked Pilate to crucify Him. After His crucifixion they took Him down from the cross and buried Him (vv. 23-29).

Paul was warming to the great burden of his sermon. The words were coming faster. His voice was rising, and a spiritual fervor took hold of him as he triumphantly shouted:

But God raised Him up from the dead and He was seen for many days by his disciples, who are now witnesses of these things to the people.

We bring you good news. God has kept His promise to us and to our children in raising up Christ. We therefore want you all to know that through this man Jesus we now proclaim the forgiveness of sins. Everyone that accepts Him is made just, a fact that could never be accomplished by the law of Moses (vv. 30-33, 38-39).

Paul's sermon was done. The people sat spellbound. He was a daring preacher, and the people were overwhelmed by his zeal and courage.

There arose a murmuring in the congregation from some of the rulers, but scores of Jews and Gentile believers went out that day asking themselves the question: "Could it be true? Could it be true?"

Out on the narrow street, as Paul and Barnabas made their way homeward, they were met by little groups of men who followed them home, asking at every step to hear more about this new teaching. They stayed and listened, hungry to hear about Jesus, and that night as the sun went down and the candles were lit in the houses of Antioch, there were many Jews and Gentiles whose eyes were opened to the Saviour and whose faces were turned toward heaven.

The next day Paul's address in the synagogue was the topic of conversation in every Jewish home. And the Gentiles heard about it, too. They did not believe in a future life, but when these people heard that Paul spoke of a life after death, they pleaded with him to repeat his sermon on the next Sabbath.

As the appointed day dawned, people came along the narrow streets from every direction. The gloomy synagogue with its single lamp burning was filled as it never had been before. People stood in the doorway and some were crowded into the street. So many were there that Luke, who later wrote the story, called it a multitude and mentioned that almost the whole city came together to hear the Word of God. Paul repeated the sermon, and the people listened. But when he got to the place where he declared that Jesus was the Christ, voices were raised against him. Some of the Jews, moved with envy, openly contradicted him. It was the custom to interrupt a speaker in the synagogue. Paul was used to it and expected it. He would reply to the interruption and go on, for he gloried in this opportunity to make plain the gospel.

There were shouts from the Jewish leaders. They grew so

violent that they lashed out savagely at Paul, punctuating their words with swearing and blasphemy. The two disciples raised their voices above the hubbub and called on the audience to listen to reason. But the Jews shouted in rising anger that Paul should keep silent.

Turning to the leaders Paul said,

> It was necessary that the Word of God be spoken to you Jews first, but since you will not listen, and have by your attitude closed the gates of heaven, behold now we turn to the Gentiles as the Lord commanded us (v. 46).

PAUL'S MINISTRY BLESSED

Crowding into the door and reaching into the street was a vast throng, eager to catch some word about eternal life. As Paul and Barnabas left the synagogue amid the hissing and cursing of the Jews, a great glad shout greeted them at the door. The Gentiles, tired of the emptiness of their religion, heard for the first time of Jesus, of the promise of resurrection, and of the hope of eternal life. That was a busy day for the apostles. When evening came they were weary in body, but they rejoiced that the Lord had found so many hearts in this Gentile city.

Through the week their house and workshop became the center for a throng of inquiring people. They came from every walk of life. Many came because their hearts were empty and because they found in Christ the answer to their great need. The home of the tentmaker and his friend Barnabas became the home of a new church. As the winter days came upon them, the rich testimony to the saving grace of Jesus was given daily in the bazaars, and out into the country towns the believers went, carrying on their trade and at the same time telling the good news of how sins are forgiven in Christ. Before a year had passed, the Word of God was preached throughout all the region, and many groups of believers were gathering on the Lord's day to worship God and to lay hold on the blessings of eternal life.

With the coming of spring and the opening of the roads through the mountain passes, trade took on new life, and the bazaars were filled with strangers from distant parts. The preachers never relaxed in their efforts to win men and women to Christ. The Jews were still angry over the sermon Paul had preached to them, and they vigorously opposed the formation of these Christian churches in their city. They could not rest until they had brought an end to this preaching.

Worship in the temple of Bacchus and in the temples of the moon-god was chiefly for the benefit of the men. The women were the real sufferers when their husbands devoted themselves to the drunken orgies of Bacchus. Pagan worship, therefore, was never popular with the women. Because of this, many of them had attached themselves to the synagogue and had become proselytes to the Jewish religion, finding in it something infinitely better than they had ever known. Now the leaders of the synagogue stirred up these women, and those who were married to leading citizens in Antioch were urged to convince their husbands they should ban the preaching of the disciples and expel them from the region altogether.

PAUL AND BARNABAS FORCED TO LEAVE ANTIOCH

And so it came to pass that Paul and Barnabas were summoned before the city magistrates and commanded to leave. And the authorities meant to see that their orders were followed. They sent a guard to accompany the two men from their home to a place well outside the gates of Antioch, where they warned them to get out of the province and not come back if they valued their lives. Accompanying the guards were the leaders of the Jews, happy now that they were rid of these Christian teachers. As the Lord had told his disciples to do in any city that would not receive them, the two travelers stooped and loosened their shoes, emptying them of every grain of the dust of Pisidian Antioch as a symbol of the disdain in which they held the city which had cast them out.

Before they left, however, they gathered many of the leaders of the new church and urged them to be faithful in spite of persecution. As the towers of Antioch disappeared in the distance, a glow of joy came into the hearts of the deportees. The trip to Antioch had not been in vain. God had honored the work there, and hundreds of the believers were witnessing for Christ all over the city and out into the hamlets and towns of the whole region. Surely the Spirit of God had been leading them, and the good seed had been sown.

The road to the east was winding and steep but well paved, for it was the main trade route connecting Syria with the cities on the Aegean Sea.

THE FRUITFUL DAYS IN ICONIUM

It was over sixty miles to Iconium, and there the two disciples purposed to go. Iconium, the capital of Lycaonia, was an old walled city made prosperous by the fertility of the surrounding plains. The journey was tedious, for it led through wild country troubled by robber bands.

The walls of Iconium could be seen miles away as the caravan moved down out of the mountains. The country was rich, and the vineyards and gardens had burst into the bloom of spring.

In Iconium the particular idols the people worshiped were Adonis and Cybele. Adonis was the beautiful youth who was loved by the mythological Venus and slain by a wild boar on a hunting trip. Cybele was supposed to be the daughter of Aranus. She was represented as sitting on a throne with huge lions at her side. She had, it was believed, brought Adonis to life again.

Paul and Barnabas planned to spend some time in Iconium, so they sought out a lodging place and went about to resume their trade as they had often done before. Thousands of Jews lived at Iconium, and to find shelter in that section of the city was an easy matter. Their purpose was the same as it had been in Antioch. When the Sabbath came, they went to the synagogue and sought an opportunity to speak. No doubt the sermon was similar to the one at Antioch, for that was the great burden of Paul's heart. There was something divinely compelling about the way they spoke, and their message was so appealing that many of the Jews and Greeks believed in Jesus as time went on.

THE FOUNDING OF THE ICONIUM CHURCH

At first the rulers of the synagogue did not oppose Paul and Barnabas, as they were mildly interested in the new point of view. But when they saw how many of their congregation believed, and how many of the Gentiles were acknowledging Christ, they were angered by Paul's preaching. They forbade the disciples to appear in the synagogue, but they could not prevent them speaking on the streets. The Lord so blessed their work in Iconium that great throngs of people believed, and soon a strong church was founded.

Back in those early days of the church, when there was no New Testament record and when the story of Jesus belonged only to the few eyewitnesses, God granted to His servants the power to do many miraculous works to convince the people that the hand of the Lord was really with the church. This divine power was revealed in both Barnabas and Paul, and as a result, many more believed. The church's faith was confirmed because of what the people saw.

The greater the opposition, the more boldly the disciples spoke, and the people of the city were divided in their opinion. Some were for the new teaching and some would have none of it. Both Jew and Gentile enemies openly opposed them and several times menaced them on the streets. But the young church had grown strong in faith, and Paul knew that when he left, they would not go back to their idols again. Adonis had lost, and Christ reigned in their hearts. When word came through some of the believers that enemies planned to stone Paul and Barnabas to death, the missionaries took their leave of the Christian company and quickly left the city. They followed the paved road to Lystra and Derbe, cities of the great plain, about eighteen miles to the south.

THE MIRACLE IN LYSTRA

No sooner had they arrived in Lystra and located a lodging where they could carry on their work than opportunities to preach the gospel were presented at every street corner. In the marketplace and wherever large groups gathered, Barnabas and Paul were there, telling about Jesus the Son of God and the life that is filled with His Spirit. The contrast between this and the depraved temple orgies to which the people were accustomed was glaring indeed.

Lystra had at its center a great temple of Jupiter. Ovid, the poet, has left us a story that long ago Jupiter and Mercury came down to earth disguised as travelers. They sought lodging and food from door to door, but repeatedly they were turned away. At last they came to a humble home where an aged couple lived. Philemon and his wife, Baucis, welcomed them to their house and fed them from their scanty store. When the meal was over, the strangers revealed themselves as gods and granted the couple long life as guardians of a holy temple.

The people of Lystra listened attentively to the disciples as they preached Christ, and many were won from their idolatry and were numbered with the Christians.

One day while Paul was addressing a crowd and telling them about the true and living God, he saw in the throng a lame man. This man had been crippled from his birth and had never walked. Something in the sermon found its mark in this man's heart, and Paul could see that the Spirit of God was stirring him mightily. Suddenly Paul turned to the crippled man and with a loud voice said, "Stand upright on thy feet" (Ac 14:10).

Every eye was turned toward the unfortunate man, and in a moment he was on his feet, leaping and walking. He could not believe his own eyes. Was this a dream, and would he awake to find it was not so?

THE APOSTLES RECEIVED AS GODS

From the crowd there came a startled gasp and then a great shout. The people had seen a miracle. Greek was the language of culture there, but the people spoke in the Lycaonian dialect in their unguarded moments and sometimes in the intimacy of their homes. In their astonishment at seeing the lame man walk, they lapsed into their native dialect and shouted wildly, "The gods are come down to us in the likeness of men" (v. 11).

The news spread through the city, and thousands came to stare at the disciples. The legend of Jupiter and Mercury was being repeated before their very eyes. It was a confirmation of their religion. As the crowd gazed they called Barnabas, Jupiter, because he was so tall and manly; and they called Paul, Mercury, because he was the chief speaker.

When the priests of the temple of Jupiter in the grove beyond the city heard this thing, they brought oxen and garlands to the gates of the home where the disciples were staying. Men and women were running through the streets in excitement telling people everywhere that the gods had come down to them. A great throng gathered at the gate, led by the priests, to offer sacrifice to the newly discovered gods! The gongs were sounding, the drums were beating, and garlands of flowers were laid over the horns of the fat oxen. It was a great day in Lystra!

When it became evident to Paul and Barnabas that the people were really worshiping them, they were disturbed beyond measure. The very thought of such a thing was repugnant to them! In eastern fashion they tore their garments as a sign of great anguish, and ran among the people, shouting.

The gongs and cymbals ceased, and the throng became silent. The "gods" were speaking.

People of Lystra, Why do ye do these things? We are ordinary men like yourselves. We are not gods. We have brought you the good news of salvation. We beg of you, turn away from these useless sacrifices to the vain gods of legend, and worship the true and living God who made the earth and sky and sea and all that in them is.

God in times past left the nations to walk in their own ways, but you never have been without evidence of His constant care of you. He sends the rain. He gives the fruitful harvest. He fills your homes with food and your hearts with gladness (vv. 15-17).

Not without reason was Paul called Mercury, for Mercury was the messenger of the gods, and the people were listening to silver-tongued oratory and beauty of speech beyond anything they had ever heard before.

The crowds disbanded, mumbling in uncertainty, and the priests led the oxen back to their stalls in the temple. The excitement was soon over, but the people talked about these things for many days. Slowly the church grew as men and women came to know Jesus Christ and were persuaded of the truth of the gospel.

TIMOTHY AND HIS HOME

One of the new believers was a young man called Timothy. His mother Lois and his grandmother Eunice lived in Lystra and were hospitable to the disciples there. Paul and Barnabas spent much time at their home, and as they told the story of the Christ over and over again, young Timothy listened with misty eyes and knew somehow that he, too, must become a preacher of this gospel. The Spirit of God was speaking to him through these great disciples, and his heart was warm.

But as the months went by, it was inevitable that Jews from the synagogue at Antioch and Iconium should visit friends in Lystra or bring their wares to trade in the markets of a new city. The story of Paul and Barnabas was still vivid in their minds, and the presence of Christian churches filled with Gen-

tiles back home was still a sore spot with their rabbis. They
were annoyed that the two men continued teaching what to
them was a false religion. Very deliberately they planned to
stop it. It was not hard to stir up the Jews of Lystra against
the disciples, and with lies and outlandish reports they raised
up such a bitterness in the hearts of their countrymen that
they all determined to take the matter into their own hands
and do away with the disciples, especially the spokesman,
Paul.

The Stoning of Paul

One day as Paul stood among his Christian friends preaching the gospel, a mob of Jews, led by men from Iconium and
Antioch, joined the little group and openly disputed the truths
they were hearing. They grew loud and angry as Paul answered them with their own Scriptures until, with a shriek of
rage, they ran through the crowd to scatter it. Fists began to
fly and the shout that went up may have been, "Stone him,
stone him! He deserves to die. Any man who preaches against
the law of Moses is a traitor. Stone him!"

The stones whirled through the air from all directions. Paul
stood his ground, pleading with them in the name of the Lord
Jesus. He was cut and bleeding now, but he could still see
the mounting anger of the people. Then at last one fellow
hurled a heavier stone that struck Paul's head. Bleeding and
unconscious Paul fell to the ground. The mob gathered around
his body, turned it over with vicious kicks. Taking hold of
the outer garments, they dragged it through the streets to a
place outside the city gate, where they abandoned it in a ditch
beside the road. That was the end of Paul, they thought, and
with satisfaction they returned to their homes.

The little group of friends, overpowered by the mob, were
helpless. They followed as the body was dragged outside the
gates, and they feared the worst. The voice of the great apostle was silenced. They had seen many people dispatched like
this before, and yet they were not sure. Perhaps he still lived.

Outside the city, Barnabas gathered up the body of Paul in his strong arms and carried him to the cool shelter of a tree. Somebody brought water and dashed it in his face, washing away the blood and dirt. Their anxiety was rewarded when they saw him open his eyes as he returned to consciousness. Doubtless someone said, "Praise be to God, who hath spared His servant and delivered him from our enemies."

The hearts of the believers were cheered, and after a while Paul's friends assisted him to his feet and led him back within the gate to the home of Timothy, where the faithful Eunice and Lois bound his wounds and ministered to his every need.

Early in the morning, before the merchants filled the streets with their bundles of wares and their well-known cries, two figures passed through the south gate of the city. The shorter man of the two was limping and leaning on the arm of his tall companion. They were still on the paved road and following a well-traveled highway over hilly country. This was the way to the Cilician Gates and the country which Paul called home. The city to which they traveled, however, was Derbe, about twenty-five miles to the south. It was a customs gate where Rome collected the tax on all goods being shipped.

WINTER IN DERBE

There was no synagogue in Derbe, but there were many of Paul's countrymen, and since he spoke with the authority of a rabbi, groups of Jews heard him gladly. Winter was upon them, and the roads would soon be covered with snow. Up in the mountains the passes would be blocked for months, and no traveling would be done until the spring came and the snows had melted.

All that winter Paul and Barnabas lived quietly in Derbe. Paul made and sold his tents and used his home and the homes of many others as centers for the teaching of the new faith. Although nothing spectacular took place there, a strong church was founded, for many who listened could not resist the logic of the teaching and turned from idols to Christ.

During the long winter months the two disciples lost no opportunity to win men and women to Jesus, and the Lord gave them great success.

When the sun grew hot and the snow melted in the valleys and the breath of spring was in the air, Paul felt that the Christians of Derbe were organized into a strong church and were well able to carry on without more help from him. It had been over two years since the church back in Syria had sent the two missionaries out, and in that time seeds had been planted that would grow up into everlasting life. The way had been hard, but the Lord had been with them and had honored their work.

THE HOMEWARD JOURNEY

The journey home could have been made easily over the mountains and through the Cilician Gates to Tarsus, and then on over very familiar ground to Syria. But the furor in Lystra and Iconium and Antioch came fresh to Paul's mind. No doubt it would be much easier to go home by way of Tarsus, but what of the churches that had just been founded? How were they faring under the whip of persecution? Had they grown, or had any of the members weakened and gone back to Adonis and the empty rites of the temple? Yes, it became clearer the longer he thought about it that his duty was to visit all the new churches again and confirm the believers in their faith. They were his friends and he never ceased to pray for them, mentioning them by name. What if this decision did mean persecution? Had not the Lord brought him through safely? So Paul and Barnabas resolved to return the way they had come.

As they entered Lystra the scenes were familiar. They knew where to find the Christians now. They went to Timothy's house and were comforted to know that God's people were standing firm in spite of persecution. Paul and Barnabas now felt confident that the Christians of Lystra were strong enough to be organized. Therefore, in every church they ordained elders to have the spiritual oversight of the family of believers. Then with prayer for them all, the two disciples passed on to Iconium.

After just a few months the church in Iconium had made real progress. Its members were witnessing for Christ among their friends, and many had openly confessed Him as their Saviour. The church had grown in Iconium and it, too, was ready to be organized. This the disciples accomplished and then continued their journey home.

As they reached the gates of Antioch, out of which they had been driven some months before, they remembered how the Gentiles of that city had welcomed the gospel and received it gladly. There was a glow of joy at seeing old friends again and at learning how steadfast the Christians of Antioch had remained throughout these months.

Paul preached to them again, and before he and Barnabas left, they appointed trusted men, who had been proved through persecution, to lead the church and have the oversight.

Springtime was well advanced now, and the disciples wanted to get to the port at Perga before the heat of summer made it too oppressive. They remembered the hot days and nights when they first arrived in Perga and how welcome was the coolness of the mountains on their trip up to Antioch. Down in the plain which bordered the coast, the summer had come in all its glory, and since, on the previous visit, they had spent little time preaching in Perga, they decided to stay a while and raise up a testimony in that city. Day after day they stayed, and God used them in the founding of a church.

And as they preached, they waited for a ship that would carry them home. Ships were there from many places, but none were bound for Seleucia. So, bidding the believers farewell, they continued their journey over the plain to the sea and along the coastal road to Attalia, one of the greatest seaports in all the empire. The city of Attalia was large and important, and like every city in that part of the world, there were many Jews living there. But Paul and Barnabas were

anxious to find a ship bound for home, so they went immediately to the harbor. Their search soon ended in success, for
in this harbor there were many boats, both great and small,
and they had come from strange lands all over the world.

They paid their fare, and as the morning winds arose, the
sails were unfurled and the ship was on her way, skirting the
rocky coast to Seleucia. All that day they could see the high
mountains of Pamphylia rising above the broad coastal plain.
Up among those mountains they had spent two winters. The
work had been hard, but as the hills grew indistinct in the
distance,the two men of God remembered how the Lord had
honored His Word and how in every city there were many
who, just a year earlier, had lived in darkness but now had
turned to God from idols.

And on their knees each night, as they sailed beneath the
stars of heaven, Barnabas and Paul opened their hearts before the Lord, thanking Him upon every remembrance of the
faithful believers and commending them one by one to His
care. And thus they came to their journey's end.

9

The Great Controversy

SELEUCIA WAS A WELCOME SIGHT, not just because of its sheltering breakwater which brought rest to the quiet harbor but also because it was the harbor of Antioch and meant home to the disciples, Paul and Barnabas. They felt it was home because of the church there. It was a strong church, outnumbering now even the mother church in Jerusalem. Paul loved the Christians of Syrian Antioch and looked upon their church as a model because they had opened their hearts to the Gentiles and welcomed them along with the Jews into the kingdom of God.

The returning missionaries had scarcely made their way through the gate of the city when news of their arrival began to pass from home to home. That night a great crowd gathered in the meeting place to hear the account of the journeys of the man they had accompanied to the ship more than two years earlier. It was a thrilling night for old and young as they sat cross-legged on the floor and listened to the account of God's power in every city.

They told the whole story—first Barnabas taking the floor and then Paul—and no one wearied of the tale, but many wept for joy to know of God's ways with the Gentiles. The travelers told of the trip through Cyprus, of Sergius Paulus at Paphos, of the heat of Perga, and of the desertion of Mark, in whom they were much disappointed. They told of their first winter, spent in the other Antioch, and of how many became Christians there. The flights to Iconium and to Lystra, where Paul had been stoned and all but killed, were quickly recounted, and last of all the story of the second winter, which was spent in Derbe.

129

In every city the Jews in the synagogue had been against them and bitterly opposed the gospel, but the Gentiles in the marketplaces had heard them gladly and turned from their idols to God. So many had opened their hearts to Jesus that in every city the missionaries visited there was a little church established.

SIGNIFICANCE OF THE FIRST MISSIONARY JOURNEY

As these stories were told, a great surge of joy came into the hearts of the believers in Antioch. God had been working. Their plan to preach the gospel to the uttermost parts of the earth had met tremendous success already. Everywhere, in spite of opposition, lamps were being lit to shine out and dispel the darkness of the world. The seed had been sown and watered, not only in Jerusalem and Antioch, but also in Asia Minor and Cyprus; now it was growing up and bearing fruit. There was nothing left to do but hold a prayer meeting and get on their knees to thank God for His grace. So as the Christians met, they prayed, rejoicing that they were ambassadors in His service, winning men and women from a life of emptiness and death to a life that satisfied both here and hereafter.

For many months Paul lived in Antioch, returning to his trade of making tents while he expounded to all who listened the great truths of the gospel, especially the righteousness of God, which can be gained, not by trying to keep the law, but by receiving it as a gift of His wondrous grace. One by one, men and women came to see that all of their hopes and needs were satisfied in Jesus Christ, the Saviour.

GROWING DISSENSION WITHIN THE CHURCH

Until this time the opposition which Paul had met in preaching the gospel had come from only one source. The unbelieving Jew was so embittered at Christian teaching that he was blind with rage. There is no doubt that his disgust was augmented by the fact that Paul had once been a Pharisee and a rabbi, a friend of the synagogue, and a hater of the Nazarene sect. Every loyal Jew believed Paul was a traitor to the law of Moses and because of that had forfeited the right to any respect at all. Paul knew how they felt and sympathized with them, for had he not felt the same way before his conversion? He was ready to meet opposition and felt it a privilege to contend with all who had denied his message.

But trouble arose from another source. Within the church itself, a few narrow-minded Jewish Christians had still never opened their hearts to the Gentiles. They wanted the church to be a Jewish sect, just as Pharisaism was a sect in Israel. They were not in favor of receiving others unless they first submitted to the ceremonies of the synagogue and became proselyte Jews. Some thought that Gentile believers should become Jews and keep the Jewish laws concerning food, feasts, washings, and offerings.

Simon Peter was a friend of Paul's. Since the Lord had taught him that Gentiles were also in His plan and had led him to Cornelius, the Gentile, he was very sympathetic to Paul's point of view. Hearing about the strength of the congregation in Antioch, he determined to pay them a visit.

THE VISIT OF SIMON PETER

Paul welcomed Peter's arrival with great enthusiasm, telling over and over about the first missionary journey into Asia Minor and of the great blessings God had bestowed when he and Barnabas had preached to the Gentiles. The old fisherman's heart glowed with joy as he listened to every word. He was moved by the fellowship which he saw at Antioch. Jews and Gentiles met together around the same table, sharing their meals as if they were members of one family. This was unheard of in Jerusalem. In fact the Mosaic law forbade it, and even the believers in Christ had not forgotten this prohibition.

It was a very rich experience for the Christians of Antioch

to meet and hear Peter, the old fisherman who had known the Lord Jesus personally and who could recount the experiences during the blessed years of His ministry here on earth.

Peter was seeing and experiencing a freedom in Christ that he had never known before. In Antioch a black man and a white man sat down together. A slave and a master were one before Christ. A Jew and a Gentile, since they were both baptized by the Spirit of God into the church, were not different from one another. They were united by a bond which was stronger than anything else in the world.

THE SPREADING OF DISCORD

All this Peter saw and rejoiced in—until the day when certain self-appointed messengers arrived from Jerusalem to spread discord. They had heard all about Barnabas and Paul, and the tale of their work in the west displeased them. In fact they appointed themselves to go to Antioch and put a stop to any further efforts to bring more Gentiles into the church. Coming from the mother church at Jerusalem, they felt they were laden with authority. With boldness they warned the Gentiles that they were not Christians unless they first submitted to the commands that Moses had laid upon the Israelites.

Peter heard about it and recognized that these were Pharisees who believed in Jesus but could not give up all of Judaism. They represented many back home, and their zeal to purify the church from all Gentiles was great enough to take them on so long a journey. Peter knew better, but he decided that while they were present he would withdraw from his fellowship with Gentiles so that they could carry no stories back to Jerusalem to upset his ministry there. It was expedient at least, for some of them were influential men in the church at home, and certainly they were sincere.

THE DISTURBERS DEALT WITH BY PAUL

But neither Peter nor the visitors from Judea had any idea of the great strength of Paul's conviction. In former days Paul had been one of them, and he knew what was going on in the mind of a Pharisee. He well remembered how Christ Himself stung them to anger when He called them all hypocrites. They were the men who had tried to trap Jesus while professing to follow Him. And now Pharisees had come to Antioch professing an interest in the church, but really they were undermining it. Paul had no mercy on them. He fought them with all his might, for they were making one supreme effort to destroy the liberty which a believer enjoys through the grace of God. They were really saying that there could be no salvation without keeping the law. They were a formidable foe, for even Barnabas was so impressed with their visit that for a moment he began to doubt if he had been doing the right thing in admitting Gentiles (Gal 2:12-13).

One day at a meeting of the church, when the people were all assembled and the visitors had spoken with conviction, a gloom of uncertainty settled over the congregation.

Paul mounted the platform. He had heard and seen enough! It was time now to put these disturbers where they belonged. They had greatly upset many of the Gentile Christians by their narrow-mindedness. Either they had no understanding of the grace of God or they were enemies of the church, who creep in like wolves to scatter the flock. To Peter and the other Jews he said,

> We Jews know that a man is not justified by keeping the law, but by faith in Jesus Christ. We ourselves are justified by faith, not by obedience to commandments; and we have recognized that no one is able to achieve justification by trying to be good.
>
> Now if we grasp the real truth about justification, we will find we are as much sinners as the Gentiles. Does that mean that Christ makes us sinners? Of course not! But if I try to build up again the whole idea of justification by

keeping the law, then I really make myself a sinner. As far as the law is concerned, I am crucified with Christ and my present life is not that of the old "I" but the risen Christ within me. Consequently, I refuse to make the grace of God seem foolish by putting myself back under the law, for if righteousness were possible under the law, then Christ died for nothing (vv. 15-21).

As Paul continued his argument, Barnabas realized that he had been wrong in giving ear to these visitors from Judea, and he thought of how God had moved the hearts of Gentiles all over Asia. He was convinced that Paul was right, and he thanked God for the courage that led him to stand up and face the false teachers.

The answer was plain. The church must come to some definite decision over the question of the Gentiles. Peter felt that the controversy could not be settled in Antioch but only in Jerusalem, where so many were unwilling to see the church as anything but a Jewish sect.

THE APPEAL TO JERUSALEM

Although Paul had temporarily won his argument at the Antioch church, and all were pleased, they now realized that for the future good of the church, some definite policy must be arrived at. So in counsel the church agreed that Paul and Barnabas should be sent to Jerusalem, where they would then deliberate with the apostles and settle the great question.

It was winter, and the boats that sailed down the coast were all in port until spring. Therefore it was necessary to travel seven hundred miles overland. It meant six long weeks and possibly more, and even though the journey was not new to Paul, he thought it safer to travel in a caravan.

Provided with food, warm clothing, and money given them by the church, Paul, Barnabas, and Peter set out upon the long road that skirted the sea. The clouds were gray and heavy, but the Christians of Antioch accompanied them part of the way. Then, bidding them God-speed, these believers went back to their homes to pray that the Lord would bring their friends safely to Jerusalem and give them success in their mission.

Day after day the three rode along the paved highway. The streams were swollen with rain, but there were stone bridges to carry them across the flooded rivers. At nightfall they strove to reach the shelter of a village, where in the yard of the inn they would be able to pitch their tent and settle down to sleep.

Through the province of Phoenicia they stopped at many villages, and when they reached Tyre and Sidon, they stayed for some days, meeting with little groups of believers and confirming them in the faith. Paul rehearsed for eager ears the story of their journey to Pamphylia, Pisidia, and Lycaonia. The Christians thanked God for this evidence of His blessing, and encouraged Paul by their prayers that the Lord would prosper the group as they went on to Jerusalem to settle the Gentile question.

In Samaria there were many Christians, and in each church the disciples told the story of their work in Antioch and Asia Minor. The Christians of Samaria were glad to hear this account. They had never been bound by the rules of the Jerusalem rabbis, and when Paul told of the Gentiles coming to Christ, they rejoiced greatly and sent them on their journey with a great hope that God would honor their testimony in Jerusalem.

When Judea's hills came into sight, the three servants of the Lord were actually completing another missionary journey, for they had been strengthening and confirming the churches all along the way to the holy city. It had been just six years since Paul had visited Jerusalem, bringing gifts from the saints at Antioch. But this time he was there to defend himself and the many Gentile Christians against the attacks of the false teachers who had sought to undermine their liberty.

At the house of Mark's mother, they met many of the

leaders of the church. These men were cordial in their welcome and heard gladly the story of how God had worked through Barnabas and Paul on their great journey. Paul found that the false teachers who had troubled the believers at Antioch were not sent officially from Jerusalem; neither were they leaders of the church.

Before a great throng, Barnabas and Paul told about their travels and about God's power in saving men and women who had always worshiped idols. But others arose to speak, too, and declared that all these foreigners were not really Christians because they were not keeping the law of Moses. They were even eating meat which had not been prepared according to the law! As these men narrowed the gates of the kingdom, Paul argued that righteousness could never come to any man by obeying the law of Moses but only by faith in the Lord Jesus whose arms are opened wide to all people.

SETTLEMENT OF THE GREAT CONTROVERSY

It was not settled in a day, but after much disputing and heated argument, the apostles and the elders called for a meeting where they could consider the varying opinions and come to a decision. The meeting was attended by representatives of both parties. They felt so strongly that bitterness crept into the debate, and James, the Lord's brother, who was the recognized leader in the mother church, could keep order only with great difficulty.

Then Peter, the disciple of the Lord who had talked with Jesus about these very matters, and who had been shown the will of God in a vision repeated three times over, rose to his feet and demanded to be heard.

> Men and Brethren, you know that a good while ago God chose me from among you and that through my preaching even Gentiles hear the word of the gospel and believe. God, who knows their sincerity, bore witness to the reality of their conversion by giving them the gift of the Holy Spirit

just as He did to us Jews. God makes no difference between a Jew and a Gentile. He makes their hearts clean by faith in Jesus. Why do you dishonor God by trying to put a burden upon the necks of Gentiles when you yourselves have never been able to carry it? The truth is, brethren, and all must admit it, that it is only by the grace of God that we Jews are saved, and we are no different from them (Ac 15:7-11).

Peter sat down and the crowd was silent. All eyes turned toward Barnabas and Paul, expecting that the last word would come from them. But Paul had given his argument, and it only remained to confirm it by telling what miracles and signs God wrought when he and Barnabas preached the gospel in distant lands. And after that, no one spoke. Even the Pharisee Christians who opposed Paul so bitterly could no longer defend their position. Some of them were not yet convinced, but they could not argue against the miraculous power of God.

So when there had been silence for a few minutes, the aged James, revered because he was the brother of the Lord, summed up the real thought of the meeting.

"Brethren, hear me," he said very solemnly and with great dignity. The audience leaned forward to hear every syllable, for he was their leader and what he said would be wisdom indeed.

Brethren, hear me. Peter has told you how God first came to foreigners to take from among them a people for His name. And this is not to be marveled at, for the Scriptures foretell it. . . . Therefore, my judgment is that we do not interfere with these Gentiles who have turned to God, but that we write a letter to each church asking that as Christians they keep from eating meat that has been put before idols, from forbidden marriages, and from eating blood or the flesh of any animal that has been strangled. This we ask because for hundreds of years the books of Moses have been read in every synagogue on the Sabbath, and any conduct which would give offence to the Jew would drive him away from the Christian church rather than lead him to it."

The First Circular Letter To the Churches

To make the decision official, James and the other disciples wrote a letter, and selecting two men of their number, Judas and Silas, they sent the document in their keeping with instructions to read and explain it to the church at Antioch. The importance of the decision of this first council of the church was so great that they sent their own chief members to be bearers of the news and thus clothed it with greater dignity in the eyes of the church.

These were wise words, and all the apostles and elders agreed. Paul had won his great controversy. Foreigners from all over the world, of any race or color, could be Christians without keeping the Jewish law. The church would be rescued from the narrowness of Judaism and would one day reach around the whole world. Christians were free of the synagogue!

This was the first of all the circular letters to the churches. Paul himself, in later years, used this method of writing letters to the churches, and so did Peter and John.

Paul and Barnabas journeyed home with light hearts. Their excitement knew no bounds. Now they would be able to give a joyful report to all the churches. At last the church had taken a mighty step and cast off her chains forever. The satisfaction this would give to Gentile believers could never be measured.

As soon as Paul and Barnabas reached Antioch, the Christians were summoned to the place of meeting to hear the result of the visit to Jerusalem. A hush fell upon all when Judas and Silas were introduced. Their names were well known in the church at Jerusalem, and the fellow believers at Antioch received them with great joy and gladness.

They told of the meetings at Jerusalem and of the heated

debate on the question of the Gentiles. Then they displayed the letter signed by James, which read as follows:

> The apostles, elders, and brethren send greetings unto the brethren which are of the Gentiles in Antioch, Syria, and Cilicia. Forasmuch as we have heard that certain which went out from us have troubled you with words, subverting your souls and saying that you must be circumcised and keep the law, and forasmuch as we did not send them, it seemed good to us to settle this matter. As the result of our deliberation, we now send to you our chosen representatives accompanied by our beloved brethren, Barnabas and Paul, whom we honor, for they have risked their lives for Jesus. These men will explain the matter to you.
>
> It seemed good to the Holy Spirit and to us that the only burden we should lay upon you is this: keep from eating food that has been put before idols, or meat that has blood in it, or any animal that has been strangled; and do not commit fornication. Do this, and it shall be well with you. Remain steadfast in our Lord (vv. 23-29).

The congregation praised God for what they had heard, and they determined with greater fervor than ever to spread the news of salvation through Christ Jesus to every part of the Gentile world—yes, even to Rome itself!

And yet, although the great dispute was ended as far as the decision of the disciples was concerned, there remained many in Jerusalem who were not convinced. As the years went by, Paul encountered them often, preaching their Pharisee standards in many of the churches throughout the empire. Some argued plausibly that the liberty of the church was endangered and the work for Christ was divided.

But now at last, the apostles were free to preach to the Gentiles and baptize them into the church.

10

The Second Missionary Journey

THE WINTER IN ANTIOCH

ALL WINTER LONG Paul remained in Antioch. The roads in the mountains were filled with snow, and the sailing vessels were tied up at their docks where they would remain until the soft spring breezes filled the air and gave promise of the heat of summer. Paul's tentmaking shed was a center not only for men of the trade but also for Christians who delighted to bring their unconverted friends to hear him talk to them about Jesus. Barnabas was Paul's constant companion and friend, and between the two of them the church had stalwart leadership and grew to new strength.

Not only did Paul and Barnabas occupy places of leadership in the church at Antioch, but many able men had come from Jerusalem and were preaching in the city and in the surrounding villages. Silas was the most recent addition to their membership. After his mission to the church at Antioch was fulfilled, Silas had decided to leave his former home and find work in Syria, where he could enjoy the fellowship of his newly-made friends.

SEPARATION OF PAUL AND BARNABAS

As the season for traveling came, it was Paul who first felt the longing for another journey to revisit the churches in the west and learn of their welfare. They were infant churches, and their need for guidance was obvious. Paul had a growing burden in his heart for these new Christians, and as the plan grew in his mind, he sought his good friend Barnabas in the hope that they might travel together again.

"Let us go again and visit our brethren in every city where we have preached the word of the Lord, and let us see how they do" (Ac 15:36).

To this Barnabas heartily agreed, and preparations were made for their departure. However, Barnabas thought they should take John Mark, his nephew, as their helper in the work. Paul was firm in his refusal. Mark had been given a chance and had deserted them in the mountains of Pamphylia, just when they needed him most. Since Mark was a lover of ease, Paul was not willing to have a repetition of the former experience. Surely the hand of God had not been upon Mark's first association with the two apostles, and why was there any reason to suppose that it would be any different now?

But Uncle Barnabas was determined, even to the point of risking the success of the journey. His determination was matched by point-blank refusal, and a quarrel sprang up between Barnabas and Paul. It was the first time they had ever come to this, and though they often had differences of opinion, their friendship for each other bound them together. Their words were so sharp that their plans to go together had to be given up. It was such a small thing to be the wedge to separate fast friends who had faced so many perils together; but each man was sure he was right, and neither would yield.

Bitterness crept into the argument, and at last the two friends decided to part. Out of evil, God brought ultimate good, for the result was that two parties started out instead of one. Barnabas took his nephew Mark and sailed for Cyprus, and Paul invited Silas to accompany him to the churches of Asia Minor.

The quarrel was fierce and sharp, but it did not last. As the years went by, Mark fully justified his uncle's confidence in him, and even Paul was glad to receive him and use him as an honored minister. The love of God finally prevailed, and the feeling stirred up by the dispute gave way to the need for spreading the gospel.

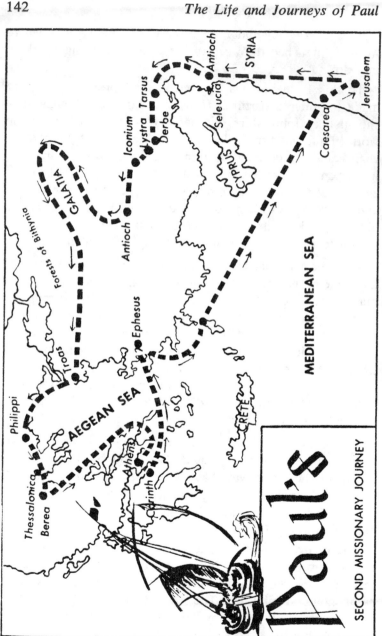

Paul's

SECOND MISSIONARY JOURNEY

The Second Missionary Journey

So Barnabas and Mark boarded a ship, while Paul and Silas started by land along the merchants' road that led through the high mountains to Lystra. The zeal of Silas, demonstrated in his preaching at Antioch, had impressed Paul and made him confident that God would honor his testimony wherever he went. Silas, like Paul, was a citizen of Rome. Together, Paul thought, they ought to be able to accomplish great things for the Lord as they visited the cities of the Gentiles.

With their packs upon their backs and the asses laden with provisions for a long journey they took leave of the brethren and set out for the Taurus mountains. This was the road along which Paul had traveled as a child when he went up to Jerusalem with his father. It was a great highway, and he felt he knew every foot of it. But for safety's sake they went in bands, joining merchants and pilgrims along the way.

Paul knew Syria and Cilicia well. He had preached in many of the villages and towns in this area while he lived in Tarsus, awaiting the call of God. So he was acquainted with many of the little Christian churches in hamlets off the highway. These had remained true, and it was Paul's purpose on this trip to visit them all, confirming them in the faith and encouraging them in their strong stand for Jesus Christ.

And the churches needed this visit. They had no New Testament to be their guidebook in the Christian life, and sometimes the waves of persecution were mountain high. To receive a visit from one of the apostles, to meet Silas from the church at Jerusalem, and to hear how the Christians fared in other cities—this was help indeed.

In Cilicia

Over rough roads and stony paths the men journeyed from town to town, sometimes following the course of the river, sometimes climbing over mountain trails. But always they

went with the knowledge that God was with them and that
His people were in need of encouragement and strengthening. Wherever they went they met friends who extended them
hospitality in the name of the Lord and who invited other
believers to their homes to meet Paul and Silas. And thus
they made their way through the high mountain pass into
Cilicia. The roads were steep in the Amanus Mountains, and
in the western part of Cilicia the towns were few, but Paul
was no stranger in this province. This was his home, and
often he had visited each village, selling his tents. Then later
he had preached the gospel to them all. Wherever they went,
friendly doors were opened, and Christians gathered to meet
the apostles, to hear Silas read the letter from Jerusalem, and
to listen to Paul as he spoke about God's plan of salvation.

AT HOME IN TARSUS

At last they left the mountain gorge and the steep rocks and
descended to the broad plain and the valley of the Cydnus.
Tarsus was still Paul's home, although both his mother and
father were dead. There was a church in Tarsus, and in it
were many of the old friends he had known in the days when
he grew up in the synagogue. They rejoiced at seeing him
again and welcomed both Paul and Silas into their homes,
glad to see men whom God had chosen to carry His gospel
to the whole world. This church had prospered, and many
Gentiles were numbered among the believers. In the fellowship of Christ there was no difference; they loved each other
as the members of one family.

As the travelers met with the Christians of Tarsus and read
the letter from James, Paul admonished the people to hold
fast to the liberty that was theirs in Christ and to keep themselves from the idolatry of the world.

IN LYCAONIA

Paul and Silas hoped to visit the most recently established
churches; therefore, saying farewell to the Christians at Tar-

sus, they joined the almost constant stream of merchants on the famous highway which led through the Cilician Gates to the north side of the Taurus Mountains and the Province of Lycaonia. Just a year earlier, Paul and Barnabas had left Derbe after spending the winter. As the city loomed before them, they looked forward to a friendly reception in the church there.

Memories of the saints at Derbe, Lystra, Iconium, and Pisidian Antioch came flooding into Paul's mind. He remembered their readiness to receive the gospel and their zeal in the face of persecution. His heart glowed with the thought of seeing them again. Would he see them all, or would some have turned back to their idols?

The two men hastened on and rejoiced to see the faithfulness of these Christian brothers and sisters. And how glad they were to see Paul once more! But he could not stay long in any of these cities. His mission was not to build up churches. That had been done already, and Paul noticed that since his first visit, the church in each city had grown; it was a great encouragement to him. After telling about the decision of the Jerusalem council and reading the letter from James, Paul and Silas took their leave and pressed on with a desire to reach new places.

No persecution came to them during this journey, because it was not their plan to preach in the marketplace. That was being done by others, and the Lord was adding to the churches daily those who took their stand for Christ.

At Lystra Paul visited the home of Timothy, remembering the kindness of Lois and Eunice, especially when he had been stoned almost to death and thrown into a ditch outside the city wall. Paul and Silas were so well pleased with the testimony of Timothy that both thought they should take him with them on their journey. He would make up for John Mark, who had failed them on the first trip.

LYSTRA AND TIMOTHY

In the year since Paul and Barnabas had been there, Timothy had worked so faithfully in the church that the older members had nothing but praise for him. He was the son of a Greek father and a Jewish mother. Timothy's father, like many a cultured Greek of that day, had found nothing satisfying in his heathen gods and goddesses and he had been quite content to allow his wife to teach her boy the religion of the Jews. Ever since childhood Timothy had heard the stories of the Jewish Bible, the Old Testament, and could recount God's dealings with His people and His promise of the Messiah. In the course of time Timothy's believing mother, Eunice, had heard the gospel from the lips of Paul. Both she and her aged mother, Lois, with the young lad Timothy, received Jesus as the Christ and were received into the church.

And now, quite willingly, Eunice surrendered her boy to God, to journey in the company of these missionaries to distant cities and perhaps to foreign lands, carrying the good news of salvation from sin. Paul loved the lad and often called him his son. The church at Lystra was proud that one of their boys should be raised up of God to be a minister, and they held a special meeting at which the elders of the church, with Paul and Silas, laid their hands on Timothy's head and in solemn prayer set him apart as a preacher of the gospel.

THE ICONIUM MESSAGE

The city of Iconium was only twenty-five miles away, and the Christians there had heard of Paul's coming. When the little band of travelers arrived, the word went out as if by magic, and that night many believers met to greet Paul. They remembered his first visit and also that many miracles had been performed by him on that occasion. They loved the apostle and owed their salvation to his tireless devotion in the preaching of the gospel. Silas read the letter from James, and both Jewish and Gentile Christians rejoiced to know that they were one in Christ and members of the same body. It was not often they had the opportunity to listen to such men as these, so they stayed late and asked all the questions that had perplexed them in the first year of their church life. Paul was glad to help them, and with words of exhortation he strengthened them, encouraging them to hold fast to the faith which they had in Christ Jesus and to preach Him among men wherever they went.

In Pisidian Antioch

In Antioch they repeated this same admonition and encouraged the hearts of the believers by their visit and their news of other churches. Everywhere there was rejoicing over James' letter. It was as if a great burden had been lifted from the necks of many Christians. They had been unhappy because of the uncertainty of their position in the church. The church itself was restless in the thought that some of the disciples in Jerusalem would not admit Gentiles to their fellowship. But now that was all settled, and the church enjoyed great peace.

Sensitivity to God's Leading

Paul and Silas, with their new friend Timothy, enjoyed these visits, but they longed to move into territory where the gospel had never been heard before. When they felt they had stayed long enough in Antioch of Pisidia, they told their friends farewell and, joining a group of travelers, they struck out to the northeast, into the province of Galatia. It was their hope to go as far as the Jewish colonies on the Black Sea.

The road was good and not too steep and dangerous as it emerged from the Sultan Mountains and stretched over the sloping wooded plains through the gentle valleys to the distant sea. But travel alone was not advisable, for wolves, leopards, and lions were common in the plateau country beyond the mountains. These animals would not molest a large group of people, but many who traveled alone or by twos or threes never reached their destination and were never seen afterward.

After they had gone about one hundred miles, they reached the rich forests of Bithynia, where the land sloped gracefully to the Black Sea. They were near their goal and the journey looked inviting, but quite suddenly Paul realized that God did not want them to go to Bithynia. Whether it was by a dream or a vision, it was increasingly clear that they should turn back. Paul was sensitive to the leading of God, and one who lived as near to the Lord as Paul did never began any journey without first placing his plans before God and waiting for His guidance. Somehow it became clear that he must abandon this trip and go in the other direction.

PAUL'S ILLNESS IN GALATIA

They held a consultation and decided to go west to Asia, preaching along the way, but the Spirit of God spoke to them very plainly, saying they should not linger to preach in Asia. They were perplexed and wondered where God would finally lead them. Feeling their way back along the road which led them to the west, Paul became ill, and the party had to stop in one of the towns of Galatia. To think of going on was impossible. So Paul had to rest because of sheer weakness and pain. The gracious people of the church there ministered to him and did their best to restore his health. They treated him as "an angel of God."

When Paul wrote a letter to them much later, he rehearsed the whole story, saying,

> You know how handicapped I was by illness when I first came among you to preach the gospel. You didn't shrink from me, or let yourselves be revolted at the disease which was such a trial to me. No, you welcomed me as though I were a messenger of God, or even as though I were Jesus Christ Himself! I believe that if you could, you would have plucked out your own eyes and given them to me, if by so doing you could have relieved my pain (Gal 4:13-15).

Apparently Paul had always had trouble with his eyes, and his present illness was a recurrence that had brought on an inflammation. Because he considered this a real hindrance to his life's work, he prayed to the Lord earnestly on three occasions to remove this malady for good. But even though God heard Paul's prayers for the healing of himself and others, His answer to this prayer was No. Instead of removing this weakness, God gave Paul strength to rise above it and to prove that pain and weakness can be endured nobly.

IN TROAS

By God's help Paul recovered sufficiently to continue his journey. Not realizing what the Lord had for them, he and Silas and Timothy traveled west through the Province of Mysia, where they were given no opportunity to preach; and one day they found themselves at the port of Troas on the edge of the blue Aegean Sea. Troas was a famous port. It was the Troy of Homer's poetry and a place of many battles. The story of the wooden horse of Troy is told with as much interest today as it was in the days of Homer.

But Paul had no thoughts for the past. He was thinking of the present and the future, and from the low hills that surrounded the city he could see the Isles of Greece, extending like stepping-stones for some giant to make his way dryshod across the sea. Beyond them, the travelers knew, the great continent of Europe stretched to the very limit of man's knowledge of the earth. There lay a dark abyss of heathen ignorance. There lay the center of the culture of Greece, and beyond that, the great city of Rome and the land of the Caesars.

Here was a civilization rich in marble statues, temples, and lordly palaces. The people worshiped at the shrines of luxury and pleasure, but really they rendered indifferent obedience to Jupiter, Saturn, and Juno, and to a host of lesser gods.

Paul and Silas lingered there, wondering where the Lord

might want them to go. They longed to be engaged in the work of preaching the gospel. They were strangely perplexed that all through the towns and cities of northern Asia Minor, God opened no door to them. Instead, He forbade their preaching. Now they were at Troas, a Roman-fortress city; would this be the place of God's choosing, or would they have to go still farther?

Day by day Paul and Silas waited, and as they waited they found a small group of Christians there. Paul did not minister to them, but he did find among them one who turned out to be his best friend. Luke, the beloved physician, the writer of the gospel that bore his name and eventually of the Acts of the Apostles, joined the three travelers at Troas. He was already a Christian, and although he was much loved as a doctor, he was willing to spend his life in the curing of souls.

THE CALL TO MACEDONIA

One night as Paul lay sleeping, God spoke to him in a dream. Paul could see the Isles of Greece stretching like a bridge across the Aegean Sea to the distant hills, and a man from Macedonia appeared plainly to him, standing with arms outstretched, begging him to come over the sea to help him and his countrymen. The long-awaited call had come at last. The suspense was over. In the morning he told the dream to Silas, Timothy and Luke, and they were agreed that the Lord intended them to go to Europe. No time was to be lost, and that very morning, with their bundles on their backs, they set out to find a ship that was engaged in the western trade. As the coolness of the night descended upon the city, the winds from the south arose, and the ship set sail on its journey of one hundred miles that would take the apostles to Philippi in Macedonia.

The following day they touched at the island of Samothracia, and by the next night came to Neapolis, where they disembarked. After a night's rest they made a short journey over the good paved road which followed the river inland to the city of Philippi.

PAUL'S WORK IN PHILIPPI

"Come over and help us!" had been the cry of Macedonia. Surely they didn't need help in education. They had schools far beyond anything that could be found in Judea. Surely they needed no help to become strong and rich. Philippi had wealth, and these four men could add nothing. But the one thing that neither Roman nor Greek possessed was real happiness. They had pleasures in abundance, but without Christ they were not satisfied. Years earlier, Philippi had been captured by Rome, and Romans had come there to live. It had become a part of the great Roman Empire that stretched over the earth from Britain to Palestine. Now it was a colony enjoying freedom from taxation and having in its population many Roman citizens of high rank.

There was no synagogue here, because the number of Jewish residents was small. Those who lived in Philippi met together each Sabbath day for prayer in a secluded spot outside the city on the pleasant bank of a river. The group was small and made up, for the most part, of women. Some of them were proselytes who had forsaken their idolatry and had found in the religion of Israel something infinitely better than they had ever known.

LYDIA, THE SELLER OF PURPLE

The four men were conspicuous among so many women, but when Paul began to preach, the heart of one Gentile woman in particular was greatly moved. She was Lydia, a business woman from Thyatira across the sea. She was a widow who was forced to carry on her own trade as a seller of purple dress goods and cloth. Thyatira was famous for its purple dye, and Lydia had made much money selling her wares to the Roman ladies of the city.

Her heart was touched by the sermon. She believed in the

God of the Jews, and with them she looked for the coming Messiah. Paul preached, the Spirit of God opened the heart of this great lady, and she gave her allegiance to Jesus, accepting Him as her Saviour. By the riverside, with all the other women looking on, Lydia was baptized, and all her household followed her example.

She became Paul's best friend in Philippi, and so great was her hospitality that she insisted that Paul and his companions stay at her home. At first they refused to put such a burden on her. Paul's plan had always been to maintain himself in the tent-making business, but Lydia would not listen to any refusal and constrained them to make her house their home.

And so as the weeks went by, the four men lost no opportunity to witness for Christ. Each Sabbath day they met at the Jews' place of prayer by the river bank, and preached to all who gathered there about the unsearchable riches of the gospel. It was not very encouraging. Only a few women became Christians. Euodias and Syntyche believed, along with two men, Epaphroditus and Clement, and a few others whose names are in the book of life. But even if the results were small, they were real, and Paul was encouraged to stay and to preach not only at the river bank but also in the bazaars and market places.

THE POOR SLAVE GIRL

All seemed to be going well when opposition arose from an unexpected source. There was a poor slave girl who was possessed of an evil spirit and who, in certain moods, could tell fortunes. People came to her to know the future, and the men who were her masters reaped a rich profit from the fees charged for consulting her. She was clad in gaudy clothing, with cheap brass rings on arms and ankles, and her young face was hardening with the lines of sin. She attracted those unstable men who would not venture into business or love without consulting a medium who claimed to hold converse with the spirit world.

Like the evil spirit who recognized Jesus as the Son of God, the spirit in this girl perceived that these men were sent of the Lord and, following them day by day through the streets and in the marketplace, she shouted to passersby, "These men are the servants of the most high God" (Ac 16:17). Her masters were annoyed, but she did not care, because she hated them anyway. She became so attracted to the message of Paul that she waited in the streets each day for the men to appear.

But Paul did not welcome the testimony of demons, and being vexed at this daily annoyance, he turned to her and, speaking to the evil spirit within her, he commanded in the name of the Lord Jesus that the spirit come out of her. The girl stood still and astonished, but she was free at last, the mistress of her own reason. She had found a happiness she had never known before, and she went on her way rejoicing.

PAUL AND SILAS IMPRISONED

However, those who profited by her bondage were angry. Their means of livelihood had been snatched away by these Jews, and in rage they planned their revenge. Seizing Paul and Silas by their garments, they dragged and pushed them through the streets, shouting to all who passed by. A great crowd followed, believing that a thief had been caught. Into the marketplace Paul and Silas were dragged, accompanied by the cry that these Jews were disturbers of the peace. It was easy to turn people against the Jews. They were hated anyway. Had not Emperor Claudius ordered all Jews to be banished from Rome?

At the end of the market square, two Roman magistrates sat on a high platform covered by a canopy to shield them from the sun. Their business was to hear and judge the grievances brought by the people. This was the first court of justice. Dragging the apostles literally by the garments, by the hair, and by wherever they might get hold of them, their persecutors took the two men of God to the magistrates, shouting their accusation.

"These men are Jews!" they protested, "And they are troubling our fair city, teaching customs which are not lawful for us as Roman citizens."

Then the crowd shouted, "Away with them! Down with the Jews!"

The magistrates were convinced. They allowed the prisoners no trial or defense. Had they realized that Paul was a Roman citizen, they would have treated him with respect, but they never asked. The judges commanded that they be beaten publicly. Their backs were bared. The lictors stepped forward and raised their rods, and as the apostles cringed under the pain of scourging, the crowd shouted, "To prison with the Jews!"

Scarred and bleeding, Paul and Silas were led to the prison and handed over to the jailor with instructions to take special care and keep them safely. Accordingly he led them to the inner dungeon and fastened their feet in the stocks. As he left them in that damp, cold place, he wondered why these men, who did not look like criminals, should be thought so dangerous.

In the home of Lydia, Timothy and Luke spent an anxious night, and with Lydia and the Christians of her household they prayed. They were not the only ones praying, for Paul and Silas themselves could not sleep. Their backs were stiff and painful from the beating, and the stocks made it impossible for them to sleep. But they could pray, and as they did, a quietness and a peace came upon them, and they began to sing some of the psalms they had known from childhood— psalms of praise to God.

> The Lord is my light and my salvation; whom shall I fear? the Lord is the strength of my life; of whom shall I be afraid? (Ps 27:1).

CONVERSION OF THE JAILER

These were strange sounds at midnight. The other prisoners were accustomed to moans and curses, but never had they heard this before. What could it mean? They were still and listening for more when suddenly a low rumbling sound was heard. It seemed like thunder in the distance, but it grew louder and louder and the very ground began to tremble. It was an earthquake! The floor seemed to heave and rock, and with a crashing sound part of the ceiling fell. The doors were wrenched from their hinges, and some of the stocks loosened as the walls crumbled. The very foundations of the great dungeon were moved.

The jailor awoke with the shock, and leaping from his bed, his first thought was for the prisoners under his care. Had any of them escaped? If so, how would he answer to Rome? His first glance told him that his prisoners were gone. There lay the great wooden door, broken from the hinges, and with a torch in his hand he ran into the corridor.

The cells within were so damaged that each door was wrenched ajar. Quickly he grasped his sword. He might as well end it all now and escape the misery of a trial and public execution later. In the glow of the torchlight, Paul saw him put his sword to his throat to take his life. A voice out of the darkness startled him. It was loud and clear: "Do thyself no harm: for we are all here" (Ac 16:28).

Trembling, he reached for the torch and sprang into the dungeon, where he fell headlong at the feet of Paul and Silas. He was greatly shaken. He could not understand why they had not fled for their freedom. Paul told him they were Roman citizens and had no need to flee; and besides that, they were servants of the Lord God bringing the gospel of salvation to the Gentiles.

As though he had found the road he had been seeking all his life, the jailor exclaimed, "What must I do to be saved?" (v. 30).

Without any hesitation Paul replied, "Believe on the Lord Jesus Christ, and thou shalt be saved, and thy house" (v. 31).

And so in the prison courtyard, with the dust of the earthquake thick in the air and the noise of confusion in the dark streets without, Paul preached the good tidings of great joy, explaining what it meant to believe, and the once brutal jailor passed from death to life.

Taking them from the court of the prison to his home, where his wife and children were, the jailor washed the backs of the apostles, and when the blood was cleansed away, with his own hands he rubbed healing oil into the wounds so recently made by the lictor's rods. That night Paul talked to them all about Jesus, and before the day dawned, a whole family had become Christians and were baptized one by one, in the manner of the believers.

As the morning dawned, messengers from the magistrates stood knocking at the prison door. They bore a frightened message from their masters, "Let these men go."

In the minds of the magistrates, it was clear that the catastrophe of the night before was a stroke from God in retaliation for their having put two of His servants in prison. But when the jailor took the glad news of their release to Paul and Silas, they were not disposed to accept it with joy.

"Tell your masters," Paul said, "that we are Romans, and they cannot dismiss their injustice to us by getting rid of us privately."

Paul knew the rights of Roman citizenship and that he could appeal this case to Rome itself if he wished to do so. He knew that the magistrates were now at his mercy. "Tell your masters to come themselves and fetch us out."

And so the once proud magistrates, seized with a panic of fear that they would be unseated as judges, found that there was nothing to do but to cast themselves on the mercy of the two prisoners. Without losing any time they presented their very humble apologies in person, beseeching these men to say nothing more of the blunder that had been made but to leave the city as soon as possible. Publicly they led them forth into the streets and set them free.

The apostles did not leave the city immediately but sought the peace and quiet of Lydia's home until their wounds were healed and they were able to travel. There Timothy and Doctor Luke ministered to them, and the few who had come to know Christ visited them.

THE FIRST CHURCH IN EUROPE

During those days of recuperation Paul and Silas had the joy of welcoming into the fellowship of the new Philippian church the man who had fastened their feet in the stocks such a short time ago, along with his family. Through suffering and faithfulness the little company grew until it became one of the strongest of all the churches.

When Paul and Silas felt strong enough to leave Philippi, they said farewell to the believers and, leaving Luke and Timothy there for a while to strengthen the church, departed for Thessalonica, the capital city of Macedonia. The road was the best in the province, being paved with marble blocks. One hundred miles they traveled and along the way came to Amphipolis, a larger city than Philippi. But they did not remain there, and in their anxiety they pushed southward and westward, past Apollonia and down the great Egnation Way to the city which Alexander the Great had named after his sister, Thessalonica.

PAUL IN THESSALONICA

Coming out of the hills they looked down upon the blue waters of the gulf and entered the city through a great marble arch carved with five bull heads laden with wreaths of flowers —a perpetual reminder that Octavius and Anthony had won the battle of Philippi. Thessalonica, because it had supported the conquering generals, had been made a free city. This meant that it could choose its own magistrates, enjoy freedom from the Roman garrison, and in no way be subject to the Roman governor of Macedonia.

There was a Jewish synagogue in Thessalonica, and the apostles preached their first sermons there. They stayed at the home of Jason, a cousin of Paul, and for three Sabbath days they witnessed in the synagogue. Paul would begin with the prophecies of the Old Testament and demonstrate to his countrymen that they were fulfilled in Jesus of Nazareth. After his impassioned appeals, some murmured, and the leaders of the synagogue disputed his doctrine and proclaimed that it was false. However, some believed and became friends of Paul, following him wherever he went and encouraging him in his preaching. Most of those who became believers were Greek proselytes and especially wives of the city officials who had forsaken the immoral rites of idol worship because they found in Judaism a religion where womanhood was held in greater respect.

But Paul and Silas did not preach only in the synagogue; they used every opportunity to witness for Jesus, and in three weeks they were able to gather together enough believers to form a church. They did not waste any time. Each evening the Christians met, and both Paul and Silas opened to them the truths of the gospel. And as others came to the light, they, too, were welcomed into the church. It was a colossal task to establish a church in three weeks, but that is what Paul and Silas did, not only bringing converts to Christ but also instructing them in the whole program of the ages. Before those brief weeks went by, Paul spoke to them about the coming of the Lord and the signs of the times. He warned them of the falling away from the faith that should precede the coming of Antichrist.

PAUL FORCED TO LEAVE THESSALONICA

Paul was a tireless worker—a rare individual who was able to weld together a strong fellowship of Christians almost overnight. But as usual, the unbelieving Jews stirred up a great mob of ruffians, who gathered around the house of Jason, throwing stones into the open court and shouting for Paul and Silas to be turned over to them. With a roar of anger they broke down the door and searched every part of the house, only to find that they were not tnere. Jason nad seen to it that they made their escape in time. But Jason did not escape. The crowd seized him and a few of the others who had become Christians and dragged them to the marketplace, where the city fathers held court.

> These men are harboring strangers who have the reputation of turning the world upside down. They have disturbed every city into which they have gone; and, against our Roman laws, they teach that there is another king—one called Jesus. These men are plotting against the Emperor (Ac 17:6-7).

The charge was serious and could not be lightly put aside. The magistrates wrote down the accusation and were much disturbed because this could lead to great trouble. Then they ordered Jason and his friends to pledge money and property, binding them to appear again on the day of the trial.

Since Jason was a man of wealth, the bond was paid; and all were allowed to go home. But that very night, after the brethren talked it over, they searched out Paul and Silas and showed them how harmful it might be for them to stay. So while the city slept, they made their way, disguised, through the gates and southward to the walled city of Berea.

HIS WELCOME IN BEREA

It was in Berea that Timothy joined Paul and Silas. He had come down from Philippi, where he and Luke had stayed to strengthen the church. He found them at the synagogue. Timothy knew that it was Paul's habit to go there, so he waited for him. When the apostles arrived, they taught in the synagogue that Jesus was the Christ, and they proved it from the Scriptures. Paul was surprised and pleased to see that the Jews listened to him without opposition. In fact, they showed real interest. Then, devouring every word that Paul preached, they went to the great scrolls which were kept in the box behind the blue curtain. They pored over the words of Isaiah and many of the other prophets and over the laws of Moses, and they traced the story of the Messiah even in their book of hymns. They would not receive this message until they had proved from the Scriptures that it was so; but when they discovered that Paul had quoted without any error, they received the message gladly and believed in Jesus.

All was going well until news of Paul's preaching got back to Thessalonica, carried by some unsuspecting Jew who meant the apostle no harm. Almost at once a flood of opposition descended upon the newly-formed church. A band of zealous Israelites hurried down from Thessalonica, and by a twisting of truth and falsehood they stirred up the people at the synagogue against Paul. The fury of their assault was aimed at Paul alone, and lest he should be the victim of vicious attack, he left the city upon the advice of the Christians there.

ATHENS, THE CITY OF IDOLATRY

In fact, a group of Christians conducted him to the port at Dium where he took ship for Athens, the greatest city in Greece. All the way to Athens his friends accompanied him, and at last, after reaching the city, they returned home and left him alone.

Silas and Timothy remained at Berea to strengthen the believers, but when their work was done they had instructions to meet Paul at Athens. The enemies thought that since Paul was the leader, they did not need to concern themselves with the others, so the two remained at Berea in comparative safety.

After Paul's friends left him, he was absolutely alone in one of the most beautiful cities of the world. Athens was called "The Mother of Greece." Dominating the city was the Acropolis, a hill with a flat, rock top which was the foundation for many great temples. Five hundred years earlier, Athens had been at the height of its greatness, but since then it had been plundered by Rome and was under its domination. Paul had been in many cities, but never had he visited a place so beautiful. It was a city of marble sculptures gleaming in the sun. The buildings were all graceful and of classic design. The people were cultured and proud that they stood for free discussion and free thought. Great architecture, great paintings, great art, and great libraries were found everywhere in the city. Along every street and in every square could be seen statues and altars—shrines built for the worship of many gods. Paul marveled as he read the inscriptions. His heart was stirred as he admired the beauty of the statuary, some of it the work of Phidias, the greatest of all workmen in marble; but his heart was stirred with pity as he thought of the blindness of the Athenian people.

Here in these very streets, and in this very marketplace at the foot of the Acropolis, Socrates had once stood and taught the people; Plato had taught his followers from this same spot; Demosthenes, the great orator, was a memory of the past; but all these had left their stamp of culture on the proud people of the city. Beneath the temples on the Acropolis, the theater of Dionysius with its marble seats sprawled over the valley and was still the meeting place where crowds gathered nightly to see the great plays. There was no doubt that these people were the most clever and refined and self-satisfied that Paul had ever met.

Near the synagogue Paul found lodging and determined to remain there until Silas and Timothy arrived. But he was not happy. These idols and their temples did not arouse him to admiration but to pity and concern. He wished in God's name that they might all be torn down and that, instead of the confusion of gods, the people might see the true and living God. All these statues were dishonoring to the Lord, and he longed to see a church established in Athens that would one day blot each idol out of Athenian hearts.

On the Sabbath day he went to the synagogue to preach
the gospel to his own countrymen first, but he was not able
to win any of them to Jesus. Discouraged, he left the synagogue and began to preach in the streets and at the marketplaces where the crowds gathered. And crowds listened, for
there were many in the streets who loved an argument and
spent the day going from one philosopher to another in an
attempt to hear some new doctrine that could become the
rage of Athens for a season.

Everywhere were the signs of idolatry. Before each image
a censer burned with incense, and women held their children
up to the idol and offered their sacrifices on the altar nearby.
Paul was sick at heart as he beheld how completely the city
was given over to idolatry.

One day he walked the length of just one street and found
temples to Minerva, Diana, Victory, and Venus. Besides this
there were altars to War, Fame, Pity, and Modesty. In all of
Athens there were three thousand statues and altars where
the citizens offered their empty worship. Paul read many of
the inscriptions as he walked up and down the streets, and
he wondered how people so religious could be so blind. He
searched the faces of the people and saw that they were weary
of their gods.

Certain philosophers of the Stoics and the Epicureans
found Paul in a marketplace, and they said,

> This babbler seems to be a setter-forth of strange gods; let
> us hear him speak. What is this new doctrine whereof thou
> speakest? Thou bringest certain things to our ears. Tell us
> what they mean (Ac 17:18-20).

THE MARS HILL SERMON

Just past the noise-filled market and half way up to the
temples on the Acropolis was a rocky semicircle known as the
hill of Mars. Here they led Paul and asked him to tell his
story. So Paul began:

Men of Athens, I perceive that in everything in your lives you are unusually religious, for as I passed along your streets and saw the gods you worship, I came to an altar with these words written, "To the unknown god." Now this god whom you worship ignorantly, is the God I declare unto you (vv. 22-23).

They were captivated immediately and leaned forward to hear more from the lips of the orator.

With a glance at the clustered temples up the hill and even at the Parthenon itself, which was the most perfect building to be found in all the world, Paul continued his talk:

God, who made the world and everything in it, since He is Lord of heaven and earth, does not live in temples of stone, fashioned by men's hands, nor can He be served by sacrifices offered from men's hands. He does not need such things, seeing that He is the giver of life and breath to men. And since He made all nations of one blood, and fixed their times and their seasons, and determined where they should dwell; and since He ordained that they should seek God who is not far from any one of us; and since we live and move and have our being in Him, we ought not to think of Him as a figure carved in marble, or made of silver or gold. Even some of your own poets have said that we are His offspring (vv. 24-29).

The audience was pleased with the speech so far and eagerly waited for more. There was no doubt in their minds that this was a man of wide learning. He was a Jew, but he had proved himself familiar with their poets. So Paul continued:

In past ages God excused the ignorance of men, but now He commands them everywhere to repent and cease from such things. For God has fixed a day when He will call the world to account and will judge all mankind by His son Jesus Christ; and the proof that God is able to do this is the fact that He raised Him from the dead (vv. 30-31).

A ripple of laughter went through the crowd as he spoke

about being raised from the dead. "This man must be mad to preach such nonsense!" They would hear no more.

Some of those who were more polite suggested that they hear him again at some future time, but Paul recognized that it was a courteous way of getting rid of him.

Paul had met opposition in every form but this was the first time he had encountered mild amusement. It silenced him more completely than stones and insults could have done. With a sense of failure he left Mars' hill, going down into the markets below and losing himself in the crowd. As he fought the mounting feeling of discouragement, he heard footsteps behind him and, turning around, he saw a little group of men and women hurrying after him. Their faces were friendly, for they had come to enquire further about the new doctrine. Dionysius, a member of the supreme court of Athens and a woman named Damaris, together with a few unnamed Athenians, clung to him and became believers in the Lord Jesus.

But Paul grew restless in Athens. He thought of the believers in Berea, where Silas and Timothy were, and wondered why he had not heard from them. He was tempted to make the trip up north again, and even planned to go to Thessalonica, but circumstances prevented him. Could this long silence mean that Silas or Timothy had met with hostility? Had the Thessalonian Jews been giving them more trouble? Paul feared for that church at Thessalonica. Persecution had fallen heavily upon the believers there, and he wondered if their faith would bear the test, especially since he had been with them only three weeks.

PAUL IN CORINTH

The long weeks of waiting were hard to bear; so, sending one of the Christians of Athens to Thessalonica to inquire about the welfare of those believers, Paul left word with friends that he was gong to Corinth; if Timothy or Silas should come, they were to be sent to the capital city, where Paul would await them.

With a sense of freedom he left the Athenians' city of marble temples behind. The memory of the Athenians' laughter when he preached Christ still burned in him, and he wondered why the Lord had not given him more souls in that great city.

Out he went on the short road to Peiraeus, where he found a little ship bound for Corinth, the capital of Achaia. Depressed in spirit, and with the knowledge that his money was running out, he began to wonder what the vision of the man of Macedonia really meant. So far it had meant a series of disappointments, for in every city he had fled for his safety, leaving his traveling companions to establish and work out the details of the new church.

AQUILA AND PRISCILLA

In his discouragement he looked for a job where he could use the trade that he had learned in Tarsus. He found the street where the tentmakers had their low sheds and entered the workshop of Aquila. It seemed that the Lord led him to that very place, for Aquila was a Jewish refugee who had left Rome when the Emperor Claudius put a ban upon all Jews. Aquila and his wife, Priscilla, had established themselves in the tentmaking business in Corinth only a few weeks before Paul's arrival.

Aquila was glad to have extra help and, because Paul was a Jew, Priscilla gave him lodging at their home. After some days together, Aquila grew to like Paul and to admire his skill in weaving cloth and sewing tents. And Paul spent many an hour telling of the wonderful experiences he had passed through and how God had brought him safely over the rough places and delivered him from prison. Aquila and his wife were amazed that this same tentmaker was once a rabbi who bitterly persecuted the sect of the Nazarenes, but they grew to admire him very much, and little by little they opened their hearts to the Lord and became disciples of Jesus.

Corinth was a city of great beauty. The ancient Corinth

was older than Athens, but so many battles had been fought
in the streets that it had fallen into a heap of ruins. It was
Julius Caesar who had ordered that the city be rebuilt, and
for one hundred years it had occupied a position of prominence in Greece. It was the center of trade and commerce
and thus attracted many Jews who lived in their quarter.
Here was the center of the worship of Venus, the goddess of
love. Corinth was a city famous for its riches and its love of
ease and pleasure. Inevitably it became a symbol for sin.
Sailors and merchants from all over the world carried the
story of Corinth back home with them and thus made it a
center of infamy as well as glamour.

In the synagogue Paul was introduced as a Jew who had
been at the temple at Jerusalem, and he was given permission
to address the worshipers. This he did with a sense of waning
power. Even though he reasoned and proved and persuaded
both Jews and Greeks, he had to fight a growing wave of
discouragement that was sweeping over him.

SILAS, TIMOTHY, AND PAUL IN CORINTH

And then Silas and Timothy came. They had been to
Athens and had learned that Paul was in Corinth. What a
relief it was to see them and to hear the news! He knew now
that they were not in jail and that all was well. What of the
churches at Berea and Thessalonica? Had they heard from
Luke at Philippi? Were the Christians standing firm?

The news was good. The churches everywhere were standing strong in the faith. Not only that, they were witnessing
all over Macedonia and many had surrendered to Christ in
the weeks that had just passed. God was working in the
churches and blessing the testimony of all His followers. They
had not forgotten Paul but had remembered him daily in their
prayer, even as he remembered them. And to show their
love, they had sent a gift of money to support Paul and free
him from the necessity of labor, so that he could give all his
time to the ministry. Paul's heart was warmed with great joy

as he heard these reports. His discouragement vanished as the morning mist before the rising sun. The old zeal returned to him, and with great vigor he launched upon a campaign to win the Corinthians to Christ.

But when the Jews withstood him and raised great opposition to him, blaspheming the name of Jesus, he turned from them with the warning that their blood would be upon their own heads.

"From henceforth," he said, "I will go unto the Gentiles" (Ac 18:6).

And indeed he did, and many of the Corinthians believed and were baptized. However, before he left he had the great joy of winning Crispus, the chief ruler of the synagogue, to Christ. It was heartening to see him come with his wife and children to be baptized publicly as a sign to his friends that he had surrendered to Jesus.

Since Silas and Timothy had come, the home of Aquila could not contain them all, so they took up their lodging next door to the synagogue in a house owned by a believer named Justus. But Paul continued at his trade whenever necessary.

And as the days went by, the awful task of witnessing to this Christless city lay heavy upon his mind. As he thought of it, there was sometimes a lurking fear in his heart. Corinth was unquestionably the most wicked city in the world, and Paul wondered if there were any hope of success.

And then one night as he lay in his bed in Justus' house, a vision of the Lord appeared to him. It was just like the vision that Joshua had seen as his heart grew faint so many years earlier. "Be not afraid," the Lord said, "but speak, and hold not thy peace: for I am with thee, and no man shall set on thee to hurt thee: for I have much people in this city" (Ac 17:9-10).

That was all he needed to know. It made him recall the day when he stood face to face with Jesus outside Damascus, and he could hear again those words, "He is a chosen vessel unto me, to bear my name before the Gentiles, and kings, and

the children of Israel: for I will show him how great things
he must suffer for my name's sake" (9:15-16).

With renewed zeal Paul preached. For a year and a half
they labored, seeking to win men and women, both Jew and
Gentile, from the paths of sin and darkness to the family of
God. Many came to know the truth and separated themselves from the filth of their old religion, gaining a new life
in Christ.

THE FIRST EPISTLE TO THE THESSALONIANS

The gift from Thessalonica and the good report of them so
stirred the heart of Paul that he wrote a letter to them from
Corinth. It was his first epistle. It was addressed to all the
disciples at Thessalonica, and it commended them for their
steadfastness of faith in the face of persecution. Paul, grateful
for their help, wrote them a fatherly letter of advice, reminding them about the teaching which he had sought to bring
them while he was there and urging them to grow in grace
and walk as children of God should. They were to abound
more and more in the richness of their testimony and in their
daily lives. And this was even more important in the light of
the coming day when the Lord would return and gather His
Church into His presence—both those believers who will have
died and those who will be alive at His coming. It was a
beautiful letter, and it showed Paul's affection for those who
were his children in the faith.

Paul and his friends stayed a long time in Corinth, and
his teaching met with greater success there than at any other
place. The body of believers grew each day as many of the
people of humble rank became Christians. But it was not all
ease and success, for some of the Jews hated Paul for his
message and lay in wait for an opportune time to vent their
hatred upon him. One day, according to plan, they aroused
a mob of idle people who laid hands on him while he was
preaching, and brought him before the judgment seat of
Gallio, the new Roman governor. Gallio was a kindly, even-

tempered man who had been entrusted with this office because
Claudius the emperor believed him to be wise and able.
Standing before Gallio with their unresisting prisoner, the
Jews found themselves without a sufficient accusation. The
only charge they brought sounded weak even in their own
ears. They could not accuse Paul of disturbing the peace or
of inciting a riot, so they said lamely, "This fellow persuadeth
men to worship God contrary to the law" (Ac 18:13).

As Paul girded himself to answer their charge, Gallio rose
from his seat and said,

> I refuse to have anything to do with this affair. I am here
> to judge lawlessness, crime, and wrongdoing, not to decide
> questions of words and names and matters of Jewish law.
> These things you must settle among yourselves (vv. 14-15).

Then in impatient anger he had them driven from the court
room. A great crowd of Greeks who witnessed the scene felt
resentment toward the Jews. They laid hands on Sosthenes,
the chief ruler of the synagogue, and gave him a public beating before the judgment seat. Gallio sat stolidly, with neither
praise nor blame for their conduct; as long as their bitterness
was not aimed at Rome, he was indifferent to it all.

Poor Sosthenes! He later became a follower of the Lord
Jesus and was with Paul in Ephesus when the apostle wrote
his first letter to the Corinthian church.

After several months had passed, the man who had carried
Paul's first letter to the church at Thessalonica returned and
reported how the epistle was received. It had set at rest some
of their difficulties but had apparently stirred up others, especially with regard to the expectation of the coming of the
Lord. There was some who felt from Paul's letter that the
time was so short that they could now stop working and live
on their savings, for in a matter of days the heavens would
receive them and they would be with the Lord.

THE SECOND EPISTLE TO THE THESSALONIANS

Paul talked over the situation with Silas and Timothy and

decided to send a second letter. With pen in hand, he commended them for their patience in tribulation and pleaded with them not to be shaken in mind nor troubled by men's words or by false letters pretending to be from him, saying that the coming of Christ was near. Evidently they had received a forged letter, claiming to be from Paul. He recalled to their minds his teaching about God's great program, about the falling away from the Lord in the last days, and about how the man of sin would come to oppose all that was of God.

Paul assured the Thessalonians that the present persecutions through which they were passing were not the great tribulation at all: Therefore, brethren, stand fast, and hold to the teachings which ye have been taught both in my ministry among you and by these letters.

And be not weary in well doing. If any among you refuses to obey our admonitions in this letter, take note of him and avoid him that he may be put to shame (2 Th 2:15; 3:13-14).

PAUL'S RETURN TO SYRIAN ANTIOCH

It was not long after this that the great apostle felt that the church at Corinth was strong enough that he could leave it and carry on other work. Somehow he felt impelled to return to Antioch in Syria. Then again, he wished to visit Jerusalem at the time of the feast. Aquila and Priscilla were sailing for Ephesus, and Paul decided to go with them. Silas and Timothy did not accompany them but stayed at Corinth to continue the work.

The voyage across the sea from Cenchrea, the seaport of Corinth, was pleasant and accomplished without incident. The ship remained long enough in Ephesus for Paul to visit the synagogue where he reasoned with the Jews and pointed them to Jesus, the Christ of the Scriptures. They did not oppose him or his message, in fact they begged him to stay longer, but this he was unable to do, and with a promise to visit them again very soon, he left Aquila and Priscilla to carry on the testimony at Ephesus. He returned to the ship which carried him safely to Caesarea, the nearest port to Jerusalem.

Paul was not long in Jerusalem. His chief concern there was to visit the mother church again. It was the feast time, and the streets were filled with pilgrims. He greeted the believers, and after renewing his friendship with James and Simon Peter and all the disciples who met at Mary's house, he returned to Antioch and the church which had sent him out on all his journeys.

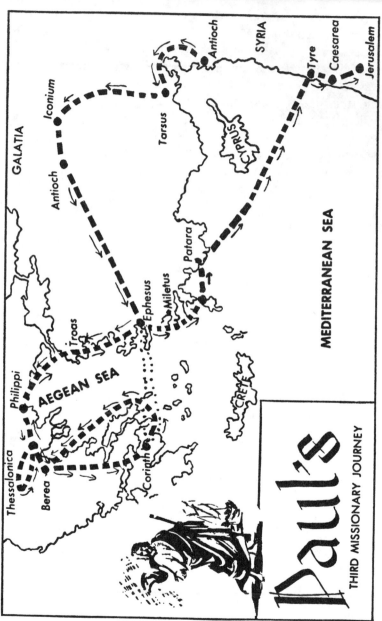

Paul's
THIRD MISSIONARY JOURNEY

11

The Third Missionary Journey

THE LAST FAREWELL TO ANTIOCH

IT HAD BEEN A YEAR since Paul had made his promise to the Jews of Ephesus to return one day and continue his ministry to them. He had often thought of them and of how he had left Aquila and Priscilla to carry on a testimony for Christ in that city. All through the winter and late into the next summer he stayed at Antioch, and he knew that if he was going to travel to Asia Minor, he would have to start before the winter snows blocked the mountain passes.

THE THIRD MISSIONARY JOURNEY

When the Christians at Antioch learned that the apostle was planning a third journey, they were not surprised. They were sorrowful, however, that they would have to say farewell once more. By this time they realized that God had fitted this man beyond any other to carry the gospel into far distant cities. So at a farewell meeting they commended him to the Lord's care, and after providing him with funds and provisions to take him on his way, they led him to the gates of the city. They watched and waved their farewells until he disappeared over a hill and was seen no more. They did not realize it then, but Paul was coming to that age where his visits had to be final visits. Never again did they see his face at his beloved church at Antioch. This proved to be their last farewell.

For the third time Paul turned his face toward the Cilician Gates, which led him through Tarsus and on to Derbe, Lystra, and Iconium. It was not as it had been in years gone by.

Each city now had its established churches, and many new converts had been won to Christ. It was a great joy to the apostle to see the progress these believers had made. He thought of those early days when not a single voice was raised for the Lord in the whole city; and as he left each place, he lifted his heart in a fervent prayer of thanksgiving for every church and every believer.

REVISITING THE EARLY CHURCHES

The work now was not so much a matter of planting the seed as it was of rooting up the tares. Many times voices were raised to deflect these early Christians from the purity of the faith. Especially were they troubled with itinerant preachers who, by their teaching, sought to upset the gospel of grace and to bring the Gentile believers back under the Mosaic law. Wherever Paul went he had to fight this influence, and in many instances false teachers had undermined his ministry by doubting his apostleship and belittling his authority.

In Derbe, Iconium, and all through the regions of Galatia where he and Silas had gone on the second great mission, he said,

> I am amazed that you should have turned away from what I taught you. The thing you are now following is not the gospel. The men who are troubling you with their false teachings are wishing to spoil the true gospel of Jesus. I tell you, brethren, the gospel which I preached to you was not of men, but of God. I was not taught it by men, but by direct revelation from Christ. So if any man preach any other gospel than this which I have preached unto you, let him be as an accursed man, and let him be put out of your church (Gal 1:6-9).

Paul revisited all of his earliest churches in order, settling their difficulties, answering their questions, counteracting the false teaching, warning, rebuking, encouraging, and confirming. This was the ministry they needed to keep them fast in the faith.

Apollos, A New Missionary

While Paul had carried on this patient work in the cities of the interior, a Christian Jew named Apollos had come to Ephesus. He had been born in Alexandria, at the mouth of the Nile, and was both well-educated and eloquent. His knowledge of the Old Testament Scriptures was comparable to Paul's for he had been raised carefully by his Hebrew parents. But now, with his eyes open to Jesus, the Messiah, he was zealous to spread the great truth everywhere.

Apollos had never seen Jesus, nor had he spoken to any of the disciples, but he had heard of John the Baptist and of how John had announced that Jesus was the Christ, in fulfillment of the prophecies. Those facts had mastered him, and he went out with his great heart full of the message, anxious to spread it to all his countrymen.

Aquila and his wife heard him in the synagogue at Ephesus and marveled at his ability. He was mighty in the Scriptures. They were quick to realize that if this man should ever enter into the fullness of the gospel as Paul had taught it to them, he would be one of the greatest men in the church and could be used of God beyond anything he had yet known.

Graciously they invited him to their home, and graciously he accepted. Quietly and without any offense to him they went over some of the things he had said in his sermon, commending him, but showing him that John's preaching about repentance was not the gospel in its fullness. They also showed him that the baptism of John was not the same baptism that Christ commanded.

They led his mind from the legalism of the synagogue to the great liberty of Christ's gospel, and Apollos listened and marveled. Day by day the scholar and orator sat beside the tentmaker and his wife as they took him one step at a time into the deeper things of the faith. And with true Christian humility, the great orator from Egypt heard the truths of God and rejoiced in them. Each day as he appeared at the synagogue, his message grew stronger, and Aquila and his faithful wife prayed that the Lord would fill this yielded vessel with mighty power.

Armed with a truth which he did not formerly possess, Apollos went on to Corinth, that great city of Achaia, to preach with all the fervor and boldness of his youth. And so, while Pharisee Jews from Jerusalem were going about seeking to do all in their power against Paul and his gospel, another Jew whom he had never seen, was visiting some of the churches he had founded and winning men and women to Christ.

ORGANIZATION OF THE CHURCH IN EPHESUS

It was just a few days after Apollos had left for Corinth that Paul arrived in Ephesus and heard about him. Paul's first step was to look up his old friend Aquila, the tentmaker, and learn of all that had happened during the months since he had left the city. He heard about certain believers who had been converted under the preaching of Apollos, and when he found that Apollos baptized them with the baptism of John, he questioned twelve men who said they were believers.

"Did you receive the Holy Spirit when you believed?" asked Paul.

But the twelve stared at him blankly and said, "We have never even heard that there is a Holy Spirit."

Evidently there was much to be corrected, and Paul set about in great kindness to do it.

After he had instructed them, he rebaptized them, both men and women, in the name of the Lord Jesus and laid his hands on them, praying that the third person of the Trinity would come upon them in all His power. And that day a new church was formed, consisting of believers who, like those at Pentecost, were baptized by the Holy Spirit.

For three months Paul attended the services at the synagogue in Ephesus and boldly preached that Jesus was the Son of God. But some arose to dispute his message, and their contention grew so bitter that the little group of Christians despaired of any good coming out of further witnessing in the synagogue. Many of the Jews had heard the gospel of Christ week after week from the lips of Aquila and Apollos and now from Paul. Not only did they refuse to believe, but they had hardened their hearts against Jesus and also had spoken in derision of Paul, warning the people that Christianity was the enemy of the Jews.

Sadly, Paul turned from the synagogue, never to enter it again as long as he was in Ephesus. In order to carry on his teaching, however, he obtained permission to rent, for a fee, the lecture room in the school building belonging to Tyrannus. This man was a teacher of rhetoric and philosophy who held his classes each morning. So Paul gathered his followers each afternoon, reasoning with them daily and discussing not only the claims of Jesus but also the many questions relating to Christianity and their pagan lives. Paul talked to his hearers about marriage, divorce, slavery, and the use of meat offered to idols. And in the space of two years the church in Ephesus flourished and grew until the gospel of Christ Jesus had been preached all over Roman Asia.

FIGHTING AGAINST IDOL WORSHIP

Ephesus was the center of a great province. For a thousand years it had been the site of the temple of Diana. When Alexander the Great was born, the temple burned to the ground, and the men of Asia gathered gold and silver to rebuild it. Each family in the province made its offering, and the new temple was so magnificent that it was regarded as one of the seven wonders of the world. When the temple was opened, a Persian Prince shot an arrow from its highest tower and then declared that whoever came within that distance from the great building would find sanctuary and be free from pursuit.

The huge building was of marble, with double rows of fluted pillars. All around the building were fourteen marble steps rising in tiers like the layers of a wedding cake, and at the base of each pillar, carved deep in the rock, were the life-like figures of men and women. There, in the center of the great temple, was a secret chamber formed by pillars of green jasper. The walls were hung with precious gifts sent from every neighboring province, and near the entrance was an altar carved by Praxiteles. From the roof hung a great purple curtain, and behind the curtain was the wooden figure of a woman, black with age. This was Diana, the goddess of the Ephesians, who, it was said, fell from the sky. The idol was hideous, but concealed behind the mystic curtain it became the object of worship for millions of people.

Little copies of the image were made of brass or silver and sometimes of gold showing Diana to be a beautiful woman wearing a crown which looked like a castle rising tier upon tier upon her head. Every household had a statue of Diana, for it was felt that she had power to ward off evil from all who lived within that home.

Diana's temple became the center of Ephesian life. Pilgrims came to visit it from all over the world. Merchants left their money with its priests, believing that the safest spot on earth was the treasury of the temple. Many were the craftsmen who gained a livelihood by exploiting the superstition of the people and manufacturing images to be used as charms.

The Power of God

Here in this town of magic and idolatry, Paul and his friends preached Christ, and hundreds abandoned their empty idolatry, finding peace in the salvation of Christ. God also allowed His apostle to do many miraculous things in Ephesus to manifest to these wonder-loving people that the power of the Almighty One was greater than the magic of Diana or any of her followers. Just as Moses in the land of Egypt had been able, by God's power, to outdo the magicians of Pharaoh, so Paul, the servant of God, was given authority to work special miracles of healing. Instead of amulets, beads and parchments on which were inscribed many incantations, Paul demonstrated that the mighty power of God flowed through him to the people. It was not only by means of his preaching, but in some cases through articles of clothing such as an apron which he wore when he worked at tentmaking or a handkerchief with which he wiped his brow.

In such a land there were always imposters, who made their living by the superstitions of the people. In one Jewish family, seven brothers, sons of Sceva the priest, were so degraded as to make their living by professing to cure diseases through charms and magic formulas. One day they saw Paul cast an evil spirit out of a man, and quickly they learned the words he used. At the first opportunity they tried to imitate him.

"We command you to come out of this man," they said, "in the name of Jesus, whom Paul preaches."

But the power of God was not in their words and instead of the man being relieved of his demon-possession, he spoke under the mastery of Satan and said, "Jesus I know, and Paul I know; but who are ye?" (Ac 19:15).

And with the superhuman strength of a madman, he flung himself upon the seven magicians and tore their clothes from their backs, bruising and beating them in the fury of his attack.

The news spread like wildfire through the town. Many had seen it with their own eyes and gave up any belief in the power of their magicians. Great throngs of former wonder-workers confessed that their art had been trickery and brought their books of magic, their amulets, and hoards of charms to a public place, where they heaped them high and set fire to the huge pile. Now that they had become Christians, God had filled their hearts with a new power; and before the power of God, the tricks of Satan must go. It was a mighty demonstration, for they burned books and charms worth about ten thousand dollars.

PAUL'S HELPERS AT EPHESUS

And so the work of the Lord prospered, and the testimony of the church at Ephesus became strong in all of Asia. Timothy came from Europe, joining himself to Paul again, and Erastus, another believer, followed in Timothy's footsteps and became one of Paul's helpers at Ephesus. In fact, this church became a center for the spreading of the gospel, just like Pisidian Antioch. Between Ephesus and Corinth there was a direct trade route. Merchants were coming and going, and frequently the believers in Christ Jesus made visits to other churches.

It was after Paul's second year in Ephesus that Apollos came back from Corinth and first met Paul. It was a glad meeting, and he had news to tell about the Corinthian converts. There was much hope and joy, but also much sorrow. Many of the Christians had fallen back into the worldliness of their pagan days, and the impurity of their former lives existed in the church and was accepted without criticism.

THE VISIT TO CORINTH

As Paul heard of it, he determined to make the journey himself and correct the growing mischief which would bring dishonor to the name of the Lord. His visit was a sad and painful one, for on his arrival he found things were worse than he supposed. He was personally humiliated that so many of his own converts had become lax in their living.

Paul's stay was brief, and he used every moment to warn the believers in Corinth that impurity in any form could not be permitted in the lives of Christians. He reminded them that the purpose of their baptism was to demonstrate that they had died to sin and had been raised to a life of righteousness. He threatened them with exclusion from the church if they did not cease to defile its name. He scolded them like a father and said that if things were no better when he came again, he would not spare them. All this was said in Christian love and with mildness and meekness, but no sooner had he sailed back to Ephesus than the Corinthians mistook his attitude for weakness and said that he was afraid of them. They went on in their sinfulness in defiance of the Lord and His apostle.

THE FIRST EPISTLE TO THE CORINTHIANS

It was just a short while later that Stephanus, Fortunatus and Achaicus, three of Paul's own converts, came to Ephesus with a full report of the unruly church at Corinth. They brought bad news. The loose worldliness which infected the community had increased. Paul immediately wrote a sharp letter to the Corinthians, ordering the church to cease from all fellowship with those who were disobedient and to exclude them from its membership. This letter, or epistle, is known as First Corinthians.

Then he waited to see how they would receive this letter. He wished to give them time to repent before he made a third visit to them.

Meanwhile, some members of the household of Chloe, a distinguished Christian family of Corinth, arrived at Ephesus with fuller information about the Corinthian church. First of all, the believers were split into four factions, following local preachers and wrangling with each other in such a way that distinct and separate groups were formed, each contending with the other. The whole church was a hotbed of unrest. Open immorality, such as was common in the pagan temples, was tolerated without any sense of shame. Frequently Christians were bringing each other before the secular courts in lawsuits. Even the Lord's Supper was turned into an occasion for drunkenness and gluttony.

So Paul found it necessary to send Timothy and Erastus to them to check this great evil. He also wrote them another stern letter, answering the attitude which was reported to be in them and correcting the evils which weakened their Christian testimony. This letter he dispatched by the hand of Titus, the young man who had accompanied him to Jerusalem several years earlier.

Not only was he grieved at the disorder in the church at Corinth, but a severe illness brought him to the point where the Ephesians despaired of his life. It was discouraging, but he held on. Not only did he have to contend with this church, he had also received word that in Galatia many of the churches were forsaking the simple truths of salvation and returning to the idea that the way into the church was by the synagogue and the law of Moses.

THE NEW ENEMY

As if there were not enough problems, a new enemy arose in Ephesus. The gospel had been preached so effectively in all the towns and villages near Ephesus and through the province of Asia, and so many converts had been made, that the tradesmen who sold silver images of Diana began to feel the decline in their business. With great alarm they held a meeting. The chief spokesman was Demetrius. He was a dealer, and bought his images from the craftsmen. In his speech he explained to the guild members the reason for their loss of trade and aroused their anger by suggesting that the great temple itself was in danger.

The speech so aroused the silversmiths that they caught Gaius and Aristarchus, two faithful friends of Paul, and dragged them into the great open theater which was reputed to be the largest in the world.

A great crowd assembled because of the shouting, and although they did not know what was going on, they took up the cry of the guild and rushed through the streets in confusion shouting, "Great is Diana of the Ephesians" (Ac 19:28).

Everybody seemed to be running. The streets were full of people hurrying to the theater to see what the excitement was about. Paul himself escaped the mob, and when he sought to enter the theater to join his friends, the disciples held him back. Even some of the leaders in the political life of Asia sent word that he should be kept hidden from the silversmiths.

In the midst of the crowd was a group of Jews who would be willing to do anything to hush Paul's voice. They regarded him as an enemy of the synagogue. Taking advantage of the tumult at the theater, one of their number, Alexander by name, raised his hand to get a hearing, hoping to deal a telling blow to the Christian church by urging the capture of Paul. But when the rabble throng recognized his Jewish face and dress, they would not listen. Instead, they shouted the more loudly, "Great is Diana of the Ephesians" (v. 34).

Alexander was glad to get away with his life, so he wasted no time in losing himself in the crowd.

For two hours the tumult continued. Somehow the power of Diana had been questioned, and her supporters were incensed. The demonstration on the street that day would show any rival religion how the populace felt about their great temple and their goddess. And when their shouts died down and their voices were exhausted, the town clerk appeased their wrath and sent them back home.

"Men of Ephesus," he said,

> the whole world knows that our city is the humble slave and worshiper of the great goddess Diana, whose image fell from Jupiter. But these men whom you have dragged here are not thieves attempting to steal the treasures of our temple, nor have they spoken evil against the goddess. Now if Demetrius or any other thinks he has a grievance against any person, the courts are open and the judges are even now sitting. Anyone may take his case before them and be judged in a proper manner. I warn you that such an uproar as this is illegal and may bring down upon us the punishment of Rome. This is a riot, and we will be held accountable. I advise you all to go home quickly and think over what I have said (vv. 35-41).

PAUL'S RETURN TO MACEDONIA

That same evening Paul asked the church to meet, and when they had come together, he told them that the time had arrived for him to go on to Macedonia. While the smoke and dust cleared away, it would be better for the Ephesian church if he were not there. He preached his farewell sermon and, embracing each of them, he departed, making his way north-ward along the road to Troas.

It was his hope to find Titus there, returning from Greece and perhaps bearing news of the church at Corinth. But at Troas he was disappointed. Titus did not come. He waited for a few days, and although the people of Troas were genuine in their friendliness to him, he was restless to go. The burden of the church at Corinth was weighing heavily now, and he had also purposed to visit all the churches in Macedonia. With this desire pressing upon him, he sailed for Macedonia and came to Philippi, where he knew he had many warm friends.

At the home of Lydia he was welcomed cordially, and that day was spent in greeting many of the Christians he had not seen for a very long time but had remembered in his prayers. The jailor and his family were there, and the meeting with the church was a happy time for Paul and all those who were his children in the faith. It was in the fellowship of the church here that he met Timothy again and heard of his success in preaching the gospel.

But the burden of Corinth was still upon him, and even though he enjoyed his stay among the Philippians, he was restless until the day came when Titus arrived from Corinth. He brought good news. The letter Paul had sent, together with the ministry of Titus, had brought about a change in the situation there. The Corinthians had punished the sinful man there who was living in open contradiction of the Lord and had purified their lives from the special sins that Paul had pointed out to them. Even the division in the church was somewhat improved, for instead of four parties, there were now only two—those who were for Paul and those who were against him. Paul's enemies doubted his claim to apostleship and even criticized his speech and personal appearance, but his friends were genuinely awakened to shame and repentance.

THE SECOND EPISTLE TO THE CORINTHIANS

With this report burning in his mind, Paul wrote the most personal of all his letters—the Second Epistle to the Corinthians. It was filled with the expression of his concern for them. He was troubled by their doubt about his apostleship, and he rehearsed much about his experiences, his thoughts, his fears and his inner life. He had much to say about his sufferings and labors for the cause of Christ. He told of being in prison often, of his five public floggings, and of suffering shipwreck three times, once being in the water for twenty-four hours.

In a sense this letter is an autobiography of Paul and a strong defense of his ministry and high calling. He wrote:

> Of the Jews five times I received forty stripes save one. Thrice was I beaten with rods, once was I stoned, thrice I suffered shipwreck, a night and a day I have been in the deep. In my travels I have been in constant danger from rivers and floods, from bandits, from my own countrymen, and from pagans. I have faced danger in city streets, danger in the desert, danger on the high seas, and danger among false Christians. I have known exhaustion, pain, long vigils, hunger and thirst, going without food and without clothing (2 Co 11:24-27).

This letter to the Corinthians was a mixture of praise and blame—praise for the loyal ones and blame for the unruly.

PAUL TRULY A FOREIGN MISSIONARY

Titus volunteered to return with the letter, and with him went Luke, the beloved physician. But Paul stayed on at Philippi, using this city as a center for his journeys through the whole province. Everywhere he exhorted Christians to a life that was separated from the world. Far into the mountains west of Philippi he journeyed, preaching the gospel in villages and towns where Christ had never been proclaimed. He used to say that he never wished to build upon another man's foundation, so he sought to visit places where the gospel story was not known. He was truly a foreign missionary doing the work of a pioneer, and wherever he went, the Lord was with him doing mighty signs and wonders and winning both Greeks and Jews to Himself.

As Paul moved from town to town, he realized the awful condition of unsaved people. They were dwelling in darkness, even though they lived in beautiful cities with temples whose glory was the wonder of the world. Even now Paul was planning a journey to Rome, where he could preach the gospel at the center of the Roman Empire. It might even be that he could press on to Spain.

THE WINTER IN CORINTH

After he had spent some weeks in Macedonia, he came south to Greece or, as it was also called, Achaia. There he was anxious to see for himself the state of the Corinthian church. Corinth needed him again, and besides, it was the capital of all Achaia, a good center from which he might preach in many of the nearby towns. For three months he stayed, laboring with Titus, who had taken a liking to the Corinthian believers and was proving to be a true and wise minister in a very difficult place.

During this time Paul found time to visit all the believers and speak privately with many, strengthening them in the faith and warning them against false teachers. And so the winter days went by.

THE EPISTLE TO THE ROMANS

It was during that winter that Paul wrote his letter to the Roman church. He had never visited the church, but the desire to do so was growing in his mind. Rome was the greatest city in the world, and to preach the message of salvation there would be a privilege indeed. Besides he already had many friends there, for by this time believers from every city he had visited had made their way to Rome and were established in business.

Paul had been a Christian now for over twenty-four years, and his hair was turning white with the care of all the churches. During these years he had come through many experiences and had found great disappointments, but his mind had opened toward Jesus as a flower opens to the sun. He had grown mature in the Christian life, but the simple gospel of Jesus Christ had become more of a conviction to him than it had ever been before.

So in his letter he determined to set forth the gospel in all its fullness. He dictated his words to Tertius, who wrote into the letter that he was the penman. It was a letter written to convince them that every man, be he pagan or Gentile or Jew, needed the salvation that God provided in His Only Begotten Son. And since God provided it and offered it as a gift, man could have it for the taking. No man has any righteousness in himself that can make him acceptable to God.

"There is none righteous, no, not one" (Ro 3:10). Not even by keeping the law can one be righteous. The law was given to prove that all the world is guilty before God, but by the deeds of the law nobody can be justified in His sight (v. 20). But God's righteousness is revealed in Jesus Christ, and by His grace all may believe. We are justified by faith in what God has done for us rather than by any good deeds we could ever do (v. 28).

The writing of Paul's greatest letter went on from day to day, setting forth the foundation facts of the Christian faith so that when false teachers came to Rome, as they no doubt would, the believers there would be fortified with a strong word from his own pen, even though they had never seen him in the flesh.

From the high peaks of lofty doctrines Paul went into the lowland of practical, everyday living and talked to them about their daily walk, the paying of their taxes, and their relationship to the Roman rulers. The great letter ended with some personal greetings to a number of the men and women of Rome, whom he named one by one. The seal was affixed and the scroll wrapped in a cloth cover and delivered to Phoebe, a woman of Cenchraea, the port of Corinth, who had business which took her to Rome.

PAUL'S DECISION TO RETURN HOME

When three months had gone by, Paul planned to sail to Syria. His enemies had not dared to trouble him while he was in Corinth, but learning of the plan to board a ship at Cenchraea, they laid plans to kill him. Away from the church where his friends stood by him, they would certainly have opportunity to do him violence. But their plan failed. It was discovered by a friend who overheard the secret and immediately warned Paul to change his plan. While his enemies watched the road to the coast, he set out on the inland road to Macedonia.

Reaching Philippi, he was joined by Luke, who stayed with him through every adventure to the day of Paul's death and wrote the story of each exploit in the Acts of the Apostles.

PLANS TO TAKE GIFTS TO THE CHURCH IN JERUSALEM

Seven men, chosen from different cities, purposed to accompany Paul on his journey home. They had each been entrusted with a special offering which their churches had gathered for the relief of the brethren in Jerusalem. Paul himself carried the offering from Corinth. These seven were sent ahead by ship to Troas while Paul and Luke remained at Philippi for the feast of the Passover. The Passover meant more to Paul now and to every Christian, for it marked the time when the Saviour rose from the dead.

Five days later they reached Troas and rejoined the seven

who awaited them. These men had not been idle. They had searched out all the Christians and told them that the great apostle was going to pay them a visit.

Upon Paul's arrival, therefore, the Christians of the city gathered together to celebrate the Lord's Supper and to listen to instruction in Christian doctrine. Paul's heart was full as he rose to address them. He remembered how in this city he had received his vision of Macedonia and how, and in his haste to go, he had slighted them: He also remembered that more recently, in his anxious fears for Corinth, he had hastened on in spite of their pleadings to stay.

THE SERMON IN TROAS

Again Paul's plans were made, and his boat was to sail the very next day. How could he say all he should to these dear people in one night? Hour after hour he stood, preaching with all his soul, answering their questions, and strengthening their faith. The place was hot and crowded, and many hanging lamps burned in the chamber. So to gain an advantage over the crowd standing on the floor, a young man, Eutychus, climbed up into a high window and perched himself precariously there. While Paul was still preaching, a terrifying cry rent the air, and a sickening thud brought the sermon to an abrupt end. Eutychus had fallen asleep, overbalanced, and come crashing down to the pavement.

Confusion reigned in the room and when the people reached the window, they saw the apparently lifeless body huddled below. They rushed to the street. Luke, the doctor, was no doubt one of the first on the spot. He glanced at the motionless form and shrugged his shoulders as if to say, "It is of no use, he is gone."

Then Paul pushed his way into the crowd and, like Elijah the prophet, stretched his body over the young man and embraced him, praying to God with great confidence that all would be well. Then, rising to his feet, he said to the stricken crowd, "Trouble not yourselves; for his life is in him" (Ac 20:10).

As they watched, the color came back to the pale cheeks of Eutychus. Paul then turned him over to his loved ones and went upstairs again where the thankful Christians gathered to hear more.

When the light of early dawn bathed the great plain to the east of Troas, Paul was still preaching, and the believers were listening. This was their great opportunity, and they did not miss a word. But with the coming day, the men had to return to their work, and Luke, with the seven trusted believers, had to go aboard the ship for an early start.

THE TRIP TO JERUSALEM

But Paul planned to walk to Assos, a distance of about twenty miles, and board the same ship there. He needed that walk to be alone with his thoughts and make some decisions. Somehow he was not happy about his trip back to Jerusalem. His spirit was not free about it. There were forebodings of trouble. Paul never had felt welcome in Jerusalem, not even in the Christian church. His work lay definitely among the Gentiles. Therefore he was troubled in spirit about the future in Jerusalem. But he was not a coward, and if it meant imprisonment in Jerusalem, it would not be the first time he had been in jail. Had not the Lord stood with him in prison? So he decided in his solitude that day to return, no matter what awaited him. Perhaps his friends in the churches he had left were wrong in their advice to shun Jerusalem, but the advice had been repeated so often that he could not help but be troubled. He wondered if he were going against the voice of God's Spirit.

At Assos he boarded the ship, and when the cargo was safely loaded, they sailed before the north wind to the island of Lesbos.

All the next day they sailed among the islands of the Aegean, passing Chios, and later, the great gulf on which the city of Ephesus was built. The ship's master had no cargo for Ephesus, but he would have put into the port there had Paul wished him to. But Paul was anxious to reach Jerusalem in time for the feast of Pentecost, and he urged the master to sail by the city.

PREACHING TO HIS BELOVED EPHESIANS

At Miletus, some twenty-five miles to the south of Ephesus, the ship would have a longer stay, for there they unloaded merchandise and picked up more cargo for the remainder of the journey. Paul dispatched a message to his friends in Ephesus, telling them that he was waiting at Miletus and wished to see them. The feeling that this would be his last trip to them grew in his mind, and since he had been warned that bonds awaited him in Jerusalem, it was best to take every opportunity.

Eagerly they came, especially the elders of the church, for they remembered his three years as their pastor, and they loved him above all others. The meeting was joyous but tense, for they all felt it was a final farewell. Last words are always filled with solemnity and importance, and Paul spoke as one who had grown old in the faith. He urged them to stand fast and be strong whatever might come to discourage them in the future.

With great eloquence he rehearsed his three years with them, reminding them of days of sunshine and shadow:

> And now I know that you, among whom I have preached the kingdom of God, shall see my face no more. Therefore I want you all to remember that I have not shrunk from declaring to you the whole counsel of God. I have fulfilled my responsibility to you, and the burden now rests upon you. Take heed to yourselves and to all the flock over which the Lord has made you overseers. Feed the church of God, for that is the only way they can grow strong.
> And remember that the time will come after I am gone

that wild wolves will rush in upon you, not sparing the flock. And even among yourselves false teachers will arise and with falsehoods lead the people astray. And when you see that happen, remember my ministry among you and how I never ceased to warn you, even with tears in my eyes. And now I commend you to Jesus and His words of grace which are able to build you up and give you an inheritance among the believers (Ac 20:25-32).

His voice ceased and his grey head drooped and the room was filled with silence. Nobody felt like talking, and it seemed the only thing to do was to fall on their knees. One by one Paul mentioned each elder at the throne of grace, asking that the Saviour keep him loyal, true, and strong in a day of temptation. When they arose to their feet, there were tears in every eye. They were seeing the last of a great warrior who had led them fearlessly in the battle. As a mother bird scatters her nest, he was now turning over full responsibilities to them, putting them on their own. With sorrow pounding in their hearts, they accompanied him down to the ship and watched until the vessel grew indistinct in the distance.

THE VISIT TO TYRE

Two days later, after skirting the island of Cos and landing at Rhodes, the nine voyagers landed at Patara in Lycia. That was the vessel's last port of call. Good fortune attended them, however, and with no delay they were able to find another ship ready to sail to Syria. With a good wind they soon came within sight of Cyprus, and without stopping there, they headed for the open sea and the great city of Tyre. It was a Gentile city, and since there was scarcely a town where Christians did not meet together, Paul and his friends sought the place where the believers gathered. For seven days they mingled with them, preaching the kingdom of God and encouraging them with the stories of what God had done in distant cities.

It was here that Paul received a warning from certain

disciples that danger awaited him in Jerusalem. It was a confirmation of what he had already sensed, but it did not shake his purpose. He wanted to go to Jerusalem for many reasons. He had a long report to make to the disciples about the spread of the gospel. Besides, he carried money for the saints at Jerusalem, the gift of the church in Corinth, and he wanted to deliver it in person.

When the week had passed and the ship was ready to resume its journey, Paul and his friends breathed a sigh of relief that they had come to the last stage of their trip. At Ptolemais they left the vessel to finish its voyage and, realizing that they had some fourteen days to spare before the great holiday at Jerusalem, they spent one day with the Christians in that port.

THE PROPHECY OF AGABUS

After they had brought greetings to the brethren, they set out over the coastal road to Caesarea. Paul always felt at home here for he had visited often. He was sure of hospitality, for this was where Philip the evangelist lived.

It was while they were living with Philip that the prophet Agabus, who had foretold the great famine in the days of Claudius Caesar, arrived from Judea. Agabus knew the household of Philip, because Philip's four daughters had been known to have the gift of prophecy, and he sought them out upon his arrival.

Coming to the house where Paul was a guest, Agabus recognized the apostle; and, with a knowledge of the feeling that existed against Paul in Jerusalem, he warned him not to go. Like one of the prophets of the Old Testament, he made his warning vivid. He loosened the long linen girdle from Paul's waist and, stooping down, he bound his own feet and hands. While the believers gazed at him in silence, he said,

> Thus saith the Holy Spirit of God: In this same way shall the Jews of Jerusalem bind the man that owns this girdle and deliver him into the hands of the Romans (Ac 21:11).

PAUL'S INSISTENCE ON GOING INTO JERUSALEM

Immediately the whole group, including Timothy and Luke, besought him to give up his plan to go to Jerusalem. With tears in their eyes they pleaded, but their words were like waves beating upon a rock. Paul was determined. Their words grieved him. All their protests were well-meant and intended to save him from bodily harm, but that is not what he feared. He had faced that before, and the Lord had delivered him. He told them,

> Why do you weep, and why do you break my heart like this? I want to go, and I am ready not only to be bound but even to die at Jerusalem for Jesus' sake (v. 13).

In the face of such determination they ceased their pleading and each one said, "The will of the Lord be done" (v. 14).

So, knowing the danger ahead, Paul gathered his baggage together and set his face like flint to go up to Jerusalem. Several of the Christians of Caesarea joined the party, one of whom was Mnason, one of the earliest of all the believers, who owned a home in Jerusalem. At this house Paul could lodge during his stay and be shielded from danger.

12

The Last Visit to Jerusalem

WITH THE DISCIPLES IN JERUSALEM

JERUSALEM WAS PREPARING for the day of Pentecost, and already the city was filled with Jews from all over the empire. But Paul and his friends were able to stay at Mnason's home. It was a pretentious place with a high wall around it, and the Christians who enjoyed the man's hospitality had every comfort.

At the home of Mary, Paul met some of the leading men of the church. James, the brother of Jesus, was one of them. He had grown older now, and his long, white hair curled over his shoulders in the fashion of a Nazarite. Paul saluted the whole church and told them the story of his third journey. He had traveled through the Cilician Gates to Galatia, and after visiting all the churches there, he had gone to Ephesus for a stay of three years. He had sailed to Europe and preached to the saints of Philippi, witnessing for Christ in the inland regions of Illyricum. And he had gone at last to Corinth, from which city he had carried on a campaign that took him to many towns of Greece. The story of four years of labor was quickly reviewed.

The Jerusalem believers heard, too, about the unruly church at Corinth, and how it had repented and turned from its evil. And then, as if to confirm his words about Corinth, Paul brought out a heavy sack of money and presented it as the gift of the Corinthians to the mother church to care for the brethren who were reduced to poverty because of their stand for Christ.

GIFTS TO THE MOTHER CHURCH

When Paul handed over his gift, the companions who had traveled with him for this very purpose brought theirs, too. Luke from Philippi, Timothy of Lystra, Sopater of Berea, Aristarchus and Secundus of Thessalonica, Gaius of Derbe, Tychicus and Trophimus of Ephesus—all Christians from far-off cities and all the product of Paul's ministry—brought heavy money bags and gave them to the brethren to distribute according to need.

Paul's report was glorious, but while he was giving it, he sensed the narrowness of the Jerusalem brethren. Of course, the gathering praised God for the wonderful growth of the kingdom and for every Gentile who accepted Christ, but at the same time Paul could feel that they were not at all like the believers of Antioch. Even the glowing story of heroism which he told was received with mixed feelings.

THE FATAL COMPROMISE

As leader of the group, James rose to receive the gifts and to acknowledge them. There was always a certain stiffness to James, and Paul and his friends felt it now. Paul felt, too, that the elders at Jerusalem had held a discussion about him, and they were not yet convinced that his position was of God. Stories about Paul's preaching had been brought back to Jerusalem, and the elders were uneasy about what they had heard. So when Paul told of the work among the Gentiles, saying that there was no difference in the sight of God between a Jew and a Gentile and that a Gentile Christian was just as much a member of the church as a Jewish Christian, their suspicions were confirmed.

The feeling of the meeting came out when James, the spokesman for them all, said,

> You see, brother, we rejoice with you over the Gentile converts, but you must not forget the many thousands of Jews who are followers of Christ. These all hold strictly to

the customs of Moses and have heard that you teach the Jews of the provinces that they need not follow these customs. Now Jerusalem is full of devout Jews, both Christians and non-Christians; and these are sure to hear of your coming and create a disturbance.

Our advice to you, therefore, is that you prove openly to these men that you do respect the Mosaic law. Four of our Christian Jews have taken upon themselves a Nazarite vow. These men are poor and will not have the money for the necessary sacrifices. Now you take them to the temple and pay their expenses, so that the Jews will see that whatever they have heard of you is untrue (Ac 21:20-24).

Paul listened to the advice and weighed it. How he longed to bind together the opposing parties in the church! In unimportant details Paul was perfectly willing to give in. He used to say that he was willing to be all things to all men that he might gain some. Here was a chance to follow after the things which made for peace. If it was so important to his testimony among the Jews, he could go through with this request without any hurt to himself.

With misgivings he accepted the suggestion in the hope that it might bring peace between the two parties. He brought the four men to the temple, announced that they were about to begin their seven days of purification, and for each of the four paid for two rams, a sheep and a basket of unleavened cakes with a measure of wine.

The plan gave promise of healing the wound, but actually it was the first step that brought his career to an end. It was a compromise, and it proved to be a sad mistake. It was planned to be a demonstration to convince the narrow-minded Jewish Christians, but it turned out to be a weapon used against him.

RIOTING IN THE TEMPLE

In the temple a group of Jews from Asia Minor gathered to listen to one of the rabbis as he discoursed about the law.

Suddenly one of them tugged at the garment of his friend and asked, "Is not that the Christian leader, Paul, over there? What can he be doing in the temple?"

The little group turned quickly to identify the man they had opposed bitterly when he preached Christ in their synagogue. Well did they remember how this man's preaching had upset the synagogue and divided their Jewish families. He had spoken against their national worship and their customs. This is the man they had run out of town, and here he was in the temple.

Someone recalled that he had seen him before with Trophimus the Ephesian, and soon they were all sure that this man had profaned the holy place by bringing a Gentile into the temple.

"Men of Israel, help!" They rushed toward Paul, screaming out their bitter accusation: "This is the man, that teacheth all men every where against the people, and the law, and this [temple]" (v. 28).

Men were running from all directions now. The crowd was gathering, and rumors flew thick and fast. Outside the temple walls the news had spread that a traitor to Israel had been caught and was to be put to death. The streets were full of people running to the temple to see the excitement.

In the temple the surging mob had seized Paul, and beating him with sticks and delivering heavy blows with their hands, they dragged him out into the street before the temple, where they prepared to kill him.

But help was at hand, and the Roman troops who kept a special watch over the city during the religious festivals, had been quick to notice the commotion at the temple gates. Lysias, their captain, did not lose a moment. With a company of troops he ran to the place where the mob was beating Paul. At the sight of the Roman soldiers, the crowd fell back.

PAUL'S DEFENSE

Seeing that Paul was the center of all the confusion, the

Roman supposed him to be a criminal and ordered him bound with chains, and then Lysias demanded of the crowd, "Who is this, and what evil has he done?"

Instantly, from a thousand Jews came a throaty roar, and in the confusion he could make out nothing. Lysias hated these rebellious Jews and detested their religious squabbles. They seemed to be the only conquered people of the empire that needed to be heavily guarded. At every religious feast they endangered the peace of Rome. And now in the confusion of this scene some were shouting one thing and some another. Lysias could not understand the meaning of their wild cries.

With an impatient gesture to his men, he gave the signal to surround Paul and bring him to the castle on the hill. The crowd grew bold, and the shouting and jeering increased. They pressed so closely to the prisoner that the soldiers had to lift him off his feet and literally carry him to the steps of the castle. From the shouts of the rabble, Lysias thought he had captured the Egyptian rioter who had gathered a multitude on the Mount of Olives and promised that at his command the walls of Jerusalem would fall.

But as they reached the castle stairs and left the angry crowd below, Paul turned with respect to his captor and said in the Greek tongue, "May I say something to you?"

Lysias was amazed that here in Jerusalem this captive "Egyptian" should address him in Greek.

Paul explained,

> I am a Jew from Tarsus, a citizen of no mean city, and I beg of you to let me speak to this crowd of people (v. 39).

Somehow Lysias was impressed with Paul's calmness in the face of danger, and with evident admiration he gave permission. So as the soldiers guarded the steps with their heavy spears, Paul raised his hand to the angry multitude as a sign that he wanted to speak to them. His very boldness gained him a hearing, and in the language of the temple and of their

Scriptures he began his address to them. The language of the
street was Aramaic, but this man spoke in the Hebrew tongue,
and the crowd was silent.

Below him were scowling faces—here a white-robed Pharisee, there a rabbi in his long-sleeved gown, and everywhere
eyes that were burning with hatred.

His speech was unlike any of his others, for the crowd was
in no mood to listen to a sermon.

"Men, brethren, and fathers, hear ye my defence which I
make now unto you" (22:1).

The crowd was electrified—this was their beloved Hebrew
tongue.

> I am a Jew, born in Tarsus of Cilicia, but I was brought
> up in this city in the school of Gamaliel. I was zealous
> for God, as you all are today (v. 3).

Paul had learned that as a speaker he must catch the
interest of his audience by telling them the things they loved
to hear!

> I persecuted to death the followers of Jesus, binding both
> men and women and casting them into prison. Your high
> priest and the Sanhedrin know I speak the truth, for they
> gave me letters to our countrymen at Damascus. They
> clothed me with authority to search out these unruly Chris-
> tians and bring them home to Jerusalem for punishment
> (vv. 4-5).

Then he told them of the light that had shone about him
as he entered the city of Damascus and of the voice and the
appearance of the Lord. He told, too, about Ananias, about
the recovery of his sight, and about the divine commission
to go and preach Christ to the whole world. Because of his
sudden change from persecutor to disciple, the Jews of Jerusalem had refused to hear him, and while in the temple one
day, he had fallen into a trance. He heard the voice of the
Lord commanding him to leave Jerusalem and to preach to
the Gentiles.

Up to that point the crowd listened in silence but when the hated name *Gentile* was spoken, their religious pride was stung, and out of the crowd there arose a shrill scream of rage. Suddenly it became an angry roar. "Away with such a fellow from the earth: for it is not fit that he should live" (v. 22).

Then, casting off their garments, they threw handfuls of dirt into the air as an obvious token of their utter disgust and shouted for his death.

Lysias could not understand Paul's defence, for he did not know the Hebrew tongue, and with the renewal of the crowd's fury, he brought him within the castle walls. He ordered his men to flog him and get the truth out of him by torture. And as the thongs bound his hands to the post, Paul said to the officer in charge, "Is it lawful for you to scourge a man that is a Roman, and uncondemned" (v. 25).

The officer was startled at the question and, ordering the soldiers to cease for a moment, he went to find Lysias, to tell him what Paul had said. "Take heed what thou doest: for this man is a Roman" (v. 26).

Lysias returned with the officer to the place where Paul stood with bared back, chained to the post. "Tell me, are thou a Roman?" (v. 27).

And when Paul assured him that he was, Lysias ordered that the bonds be taken from him and the scourge be put away. He had almost made a great mistake.

Then he turned to Paul and said, "I had to pay a large sum of money to be made a Roman citizen."

And Paul replied, "But I am a Roman citizen by birth."

The soldiers were ordered to bring Paul's clothing and to help him into his robe and cloak. Then the apostle was taken to a stone cell, from which he fully expected to be set free by the next day. But he had passed through the door of a Roman prison, and in a real sense he was never to be free again.

PAUL BEFORE THE SANHEDRIN

Instead of being set free, Paul was brought by a troop of soldiers into the great hall of the temple. All his bonds had been removed, and he found himself face to face with the Jewish Sanhedrin. This august body had been summoned by Lysias in order that he might hear the charges of the Jews and come to some decision about the prisoner. Entering the outer court of the temple, Paul sat between his guards in the very hall where he had often stood as an accuser and given his voice against the disciples of Jesus.

Gazing into the eyes of the Sanhedrin, he knew that there were men here who had been present at a mock trial a quarter of a century ago when Jesus stood in this very place.

The last time Paul had been in this council chamber his heart had been burning with hatred. He used to attend every meeting of this court and vote against the Christians. But now it was different. His heart was filled with the peace of God, and his chief desire was to speak in such a manner that he might be an effective witness for his Saviour.

Lysias gave him permission, and with the skill of a great orator Paul began his talk. "Men and brethren, I have lived in all good conscience before God until this day" (23:1).

The members of the Sanhedrin were sure this was a lie. They considered him a traitor to their cause, and a statement like this stunned them. Ananias, the high priest, cried out, "Guard, strike him on the mouth!"

But the guard looked at Lysias, his commander, and stood at attention.

Paul was roused to anger by this stinging command and turning his near-sighted eyes upon the high priest he quickly replied,

> God shall smite thee, thou hypocrite, for thou sittest there and judgest me by the law of our nation, and at the same time thou breakest the law by commanding me to be struck (v. 3).

There was shouting of many voices, and someone cried, "How dare you speak against God's high priest?"

There was a charge against Paul immediately. He realized he had made a blunder and quickly he apologized for it.

> Brothers, I did not know that he was the high priest; for our law says, "Thou shalt not speak ill of a ruler of the people" (v. 5).

Paul's sight had never been good, and as he grew older it did not improve. He used to refer to this trouble as his thorn in the flesh.

Paul continued his speech. Feeling that the council was part Pharisee and part Sadducee, he shouted,

> Men and brethren, I am a Pharisee, and the son of a Pharisee, and as such the central hope of my faith was the resurrection of the dead. It was natural for me to believe in Christ Jesus because He is the only one in all our history who has proven that hope. It is really because of this that I am called in question (v. 6).

He knew when he spoke that what he said would divide the council, for he knew who was a Pharisee and who was a Sadducee. Since the Pharisees believed in the resurrection of the dead and the Sadducees denied it, there arose a great dissension in the council. Cutting remarks were flung by each side at the other. Men jumped to their feet, shaking their fists at each other; and the Pharisees, remembering Gamaliel's advice, took the position that if a Spirit or an angel had really spoken to Paul, they should not be in the position of fighting against God. So, forgetting their grievance against the apostle, they said, "We find no evil in this man" (v. 9).

But the Sadducees would not hear of such a decision, and the din increased. Lysias looked on in calm disgust. This was typical of all the Jews' religious squabbling. Cries and curses were hurled from one party to another as each claimed the right to decide about Paul. Some tried to lay hands on him to drag him out to his death, but the armed soldiers at a command from their captain, encircled Paul and literally saved him from being torn in pieces. Lysias gave a sharp order, and the guards conducted Paul up the hill and into the castle.

PAUL'S VISION IN THE NIGHT

That night as he lay on his pallet of straw, Paul wished he had obeyed the voice of the Holy Spirit and not come to Jerusalem. Everywhere he had failed. His plans to carry the gospel to Rome and even to Spain had come to naught. As he tried to sleep, he was uneasy and restless; and in his agony, he saw the Lord standing by his side and saying, "Be of good cheer, Paul: for as thou hast testified of me in Jerusalem, so must thou bear witness also at Rome" (v. 11).

Paul's spirit was revived and comforted. He did not know how this promise was to be fulfilled, but it was enough for God to know. Paul was content. The longing of his heart was to be granted. God was not through with him yet.

Before the next day had passed, a young man climbed the castle hill and entered the garrison with a request to visit the prisoner. He said he was a relative and was admitted. When Paul saw him he recognized his own sister's son. When Paul was a young man in Tarsus, his sister had been married to a man in Jerusalem, and they had lived there ever since and raised a family loyal to the synagogue.

THE WARNING

"Uncle Paul," he said, "there is a plot among the Jews to destroy you, and I come to warn you. More than forty of them have bound themselves by an oath that they will neither eat nor drink until they have killed you. Tomorrow the chief priests are going to ask Lysias to bring you to the council again, saying that they want to ask you certain questions. But the band of forty will lie in wait, and as soon as the guards turn you over to the temple authorities, they will spring upon you and kill you."

Paul was bound to his guard, but he asked the centurion to take his nephew to Lysias and warn him of the plot. The chief captain listened to every word and made the young man promise to keep these matters in strict secrecy.

But it was beginning to be clear to Lysias that the only way to insure the peace was to get Paul out of Jerusalem. In his mind a plan was forming. He would send his prisoner to Felix, the governor, at Caesarea. That was the Roman capital of Judea, and the danger of riot would not be as great in a distant city with a bigger Roman garrison. With his plans laid to send Paul away that very night, he chuckled to think of the Jews' disgust when they found their prisoner gone. He laughed to think of how the forty would have to break their vow or die very quickly of starvation.

That night an escort of two hundred soldiers under the command of two centurions, along with seventy horsemen and two hundred spearmen, set out for Caesarea with their prisoner. The company was large because Lysias feared an uprising of the Jews. Besides this, the garrison at Jerusalem had been strengthened during the feast of Pentecost, but now that it was over and the pilgrims had gone home, many of the soldiers should be sent back to the stations from which they had come.

At Antipatris, the soldiers turned back toward Jerusalem, and the horsemen continued with Paul, feeling that the danger from the Jews was over.

Lysias had sent a letter to Felix, outlining Paul's case and concluding, "I can find nothing against the prisoner worthy of death or of bonds, but I am telling his accusers to bring their charge before your judgment seat."

The letter gave the impression that Lysias had rescued Paul from these Jews because he was a Roman.

When Felix read it, he noted that Paul was a Roman citizen, and he asked from what province he had come. When he learned that he was from Cilicia, he commanded that he be kept safe and that a trial be arranged after his accusers arrived from Jerusalem.

But Paul had fallen into the hands of a weak man, whose habit it was to procrastinate and who, to protect his power, was unscrupulous in his injustice. The next two years of Paul's life were spent within the prison walls at Caesarea. It was discouraging, but then, he had God's promise that he would preach the gospel at Rome.

Antonius Felix was appointed procurator by the Emperor Claudius in A.D. 52. He married a Jewess, Drusilla, the daughter of Agrippa I, after taking her away from her husband. The sin made him unhappy in his high office. He had once been a slave, and now that he had been set free and exalted to great power, he was not equal to it. His reign was one of revenge and cruelty, and his dishonesty was evident in the taking and giving of bribes. He was hated by all whom he ruled, and his only remedy for the disorders of Judea was brute force.

THE TRIAL BEFORE FELIX

Five days after Paul arrived in Caesarea, the high priest, Ananias, and the elders of Jerusalem came to accuse him. Because these Jews were unacquainted with the Roman law, they brought with them a clever lawyer named Tertullus. They were not going to lose this time! Standing in the court of Felix, the orator began his speech by complimenting the governor and criticizing Lysias, the chief captain.

> Seeing that through you we enjoy great peace in our land and that by your care great things have been done for our nation, we acknowledge it everywhere with thankfulness, most noble Felix. I do not want to tire you, but hope that you will be kind enough to hear these few words (24:2-4).

Then, pointing a long finger at the apostle, who sat near the front of the hall in charge of a soldier, he continued,

> We have found this man a pestilent fellow, stirring up
> sedition among our Jewish people wherever he has gone
> in the Roman world. He is a ringleader of the sect called
> the Nazarenes, and he deliberately tried to profane our
> temple. When we captured him to judge him according
> to our law, Lysias rushed upon us with great violence and
> took him out of our hands, ordering us to appear before
> you, which we have done (vv. 5-8).

Turning to his employers with an eloquent sweep of the
hand, Tertullus asked them if these facts were not so. And
as Felix searched their faces, they nodded one by one.

These were grave charges, especially the one about inciting
riot among the Jews. If there was anything for which the
Romans were watchful, it was for the traitor who disturbed
the Roman peace. But as Paul listened to this speech, he
saw the weak points in it, and when he was given permission
to make his defense, he was quick to point them out.

PAUL'S DEFENSE

As Paul stood up before the court, Felix leaned forward
to listen attentively. He had heard of these Nazarenes and
their zeal, and since his wife was a Jewess, it was of some interest to him to hear about this Jesus who, it was claimed,
had risen from the dead.

Tertullus was an orator, but Paul had heard the men of
Athens, and God had given him an ability to speak that far
surpassed that of any of his contemporaries. He began:

> I am happy, most noble Felix, to make my defence before
> you, because I know that for many years you have been
> a judge of this nation (v. 10).

Then, launching into his argument without further delay,
he denied each charge against him, outlining with great simplicity the events that led to his arrest.

> Take note that it is only twelve days since I arrived in
> Jerusalem. I went there to worship. Thus, my accusers

did not find me disputing with any man, either in the
temple or in any synagogue or in the city. They never
found me stirring up the crowd, and they cannot prove
that of which they accuse me. One thing, however, I do
admit. I belong to the followers of Jesus, which they
regard as heresy. After the manner of the Christians, I
worship the God of my fathers. I believe all that is written in our Jewish law and in the prophets; and like these
men, I hope and look for the resurrection of the dead.
And in all my life I strive to maintain a conscience that is
clear toward God and man.

I was away from Jerusalem for many years, and only
came back to bring money to my countrymen—the offerings of the churches. And when certain Jews from Asia
saw me in the temple, having purified myself before going
in, they raised a cry which started the riot. These are the
men who should be here today to witness that I came not
with multitude or with tumult. But since they are not here,
let these who are present say if they saw me do anything
that was evil when I stood before their council (vv. 11-20).

Paul looked upon them all, and there was silence. Felix
felt in his heart that Paul was innocent. This was not the first
time he had met with Jewish spite and malice. But if a voice
told him to dismiss the case, another tempted him to wait
until he found out which side he could support to his own best
advantage.

Paul Held in Prison

The mention of money for the brethren in Jerusalem made
him wonder if a sizeable sum might be paid to him for Paul's
liberty. At any rate it was worth trying! If the church wanted
their leader's release, they would no doubt raise a fund to
obtain it. He determined to postpone his decision until another day. It would not hurt to have Paul around for a while;
there was much about the Nazarenes that interested him, and
he wished to have a private audience with the prisoner.

With an impatient wave of his hand, Felix dismissed his

court, promising to hear them again when Lysias came down from Jerusalem. Paul, the prisoner, was kept in military custody, chained to a guard, but free to receive his friends and acquaintances. The months sped on and Lysias never came down, and Ananias, with his elders and their lawyer, disgusted with the weakness of the governor, turned their faces in anger toward Jerusalem.

During the next few days Paul had many private audiences with Felix. On one occasion Felix brought his wife, Drusilla. She was a princess, beautiful and not yet twenty. Felix had told her about Paul and, being a Jewess, she wished to see this countryman of hers who had turned Christian. She understood the difference between Paul and the Jews who accused him, and she had tried to explain it to her husband. It would be interesting to see this man and hear him. Felix gave orders to bring Paul to the palace.

With guards on both sides of him, Paul entered the great room of the palace, where Felix and his young wife reclined on silken couches. She was beautiful and ambitious, and with a smile of curiosity, she turned her attention to her aging countryman, of whom she had heard so much. Drusilla, the Jewess, had a religious background; but since she had abandoned herself to a life of wickedness for the sake of power and position, she was not greatly concerned with this interview but only a little curious.

Felix had no religion. Like most of his class, he possessed a superstitious dread of the unknown, and when Paul spoke, he was fascinated by the man's conviction and authority. He was gripped by the fear that Paul might be right in what he said. Maybe there was a living God who held the future in His hands, and maybe God would punish the wicked. If so, where would he stand? But when his princess smiled upon him, he forgot it all and turned his back upon Christ with a careless shrug.

The great apostle did not mince matters. He spoke out

boldly about living clean, righteous lives and about controlling passions.

Felix's life had been uncontrolled and utterly selfish. He had gratified every feeling of hatred and revenge and desire. But now Paul's words frightened him, and he trembled as he thought of the future. Drusilla arched her pretty eyebrows and smiled a vacant smile that he could not resist. He realized that if he allowed his emotions to carry him so far as to fall under the spell of Paul, he would have to give up this beautiful but sinful woman who was the light of his lecherous life.

A feeling of fear seized him, and covering it all under the pretence of being very busy in official matters, he waved his hand as a sign that the interview had ended. "Go thy way for this time," he said. "When I have a convenient season, I will call for thee" (v. 25).

As Paul retired from the room, he heard the giggling laugh of the young princess as she and her husband quickly turned to other things.

As the days sped by, Felix sent for Paul again and again, for he liked to converse with him about eternal things, and besides this, he still entertained a hope that the Christians would offer a sum of money for their leader's liberty. But the money never came, and each day that Felix rejected the gospel, his heart grew harder. Paul went back to his life in the prison, holding conversations daily with believers who visited him.

And the life of Caesarea went on day after day while Paul lived two long years chained to a Roman guard, with his ministry at a standstill and his cause untried. His enemies were not asleep, however, and they pleaded with Felix to keep him a prisoner. So, seeking to do the Jews a favor, the governor left him bound. When appeals were made by Paul's friends, he promised to hasten matters upon the arrival of the proper witnesses to proceed with a trial. Both the friends and enemies of Paul pleaded with the governor for a decision, but he put them off and would neither put him to death nor release him.

Felix was suddenly recalled to Rome. During his term of office there had been many uprisings of the Zealots, which he had subdued with force, only to find that they broke out again in another area. Reports of this reached the ears of Caesar, who would tolerate no disorder in his realms. So Felix was removed, and another governor was sent with instructions to keep the Roman peace.

PAUL BEFORE FESTUS

No sooner had Festus come to Herod's castle and taken up the reins of authority than the Jews saw another opportunity to bring about Paul's death. When Festus made his first official visit to Jerusalem, the chief priest and some of his men waited upon him and begged that Paul be brought to Jerusalem for trial. Their plan was to murder him at some spot along the road. But they overplayed their part, and Festus guessed that something lay behind their keen interest.

"It is not the custom of Romans," he probably said, "to give up any man for punishment before he has met his accusers and has made his defense. He is being kept at Caesarea, and when I return shortly, let them that are of power among you accompany me and accuse the man if there is any wrong in him."

This man was not like Felix. He kept his word, and the next day he returned to Caesarea. Paul was brought to the court to face some of the same accusers who had cried out for his blood in the days of Felix. Festus had no understanding of Jewish law, and he marveled at the zeal of these men of Jerusalem in their efforts ot procure a death sentence. He listened patiently to the accusations and the arguments. It seemed to him to be a dispute about their religions which he could never settle.

He was anxious to begin well and to win the favor of those he ruled over, so giving ear to their request for many witnesses, he turned to Paul and asked, "Are you willing to go up to Jerusalem and there be judged of these things in my court?"

THE APPEAL TO CAESAR

Paul thought of the hatred of the Sanhedrin and realized that in Jerusalem he would be in the midst of his enemies. He made up his mind quickly and said,

> Against the Jews I have done no wrong, as you very well know. But if I have sinned against Roman law and have done anything that deserves death, I am ready to die. But if none of these things are true with which they accuse me, no man can give me up to them because I appeal to Caesar (25:10-11).

Festus was astonished. He had never listened to such an appeal before, but he knew that by Roman law it could not be denied, for Paul was a free citizen and this was his noblest right as a Roman. After conferring hastily with his counsel, he rose and made his pronouncement in grave tones, like the sentence of a court. "Hast thou appealed unto Caesar? Unto Caesar shalt thou go" (v. 12).

The die was cast. The cause of Christianity was to go before the highest court in the world. Festus prepared a report to his emperor and found great difficulty in knowing what to write. He had nothing definite to state against this man, but his report had to go through.

While Festus pondered, he received guests from the neighboring provinces and towns, wishing him well in his new office and saying how glad they were to welcome him to Judea. Among those who came was King Herod Agrippa II of Galilee and the region about Jordan. He was a brother of the young and beautiful Drusilla and a great-grandson of Herod the Great.

The Herods were all fond of show, and Festus did his best to feed his guest's vanity and court his favor. In the course of conversation he told his guest about his puzzling prisoner, asking his advice about how to frame a letter of appeal to Caesar Augustus.

PAUL BEFORE AGRIPPA

The king asked to hear the apostle himself, promising that after he had heard him, he would help Festus to report to Caesar. Agrippa's own brother-in-law had had long dealings with Paul, and this would be an opportunity to hear a man who was known as a great orator as he spoke on a subject that had troubled Israel.

The request was granted, and the next day Agrippa came with a show of royal splendor. Bernice was with him, ablaze in all her jewels, and to please the king, Festus had invited the officers of his regiments and the chief men of the city. It was a mock trial, for nothing could be decided, but Agrippa had requested it.

Into the praetorium the brilliant company came, seating themselves in the gilded chairs that Festus had placed for his visitors. Around the wall the lictors stood at attention, and the prisoner stood in the center of the grandeur, bound by the feet with a chain.

Festus stated the case as he knew it. Then Agrippa asked Paul to speak for himself, and settled back in his chair to listen. With an eloquent motion of his hand, Paul commanded their attention and began his defense.

> I think myself fortunate, King Agrippa, in that I am to make my defence before you today, regarding all the things for which I am accused by my countrymen, because I know that you thoroughly understand the religion and customs of my people. Therefore I beg you to hear me patiently (26:2-3).

Agrippa was complimented, and his attitude was friendly. Paul had made a clever beginning. He went on. His testimony, found in Acts 26, was essentially as follows:

My accusers know my life from its beginning. They know that I was brought up in Jerusalem as a strict Pharisee. In the days of our forefathers God gave our nation a promise of the Messiah, Whose coming they are still expecting. It is because I believe this promise is fulfilled that they accuse me of heresy. Every Pharisee believes in the resurrection of the dead, and yet they deny that God could raise Jesus of Nazareth. As for me I know it, for I have seen Him and heard Him.

I did not always believe in Jesus. At one time I, too, thought Him an impostor, and I persecuted His followers far and wide. But while I was on the way to Damascus on that business, I saw Jesus; and a light brighter than the sun at noonday made me blind. He it was who spoke to me and gave me my commission to be a witness to the Gentiles. Whereupon, O King Agrippa, I was not disobedient to the heavenly vision but witnessed first at Damascus, then at Jerusalem and through all the coasts of Judea, and then to the Gentiles, pleading with them to repent, turn to God, and live lives worthy of this great profession.

It is because of this that the Jews caught me in the temple and sought to kill me. But by the help of God I am alive today, witnessing both to small and great the very thing which Moses and the prophets said would come— that Messiah should suffer and rise again from the dead (vv. 4-23).

Festus had been listening closely with growing astonishment. He knew of Jesus from the Roman records. He had been crucified under Pontius Pilate; that was now history. But this prisoner talked calmly of His resurrection and of having seen and talked with Him since that event. What nonsense! The man must be insane. "Paul," he shouted with a loud voice, "thou art beside thyself; much learning doth make thee mad" (v. 24).

No, most noble Festus, I am not mad. I am speaking nothing but the truth, in soberness. And what is more, the king knows about all these things, for none of this happened in secret. King Agrippa, do you believe the prophets? (vv. 25-27).

He leaned forward for an answer. Agrippa hesitated, and no answer came. He did not like the question, for whichever way he answered it, he would be caught. Paul saw his hesitation and quickly added, "I know that thou believest."

The king was moved, but he was also very much embarrassed before the assemblage. "Almost thou persuadest me to be a Christian," he replied (v. 28).

Quick as a swordsman who moves in to make his kill, Paul flashed his ready reply: "I would to God, that not only thou but also all that hear me this day, were both almost, and altogether such as I am"; and then he added three short words which revealed forevermore what Christianity had done for him, "except these bonds" (v. 29).

And as he said it, he pointed to his chain. A few years ago he had delighted in binding men and women and throwing them into prison, but now he would not impose a chain upon anyone.

PAUL SENT TO ROME

Agrippa had had enough. He rose to his feet, and Bernice and Festus followed him to the side of the room. There they talked between themselves for a minute, and with the nodding of heads they agreed that Paul had done nothing worthy of death or of bonds. "This man might have been set at liberty," said the king, "if he had not appealed unto Caesar" (v. 32).

Festus sat down to make his report, and Paul was taken back to the prison to await the time of his journey to Rome.

13

The Voyage to Rome

SAILING NORTHWARD TO SIDON

IT WAS LATE AUTUMN when Festus gathered together a group of prisoners and sent them to Rome. They were mostly political prisoners who, for some defiance of the laws of Rome, were called criminals. They were being sent to the highest court of all, and if convicted, they would fight with wild beasts in the Coliseum and die before the cruel eyes of a holiday crowd.

Most of the ships bound for Rome had loaded their cargoes earlier and headed into the western sea. Every sailor knew that soon the boats would be forced to tie up for the winter and that the equinoctial winds made a long voyage very hazardous. Festus could not find a ship bound for Rome, but wishing to get these prisoners off his hands, he set them aboard a small craft engaged in the coastal trade from Egypt to Adramyttium, a port in Mysia near the city of Troas.

The prisoners, in charge of a centurion named Julius and a company of soldiers, were to go as far as they could in the vessel, with the expectation that in some harbor of Asia they would find another ship bound for Rome. Festus gave full instructions to Julius, charging him to guard these men with his life and deliver them to the barracks of Augustus.

The centurion knew that Paul was not a political prisoner, for Festus had told him that he was not dangerous but was being sent to Rome at his own request. It was a religious question upon which he was being tried. Julius therefore, treated him with great respect and leniency and even granted him privileges in certain of the ports at which they called.

Luke accompanied Paul as his helper and companion; Aristarchus, a believer from Thessalonica, who had brought an offering to the church at Jerusalem, was also numbered among the passengers.

When the strong wind blew from the west, the ropes were cast off and the long oars took the vessel beyond the breakwater into the sea. The sailors unfurled the white sail, and as the ship came about, the master set her course and sent her through the waves northward to the port of Sidon.

THE PORT OF MYRA

At Sidon, the ship took on cargo for the cities of Asia, and Paul was permitted to leave the boat, chained, of course, to a guard. He spent the time visiting friends and confirming the faith of the believers. It was his last word to them, and it was a warning of the dangers which faced the Christian church and of how the enemies of Christ were always busy. And when the boat was loaded, they accompanied him back to it, waving farewell as the sails were spread and the prow turned to the west, toward the beautiful island of Cyprus.

But the season was late; the winter winds were beginning to blow, and the sea was rough. The little ship was forced off its course, and for safety's sake had to hug the shore and steer for the sheltered mainland. And so through heavy seas, they journeyed past the beloved Tarsus, westward to Pamphylia, sailing when the winds were fair and anchoring when they were angry. At last they reached the port of Myra on the Lycian coast.

Julius ordered his men to leave the ship, and while the little vessel prepared for the northward journey to its home port, he inquired among the larger ships of the harbor for one which could carry them to Rome. At last he found one engaged in the Egyptian grain trade, heavy with wheat and ready to sail to Italy to remain for the winter.

Already a large number of men had engaged passage, but the master of the ship made room for the new company, hoping that he would be paid well, since Julius was on government business. All told, there were two hundred and seventy-six men aboard as the heavy ship put to sea. The extra weight was in her favor, and the captain headed her into the winds and the choppy waters, hoping that there was yet time to reach their destination.

It was now October, and the skies were grey. After the ship left Myra, a strong headwind blew them from their course. They skirted the Island of Rhodes and for many days made little progress, sheltering in the lee of the Aegean islands and drifting as far north as Cnidus and as far south as Crete. In another month no ships would be at sea, and the winter gales would have their solitary rule. It behooved them to make haste.

FAIR HAVENS

Laboriously, the creaking ship tacked her way against the wind. With great difficulty they rounded the cape of Salmone, and in the shelter of the island of Crete they made their way into Fair Havens and anchored in the bay. Fair Havens was not a great harbor and was an entirely unsuitable place to tie up for the winter. so after a change in the wind, an attempt was made to reach Phenice in the southwestern part of the island.

Anyone who knew the sea was aware of the dangers. It seemed that to reach Rome was now out of the question. All that remained was to choose some sheltered harbor and winter there. Paul's advice was to remain in Fair Havens. With his experience upon the sea where he had three times been shipwrecked, he had learned to be cautious. Addressing those in command, he said, "Sirs, I perceive that this voyage will be with hurt and much damage, not only of the lading and ship, but also of our lives" (27:10).

But the master of the ship thought otherwise, and the men, desiring to winter in some larger city, agreed to risk it as far as Phenice, some forty miles westward. A sudden shift in the wind decided the matter. The gale from the north subsided, and out of the south came soft winds, reminiscent of Alexandria and a warmer clime. It was all they needed. In calm waters the men raised the anchor and hoisted sail, purposing to skirt the shore of Crete until they reached Phenice.

THE STORM

But the plans were quickly shattered. Only a few miles out of Fair Havens the wind suddenly shifted from the south to the northeast, and down from the Cretan Mountains it blew so violently that it became a tempest. The mast groaned as the ship heeled over in the first attack of the blast. There was not even time to pull in the little boat that tossed at the stern, attached by a rope. The great waves rose behind the ship as if by magic, and nothing was left for the sailors but to yield and run before the gale.

Ahead of them lay the continent of Africa with its Bay of Syrtis. Every sailor feared this place, for there were no harbors. There were only shallow beaches where sand bars shifted with the winds and became a grave for many ships. However, the little island of Clauda was still before them, and gratefully they ran under its sheltering cliffs. Here they gained much-needed time to pull in the little waterlogged boat and prepare the ship against whatever might be ahead. Great ropes were passed under the vessel and drawn tight to protect the planking and hold the ship together, especially if it should be grounded on a sand bar.

Even the inadequate shelter of Clauda was doubtful to them, for the danger of grounding on the sand and being pounded to pieces against the beach was worse than the fear of the tempest in the open sea. And so they were blown away from the island, and having done all that brave men could do to save their lives, they lashed the great yardarm to the deck and rode before the storm with the mast bare. All they could hope to do now was to keep in the open sea until the tempest was over.

All through the night they labored, fearing the worst but hoping that tomorrow would bring some help. But the next morning the storm was no better, and so much water had come aboard and seeped through the creaking sides that the ship was riding lower in the waves. The captain ordered all personal baggage to be thrown overboard to lighten the ship. As the leaks gained and the vessel sank deeper in the valleys of the sea, the freight was cast overboard. Then the furniture and the heavy sail and the yardarm were pushed over the side along with all the tackling that could be spared.

Day and night sailors toiled wearily in their race with the waves. The little vessel bobbed up and down like a cork, with waves beating over its decks and briny water pouring through its sides. Days and nights of terror followed, during which the sky hung low and neither sun, moon nor stars appeared. Around them the hissing black waves at one moment seemed like a mountain bearing down upon them and at another, like a valley being scooped out before them, into which they were swiftly falling.

Both sailors and passengers had long since given up hope. They were now doing nothing for the ship, merely holding onto ropes and spars. They felt that each plunging motion of the deck would be the last. No one thought of taking food, for they were sure death was near.

PAUL'S VISION

But Paul believed God's promise that he would live to see Rome, and during one of his moments of sleep, when from sheer exhaustion he lay below deck, he had a vision from the Lord. There stood by him an angel of God and revealed that not only would Paul be safe, but no passenger aboard would lose his life.

And so when their spirits were at the lowest ebb, Paul rallied them with a heartening word. "Sirs," he said,

> You should have taken my advice and wintered in Fair Havens, but don't despair, because all our lives will be

saved. The only loss will be the ship. For there stood by me last night God's angel, and he gave me this message: 'Fear not, Paul, you will yet reach Rome and appear before Caesar; and God has also given you the lives of all your shipmates.' Wherefore, sirs, cheer up, for I believe God, and His promise cannot fail. However, we will be wrecked upon an island (27:21-26).

At the end of the second week, about midnight, it was apparent to the seasoned sailors that they were nearing land. They were somewhere in the Adriatic Sea. A cry from the ship's watch rent the air and put alarm into all their hearts: "Breakers! Breakers!"

The sailors listened and thought they heard the roar of waves on rocks. The sounding lines were dropped overboard, and it was found that the water was twenty fathoms deep. When they had gone a little farther, they sounded again and found it was fifteen fathoms deep. This meant that the sea was becoming shallower, and there was danger of rock or sand bars. And because it was as black as ink around them, they cast out four anchors to hold them fast, and waited impatiently for the dawn.

THE SAILOR'S CONSPIRACY

Up in the bow of the ship a conspiracy was taking place. Some of the sailors were laying a plan to escape with the small boat that had been hauled up on the deck. They planned to lower the boat and board it under the pretence of casting anchors out of the bows. Thus they would escape to land and abandon their friends to the raging sea. In the argument as to who should go, Paul became aware of their plan and quickly called the centurion and his soldiers. "Unless these men stay, we cannot be saved."

Julius sprang into action. A quick command sent one of his soldiers to the side of the ship with drawn sword. He brought it down sharply on the rope and severed it, and the little boat disappeared in the darkness. It was a reckless stroke, and without a boat they were even more helpless. But the plot was ended, and the sullen sailors huddled in groups, shivering in the cold rain until the first streak of light appeared in the east and they could see the low black rocks of the land.

No one knew what land it was, but the two hundred and seventy-six men aboard crowded to the decks to catch a glimpse of it. With a great surge of confidence, Paul urged them all to take some food, declaring that they would need the strength to carry them through. They had fasted for fourteen days, for the danger had been so great that nobody had cared to eat. Holding up bread, Paul bowed his head, and in the sight of the heathen soldiers and sailors, he gave thanks to God and ate the food. His good cheer was contagious. The hope of the others was revived, and they each took food, and in the strength of it determined to fight for their lives.

If the ship was to be lost and driven onto the beach, let her go up as near to the land as possible! All hands turned to the work again. They threw overboard the remainder of the cargo of wheat, and the ship, relieved of her burden, rode lightly on the waves. This would help them run her in closer to shore.

One thing they noticed which gave them a ray of hope was that the line of coastal rock was broken by a small creek and a sandy beach. The captain thought it might be possible to steer the ship into the mouth of the creek and beach it. He gave his orders quickly. The rudder was unlashed, the anchor ropes at the stern were cut, a light sail was hoisted to the mast, and the battered ship lumbered toward the shore. They did not get very far, for the coast was unknown to them, and in a place where two currents met, the vessel grounded on a sandbar, and with a grinding noise her bow stuck fast.

THE SHIPWRECK

As the breakers beat upon the stern of the boat, they could all see that there was no hope of her getting off the bar. The waves were still rolling in fury, and the planks of the ship were loosening. Up in the bow of the ship the Roman soldiers, knowing that their own lives would be forfeited if they lost their prisoners, went to their commander saying, "Sir, we cannot be held responsible for our prisoners any longer. No man can swim through these angry waters chained to another. Would it not be wise to kill them all now?"

But Julius had come to know and love Paul, so for his sake he ordered that the prisoners' chains be loosened and all who could swim should make for the shore. Those who could not swim caught up planks and broken pieces of wood to which they clung as they slid or jumped over the side and were carried by the waves to shore.

They were a miserable band of men, weak and exhausted, who gathered on the beach and watched the ship break up by the pounding of the mighty waves. But they were all there— to a man—bruised, tattered, half-drowned, and shivering in the rain; but they were safe at last.

Landing on the Island of Malta

Their plight had attracted the natives on the shore, and many of them ran to help the strangers, lighting fires so that they might warm themselves. It was then that the shipwrecked men learned where they were. They had landed on the island of Malta, only sixty miles from Sicily, a Roman possession.

The people of Malta were of Phoenician descent, and through long centuries they had been people of the sea. So it was with great sympathy that they had watched the vessel in distress and the efforts made to save her. And when the men were helped to shore one by one, the natives of Malta marveled, for they felt that many must die in such a shipwreck.

The Vengeance of the Gods

As soon as Paul got to shore, he joined the others in bringing sticks for the fire. With an armful of brushwood, he ap-

proached one of the fires and laid his burden in the flames.
Suddenly a viper, which had been clinging to the wood, unseen by Paul, was stung by the heat and jumped for safety,
fastening itself upon his hand. For a second it clung there,
and a cry of fear went up from the horror-stricken onlookers.
With one quick motion Paul shook it off, and it dropped back
into the fire.

Here was a prisoner, they thought, who had escaped the
sea, but the vengeance of the gods had followed him, and his
hour had come. They knew the deadly poison of the viper
and the speed with which it acts. They expected to see Paul
sicken and fall dead in a matter of minutes. With horror in
their faces they watched him. Surely he had committed some
terrible crime to meet death by so sudden a stroke.

PAUL'S RECOVERY

But in Paul's mind there was no such thought. He was not
afraid, for he believed God and was confident that he would
preach the gospel in Rome, as he had been promised. The
minutes sped by and Paul prodded the fire, moving closer to
it to dry his clothing and to warm his body. Closely they
watched him; and as each moment passed, their amazement
grew even greater. He did not seem pale, nor did he look
like a dying man.

One by one the superstitious Maltese nodded their heads
and concluded that he must be a god in disguise. This, com-
bined with what followed in the next few days, gave Paul an
opportunity to preach the gospel of the one true God, who
can protect his servants from every evil.

HEALING THE GOVERNOR'S FATHER

The islanders took the shipwrecked people to the governor,
whose residence was close to the scene of the disaster. His
house and outbuildings were large and his heart was larger,
so he made provision for them all for three days. Publius, the
Roman governor of Malta, had an aged father living in his

residence, who was sick with a fever. When Paul heard of this, he asked to see him and, receiving permission, he laid his hands on the old man. Lifting his eyes to God in heaven, the apostle prayed fervently that a miracle would be done and that this man might be healed as a testimony to the power of God and the truth of the gospel.

The Lord heard that prayer, and the governor's father was made well. Publius heard the good news, and so did many of the sick on Malta. By the score they came, hoping that this man Paul might heal them, too. And so for three winter months, while Julius and his prisoners waited until the sea became navigable again, Paul and his friends, Luke and Aristarchus, preached the gospel of Christ, and God confirmed their words by miracles.

Special honors were given to Paul and his friends. They had won the love and confidence of many people. Those of high degree and low had seen the mighty power of God, and some believed.

ON TO SYRACUSE

The three months went by quickly. With the first balmy breezes of spring, the masters of the ships in the harbor began calling back their crews and made ready to sail. Julius was restless to go, and when he made arrangements with the owner of another wheat ship of Alexandria, the soldiers with their prisoners prepared to depart. By this time Paul had many friends, and they were sorry to see him leave. In token of their love, they brought gifts and provisions and, gathering at the quay, they waved farewell. The heavy ship was paddled out into the bay and the sails were hoisted. The soft winds blew, and after a day of good sailing with sunny skies above and blue waters about them, they reached the ancient city of Syracuse, nestling on a beautiful gulf of Sicily.

For three days Paul and his companions, under Roman guard, visited the great city whose people were so proud of their skill in the chariot race. There, with the shadow of

Diana's white temple falling upon them and the priests of paganism slaughtering four hundred oxen each year upon the altar of Diana, Paul told of Jesus. And even though the time was short and the people few, the seeds of a faithful church were planted and began to grow.

But the ship sailed on. Upon her bow, as she cut through the waves, were large ornate figureheads of the twin brothers, Castor and Pollux, who in ancient mythology were the sons of Zeus. The sailors were proud to be on such a ship, for these heavenly twins were said to protect seamen on their voyages.

THE SHIMMERING BAY OF NAPLES

Far to the west, as they made their way to the mainland, they could see the burning mountain, grey by day and glowing with fire by night. Etna was a landmark to every traveler on his way to Rome. In the narrow straits of Messina they touched the first Italian port. In the beautiful harbor of Rhegium, sheltered by the high hills of Sicily and the mainland, the wind ceased and the ship lay motionless for a day. But in the morning the south wind blew, and with all the sail spread to the breeze, the narrow strait was left behind. All that day and night they ran before the wind and came the next morning into one of the great harbors of Rome. It was the city of Puteoli on the Bay of Naples. All around the friendly bay were the fashionable resorts of the wealthy citizens of Rome. Away in the distance rose Mount Vesuvius, and at her feet were the prosperous cities of Pompeii and Herculaneum.

Because of its magnificent scenery and its charming climate, the Bay of Naples was the favorite seaside resort of the nobles of Rome. The emperor had his villa on this, the most beautiful bay in the world. Here at the city of Puteoli the largest ships discharged their cargoes, and passengers disembarked and followed the Appian Way up to Rome. It was here in this very harbor that Caligula, not many years before, mad with power, boasted that he could ride in his chariot to his villa across the shining bay. At his command, boats were fastened together, and a roadway three miles long was built over them so that he might ride across and say that he could master the sea.

Paul's feet touched Italian soil first at Puteoli. Julius stayed for a while in that city, and during that time Paul was allowed to see his friends freely. There were Christians everywhere now, and when word came that Paul was there, many of them met with him and begged that he be allowed to stay with them longer.

During the seven-day layover the Christians had opportunity to send word to Rome of Paul's arrival. The believers in Rome were happy to see the man who had spent his life in the service of Christ. They had read and memorized his letter to them. Each Sunday as they met for Christian fellowship, they read parts of Paul's letter and rejoiced in their salvation. Many determined to go out on the highway to meet him and accompany him back to Rome. Some came forty miles and met him at the market of Appius, and some came thirty miles to Three Taverns.

When Paul saw the friends from the church at Rome, his heart was moved. He thought of the trial that awaited him and the possible condemnation, but when he saw the love and devotion of these friends for Christ and His servants, he thanked God and took courage. Among the believers who came were his old companions Aquila and Priscilla.

THE GATES OF ROME

Rome was just ahead. Rome, the mistress of the world! Rome, the city of palaces and temples! Rome, the center of the earth, the seat of the Emperor!

And now the gates were in sight. Julius drew his band of prisoners together in the center of the soldier escort and marched them through the streets to the imperial barracks, where he handed them over to Barrhus, the chief advisor of the Emperor, an honest old soldier who had lost one of his hands in battle. Barrhus listened with interest and kindness as Julius told about each man, and when he came to Paul, he obtained a special favor—a private room where he could live with his guard and where he could see his friends whenever he wished.

14

A Prisoner in Rome

MEETING THE OFFICERS OF THE CHURCH

THREE DAYS after Paul's arrival in Rome, his room was full of visitors. He had sent messages to the chief officers of the Jewish synagogue in the city, asking them to come and hear his story. The life of a Jew in Rome had always been hard. Under Claudius, all Jews had been driven from the city, but now there had come a relaxing of the laws. So many Jews returned to Rome that seven synagogues were built for the worshipers. Segregated from the Romans, they lived in their homes on the west bank of the Tiber River.

Realizing how many things his countrymen had suffered at the hands of the Roman emperor and that the city's enmity might be aroused on the slightest pretext, Paul did not wish his presence in Rome to bring any more trouble upon them. His appeal to Caesar could be regarded by his enemies as an attempt to bring more persecution upon the Jews by focusing attention on their religious quarrels.

When the Jewish leaders came at Paul's invitation, he explained to them that he had taken this course of appealing to Caesar only because there was no other means of obtaining his freedom. They listened and were not hostile.

> Brethren, even though I have done nothing against our people or the religious customs of our fathers, I was arrested in Jerusalem and turned over to the Roman autorities. When they had examined me, they wished to set me at liberty because they found I had done nothing worthy of death. But when our Jewish leaders cried out for the death penalty, I was forced to appeal to Caesar,

229

> as a Roman citizen. I have not done this to accuse my
> nation but to win my freedom.
>
> Now I have asked you to come here that I might see
> you and speak with you to make my position clear; it is
> because of my belief in the Messiah, the hope of Israel,
> that I am a prisoner today (Ac 28:17-20).

They knew he was a follower of Jesus, and they had heard
of his visits to many synagogues in the empire, but they were
friendly because they knew also that any demonstration would
bring the enmity of Rome upon them again.

> We know nothing at all about the matter. No letters
> have reached us about you, nor have we heard any reports
> about this from travelers or merchants. In fact, we know
> nothing about this Nazarene sect, except that everywhere
> it is spoken against. Sometime we would like to hear your
> views concerning the Messiah (vv. 21-23).

Preaching in Rome

Finally, on an appointed day, the door of opportunity
opened for the old warrior to preach on his favorite theme:
Jesus the Christ, the Saviour from sin. He had not been
given such an opportunity for three years. From morning
until evening Paul talked to these Jews, who had come in
great numbers now to hear his words about the Messiah.
The light of the gospel was in his eye and the fire of the
Lord in his voice as he led his hearers back through their
own Scriptures. All his training in the school of Gamaliel was
at his command, and he quoted passage after passage from
their scrolls. He used the words of Moses and of the prophets
to show that the only hope of Israel is in the promised
Messiah. Yes, even their own Scriptures contained it all, if
they would only believe.

And when the day was done, there was a division among
his hearers. Some were convinced and went out with a new
hope in their hearts and a new life to live, but others sneered
with disdain.

But Paul continued as they filed out of the room,

> Even your blindness and hardness of heart has been fore-
> told by Isaiah, the prophet. Did not Isaiah clearly say that
> the people would hear Messiah's message and not under-
> stand and that they shall see His form and not recognize
> Him? Be it known unto you that God's salvation is sent
> unto the Gentiles, and they will listen and accept (28:25-
> 26, 28).

And with their brows knit in anger, they left the room with
Paul's last words ringing in their ears.

THE ORBIT OF CHRISTIAN ACTIVITY

Not long after this, the church at Philippi, learning of
Paul's imprisonment, gathered a fund of money which they
sent to him for his support in Rome. It was a welcome gift
and so large that it enabled him, with the consent of his cap-
tors and upon the bond of some fellow Christians in Rome,
to move into his own rented house, where he lived for two
whole years, awaiting the day when Nero would order his
trial.

During his imprisonment he was treated with great leniency
but was chained constantly to a Roman guard. Wherever he
went through the streets of Rome, a guard accompanied him.
After two years of this, many a rough soldier heard the gospel,
and as Paul dictated his letters and preached to his friends,
some of these guards were converted. Paul was no secret
Christian, and through his Christian friends, he let it be
known that he would teach the new gospel to any who would
come to his house. And many came, until his house in Rome
became a center of Christian testimony.

Disciples of Christ from many cities came and went, seeking Paul's counsel and advice on matters of the Christian
faith and carrying his letters to the churches in the east.
Lystra and Derbe, Corinth and Ephesus, Colossae and Thessalonica, even the church in Berea had sent one of their

representatives to work under Paul's direction in spreading the gospel to the cities where Christ was unknown. Some of them were witnessing in the crowded streets of Rome and ministering to the apostle at the same time. His house became a center of activity from which the messengers of the cross went out to all the empire in an orbit which brought them, like comets, back to their starting point again.

Paul grew to love his soldier guards. They were stalwart and faithful men, and it was not long until a little group of believers was to be found among the Praetorian Guard and the men of Caesar's household. And these men, being convinced of the truth of Christianity as they heard it from Paul's lips, carried it into their homes to their sisters and brothers as well as to all the men of the barracks and found it to be satisfying and real. The aged apostle thought of his imprisonment, and a smile came upon his face as he lifted his heart to God in thankfulness that his bonds had helped Christianity rather than hindered it.

As his friends were coming and going, Paul waited for news of his trial. At the death of Claudius, Nero came to the throne. He was not the son of Claudius, but his widowed mother pushed him forward and had him crowned emperor at seventeen. Britannicus, his half brother, was the rightful heir, but through the mother's maneuvering, Nero was chosen. Before he had been Emperor one year, he had Britannicus poisoned, and as the years sped by, he grew to hate his mother and ordered his friends to put her to death. They seized her one night and tried to drown her, but finding it difficult, they stabbed her with a dagger. Nero married Claudius' gentle daughter, Octavia, but grew to hate her. When Paul came to Rome, the young Nero, now twenty-four, was devising plans to put her to death and marry Poppaea.

Wholly given to a dissolute life of passion and wickedness, he had no intention of wasting any time on a Jewish prisoner. And so Paul remained under the care of a guard, waiting while Nero pursued his reckless way.

THE COMING OF TIMOTHY

Paul's heart was greatly cheered when his faithful young friend Timothy left his home and came to Rome to be near the man who was his spiritual father and to do the Lord's work under the direction of the great apostle. Four years had passed since Paul and Timothy had come to Europe together to preach Christ. They had gone to Philippi and planted the gospel in Macedonia, beginning at a women's prayer meeting where Lydia, the seller of purple, opened her heart to Christ and her home to the believers as a place of meeting. Paul's thoughts went back to that day. He thought of how he had been publicly scourged in the marketplace and imprisoned. He remembered the jailor who became a Christian with his entire household. He remembered how the Philippian church cared for his needs as he went down to Thessalonica. Twice they had sent money to him there. And now, hearing of his bonds in Rome, they had sent money again by the hand of Epaphroditus, who came as a missionary to stand by Paul and work for Christ under his direction.

No doubt it was Lydia, the wealthy merchant, who had stirred up the church at Philippi to stand behind this man of God with their gifts. What an encouragement it was to hear from the lips of Epaphroditus that the Philippian church was standing true to the faith! What a strength it was to Paul to know that one of their members had come to be his companion in labor!

THE EPISTLE TO THE PHILIPPIANS

Epaphroditus preached the kingdom of God with great zeal and with such fervor that he cared nothing for his own safety and health. Day after day he went into the narrow streets of Rome, gathered a crowd wherever he could, and told them of Jesus and His love. After only a few months, a serious illness put a stop to his ministry and confined him to his bed, where for weeks he lay hovering near the gates of death. And then at last he began to recover, but his body was weak, and he was discouraged that he found himself unable to give himself to the work. Paul could see that he was homesick, and he made up his mind to send him back to Philippi.

With Timothy as his penman, Paul began to dictate a letter. His thoughts spanned the years and he recalled vividly each member of the church:

> I thank my God every time I think of you.
> You have been diligent in your care of me. Twice before, at the beginning of my ministry in Macedonia, you helped me with your gifts at a time when I was in need and no other church was assisting.
> I am full, and abound. All my needs are taken care of, thanks to what you have sent me by Epaphroditus. I know this offering is well pleasing to God (Phil 1:3; 4:15-16, 18).

He spoke about Epaphroditus and how he had served the Lord with such unselfish vigor that he had fallen ill and lay for long months between life and death.

> It was his zeal for Christ that brought about his illness. Therefore when he returns to you bearing this letter, receive him with gladness and honor. He has sacrificed a lot for Christ.
> Before long I hope to send Timothy to you so that I can be comforted by news from you. . . . Then perhaps later on I will come myself when I see how the trial turns out (2:29-30, 19, 24).
> I want you to rejoice, and not be downhearted, for the things which have happened to me have turned out for the good of the gospel, for through my being chained to a soldier, the attention of all the Praetorian Guard has been drawn to me and many a believer in Rome has become bold to speak the word of God without fear (1:12-14).

Looking ahead with uncertainty, Paul spoke of his trial. He had no way of knowing how it would turn out. Life was a light thing to the young emperor, and Paul had no assurance that he would be spared. In fact he had weighed the possibility of death and found it was not unpleasant, for it would mean being with Christ. And yet he had gleams of hope that he would be set free. To live would only mean more work for Jesus, but to die would be a great gain and an abundant entrance into heaven. And so the words came hot from his heart as he said:

> For to me to live is Christ, but to die is gain. I am in a place of indecision, not knowing which I would prefer. I have a desire to depart and be with Christ which is far better, but to remain and work on is better for the churches. But I feel confident that God will bring me through this experience and that we will soon be rejoicing together in a great victory. But whether I come to you or not, continue in the faith and let your lives be worthy of Jesus (1:21-27).

The letter was soon written and the seal placed upon it, and Epaphroditus carried it with him as he boarded ship for his home city. Paul had one less companion in labor now, but Timothy and Luke remained close to him, keeping him in touch with the Christians of Rome. Mark, Tychicus, Aristarchus, Demas, Trophimus and Titus placed themselves at Paul's disposal and spent their days coming and going, at the aged apostle's direction, among the churches to which Paul sent messages.

THE EPISTLE TO THE COLOSSIANS

In the forefront of the Lord's service was a man named Epaphras. He had been the missionary by whom the Colossians had first heard the gospel of Christ and had been converted to Christianity. Now he was in Rome working for the Lord as one of Paul's helpers. The church at Colossae had sent their most valued leader to preach the gospel in the greatest city of the world.

As one of Paul's companions, Epaphras spent many hours with the great apostle, planning their program and discussing the many churches upon which Paul kept a watchful eye. Day by day they prayed together for each church, remembering their faithfulness and asking God to strengthen them and use them. As Epaphras prayed, his thoughts went back to his beloved congregation at Colossae, and he asked the Lord over and over again that they might stand perfect and complete in the will of God. Paul had never seen the church at Colossae, and Epaphras, because it was near to his heart, referred to it constantly, telling of the faithful ones there and of how Archippus had been left in charge and was carrying on the testimony, using Philemon's home as a meeting place for believers.

But as Epaphras told of his beloved church, he revealed a deep concern over the appearance of certain Jews who, in a very subtle way, were leading the people into two forms of error. The first was known as "asceticism" and taught that the people ought to live lives of self-denial in order to gain salvation. They emphasized the keeping of certain days as holy days, and their preaching was full of prohibitions, calling the people to refrain from touching this and tasting that, and thus by self-denial they would become worthy of eternal life. The second error was a mystic philosophy which robbed Christ of His position as the Son of God and the Saviour of men.

Here was the old error which Paul had met so often raising its ugly head again and spoiling the Christian message. Who was better fitted to warn the Colossians against such heresy? Paul determined to write a letter to them, and with Timothy there to set down his thoughts as he dictated them, he began.

First, he told of his affection for them and of how Epaphras had told him of their condition. As to the basic things, he commended them highly. For their faith in Christ, their love for all their fellow Christians, and their hope for heaven, he praised them. Then, turning to the doctrinal admonition, he warned them against the danger of false philosophy and Jewish teaching that undermined the deity of the Lord:

Beware lest any man spoil you through philosophy and vain deceit, after the traditions of men, after the teachings of worldliness and not after Christ, for in Him dwelleth all the fulness of the Godhead bodily, and in Him you are complete.

Let no man, therefore, judge you with regard to what you eat or drink, or what days you keep holy, for all these things are only a shadow, while the real substance is in Christ (Col 2:8-9, 16-17).

Paul could not end his letter without adding to these warnings some words of practical advice for Christian living:

Put on then, as God's chosen ones, a garment of compassion, kindness, lowliness, meekness, and patience, forgiving one another; taking no action against one another, even as the Lord has set you an example.

And let the peace of God rule in your hearts, and the word of God dwell in you richly as you teach and admonish one another in all wisdom, and as you sing your psalms and hymns of gratitude to God (3:12-13, 15-16).

And then, taking the manuscript from Timothy, Paul wrote a final greeting with his own hand and signed it with his own signature lest any should doubt that he had sent it. After rereading it to see if he had left anything out, he gave it to Tychicus with orders to deliver it to the Colossian church and after a visit there, to return with news of how they fared.

The Conversion of Onesimus

Accompanying Tychicus on his journey was a man named Onesimus. He had been a slave in the household of Philemon of Colossae and his heart had been rebellious. He waited his chance to rob his master of clothing and money and fled, thinking he could lose himself in the crowded streets of Rome and begin life over again in a different way. But in Rome he came under the influence of Paul and was converted. And then, day by day, he learned more of Jesus and His love.

Gratitude and wonder filled his heart, and he realized that Jesus died to save him, a runaway slave and a thief. And as he grew in grace and in the knowledge of God, he saw that in the Lord's sight slave and free man were equal.

What an amazing difference there was between the way Paul treated him as a believer and the old life he had known back in Colossae! Confessing his sin to God, he made a full surrender. So genuine was his conversion that Paul even used him to reach others for Christ and found him eager to tell the good news to others. Half the population of Rome was slaves, and Onesimus could reach many who would not otherwise listen to the gospel.

But with a knowledge of this injustice done to Philemon, Paul realized, and Onesimus agreed, that the only course was to return to his master with a full confession. It meant punishment, and even though Philemon and his wife Apphia were kind and just, the overseer of the household would surely flog him. He had seen the beating administered to many others who had been adventuresome and disloyal, and the thought of returning home was not pleasant, especially now that he was a free man in Christ and useful to the great apostle.

But since he was now a Christian, he wanted to make every mistake of his life right, both in God's sight and in the sight of men. That is the only way of peace and usefulness. He resolved that for the Lord's sake he would even return to slavery to make amends for his sin.

The Epistle to Philemon

To soften the hardness of that return, Paul wrote a brief personal letter to Philemon with his own hand. Philemon had been one of his own converts and had come to Christ during Paul's long stay at Ephesus. Now, with a zeal for his Lord, he had shown great hospitality for the church at Colossae. In fact, they met each week in his beautiful home under the ministry of Archippus.

With boldness, therefore, and also with gentlemanly discretion, moved by strong Christian feeling, Paul wrote an appeal to his friend:

> For the sake of the love which you bear me, I ask you to be good to my son Onesimus.
>
> I would gladly have kept him with me, for I found him useful in the spreading of the gospel; but I could not do that without your consent. Don't receive him as a slave but as a beloved brother. God has changed his heart. I am confident that he will be valuable to you now not only as a servant, but as a brother beloved, and as a Christian. If you consider me a partner, receive him as you would me, and if he has robbed you, believe me, I will repay it myself.
>
> I expect any day now to be released from my bonds, so I think you may get a room ready for me, for I hope soon to be able to pay you a visit (Phile 9-10, 13-19, 22).

THE EPISTLE TO THE EPHESIANS

While Tychicus and Onesimus prepared to set out for their journey, Paul was putting the last strokes to a letter which he had been carefully setting down for many weeks. It was a general letter, not meant to correct any particular evil in a local church but to be passed around among many churches to strengthen their faith, to encourage them in the Christian life, and to deepen their understanding of their position and privileges in Christ Jesus.

He began with a hymn of praise to the three persons of the Holy Trinity—the Father, the Son, and the Holy Spirit. Then with masterful strokes he painted a picture of the church as a temple of God, built upon the foundation of Christ. Every great doctrine of the faith was touched upon in his beautiful letter. The maturity of his own Christian life is evident in every line. There were no personal references and no greetings to local families or fellow laborers. Had Paul meant it for Ephesus alone, he would have followed his custom of sending greetings to many, for he had labored three years there, longer than in any other city. Instead, Paul meant it as his final admonition to many churches. He was now Paul the aged, and his days of writing letters would soon be over. He longed to put into one circular letter the fullness of the gospel and the encouragement that would enrich and make steadfast every member of the body of Christ, and such a letter would apply to every church that he had founded. He wrote:

> Remember that you were dead in trespasses and sins, walking according to the course of this world and under Satan's power. But God, who is rich in mercy, because of His great love to us all, even when you were dead in your sins, has brought you to life in Christ.
>
> For by grace you are saved, through faith, and that salvation is not of yourselves, but it is the gift of God. It does not come by your good deeds for that would make you boastful.
>
> Remember that you were without Christ, being Gentiles and therefore aliens to Israel and strangers to the promises of God. Remember that you were without God and without hope in the world (Eph 2:1-2, 4-5, 8-9, 11-12).

By a swift and beautiful transition he descended from the lofty peaks to the deep valleys of common life. "I therefore, the prisoner of the Lord, beseech you that ye walk worthy of the vocation wherewith ye are called" (4:1).

As he dictated the last chapter of his masterpiece, he was searching for some illustration that would make these words live forever in the minds of his readers. Seated before him was the young man whom he loved. Timothy, quill in hand, was listening for every word that fell from his inspired lips. By his side stood the ever-present Roman guard, magnificent with the armour of the Empire and proud to be among Nero's chosen men. Paul's eyes focused upon him, and a smile appeared on his lips. Turning again to Timothy, he had him write:

Finally, my brethren, be strong in the Lord, and in the power of His might. Put on the whole armour of God, that ye may be able to stand against the trickery of the devil, for we are not wrestling against flesh and blood in our battle with those who hate us, but with unseen spiritual enemies who rule in the present darkness, even Satan and his angels. Therefore, take unto yourselves the whole armour of God that you may be able to make a strong stand in this evil day.

Stand, therefore, having your loins girded with truth, and having put on the breastplate of righteousness and having covered your feet with the protection of the gospel (6:10-15).

With one more glance at the equipment of the guard, he hastened to add:

Above all this, take the shield of faith, which will help you to turn back the burning darts of Satan, and take the helmet of salvation and the sword of the Spirit which is the Word of God. And after you have done all that, pray constantly in the Spirit and never give up, remembering all the saints.

Peace be to the brethren, together with love and faith. Grace be with all them that love our Lord Jesus Christ in sincerity. Amen (vv. 16-18, 23-24).

THE GOSPEL SPREAD BY CAPTIVITY

And so the letters were sent, and Paul settled down to his daily routine of teaching all who came to his house and strengthening them in the things of Christ. For two years his captivity, to the surprise of all his friends and even to himself, actually furthered the gospel. They were lenient years, and because of the indulgence of the Roman Empire, they were useful years; nor were they clouded in unhappiness because of his forced imprisonment. His mind was free from personal cares, and hope mounted forever in his heart that after the trial he would be set free. So he wrote from his home these words: "Rejoice in the Lord alway: and again I say, Rejoice" (Phil 4:4).

15

The Fight, the Race, and the Trust

PAUL SET FREE!

THE LONG-AWAITED TRIAL took place at last. It was in A.D. 63, after Paul had spent two years in captivity.

All he had hoped and anticipated came to pass. The favorable letter of Festus and the report of Julius tipped the balance in his direction. After these long months, and with his accusers so far away, the Jewish opposition had declined. And because the Jews were held under suspicion, the court was quick to discount written charges against this man. Paul was set free.

Back at his home, without a guard for the first time in over four years, he began immediately to work out a plan. He must not be inactive but must make his few remaining years count for the most. He had always purposed to visit the western rim of the Empire. In writing to the church at Rome some years earlier, he had told of his intention to go to Spain. Then again, his thoughts were always with the churches, and he turned over in his mind a plan to visit many of them in Asia and in Greece. Since he had written to Philemon at Colossae and heard the story of the church there from the lips of Epaphras, he experienced a longing to visit there. This was his opportunity. Then, too, he had written to his favorite church in Philippi, and the prospect of seeing those who had cared for him during his imprisonment at Rome put a glow of warmth into his heart.

His mind was made up and, losing no time, he found a ship bound for Spain and sailed west to meet new people and to witness anew for his Saviour. But this was only a brief visit, and after encouraging the few Christians there and strengthening their faith in Christ Jesus, he boarded a ship for his own beloved land. After many days he came at last to Ephesus, and accompanied by Luke, the faithful companion of his Roman imprisonment, he made his way inland to Colossae on the Lycus River.

IN COLOSSAE

For the first time Paul saw the church which Epaphras had founded, and to which he himself had written a letter. It was a cordial welcome they all gave him. The Christians revered him as the great leader of Christianity; Philemon, who had known Paul in Ephesus, welcomed him into his big house, where the church of Colossae met; but no welcome could have been warmer and more sincere than the beaming face of Onesimus, the runaway slave, who was one of the trophies of Paul's ministry in Rome.

Paul could not remain long in Colossae, but the church made use of his every moment, and before the time came to say farewell, he had gone over everything he had said in his letter, reminding them again of how God came down to earth in the person of His only begotten Son, how He was truly God, and how eternal life came only by receiving Him as Saviour. Then he warned them of false teachers who would deny the doctrine of Christ and take away from His deity. So, having greatly enriched their faith, Paul hastened on to Ephesus.

MINISTERING TO THE EPHESIANS

Here he felt at home. The church had prospered and was faithful. The members had been wary of false doctrine and guarded the purity of their pulpit zealously. No one was ever invited to preach before that church unless he was sound in the faith, acknowledging the deity of Jesus Christ and the gospel of His redeeming grace.

They were happy to see their old pastor once more. Earlier, the elders of Ephesus had wept when Paul's ship sailed away from the quay at Miletus, for they felt they would see his face no more; but now, after these many months, he had come again! The rigor of the years had aged him. The flashing eye and the quick, determined step were gone. Paul had suffered much since last they heard his messages, and the lines in his saintly old face told of the burdens he had borne.

Not only had he been in prison, but he had been shipwrecked and whipped and saddened in spirit because of loneliness and the hardness of peoples' hearts. Upon his aging shoulders rested the care of all the churches. Wherever a fellow Christian suffered, Paul suffered too. Wherever such a person was cast into prison, Paul's spirit seemed to enter the prison with him. In fact, Paul was so closely identified with his fellow believers that they felt a family bond drawing them together and making them one.

But the time was short, and as Paul's anxiety to visit Macedonia grew, he began to make plans to journey over the Aegean Sea to Philippi and Thessalonica and many of the villages where he had planted the banner of the cross in former years. But Ephesus needed leadership. They were a strong church, but since the city was so important in Asia Minor, it was necessary to have a testimony there that could counteract all the forces of Diana.

Paul was happy when he thought of the church at Ephesus. They had done well, but he noted that the worldliness of the big city made it hard for some of the believers to keep the freshness of their love for the Lord always to the fore. The undertow was great, and the city attracted many teachers of religion who tried to invade the purity of the church and confuse the people with the endless theories and legends.

During Paul's stay in Ephesus, he found many an occasion to preach about these things and to warn the church to be watchful, and whenever such false doctrine appeared, to put its teacher from their fellowship.

Paul thought the situation serious enough to leave Timothy

in Ephesus, asking him to take the pastorate of that important church and make it a stronghold for the true gospel of God's grace. And so, with an anxious heart, he said farewell to his beloved friend, praying that he would be a faithful minister and that his presence there would enrich the church in all spiritual blessings.

PAUL IN MACEDONIA

Across the narrow sea, on the continent of Europe, Paul's thoughts were still with Timothy. He ministered to the saints in the various cities of Macedonia, encouraging, strengthening and warning them, but he could not get his mind off the young man in Ephesus and his strategic work. He thought again of the false teachers and the inroads they had made in certain churches, especially in the province of Galatia, and he decided that Ephesus was the key to the whole of Asia.

THE EPISTLE TO TIMOTHY

With his pen in hand and parchment before him, he began to write a letter to Timothy:

> Paul, an apostle of Jesus Christ by the commandment of God our Saviour, and of Jesus Christ our hope, unto Timothy, my own son in the faith. I urged you when I was leaving for Macedonia, to remain at Ephesus that you might charge certain persons not to teach strange doctrine, nor to occupy themselves with myths and endless genealogies which stir up speculations and do not bring anyone nearer to God (1 Ti 1:1-4).

The letter was filled with instructions to the young man. Questions of organization and of church government needed to be settled, and Paul felt that his friend would profit greatly by such instructions and encouragement:

> Tmiothy, my son, I charge you that supplications, prayers, intercessions and thanksgiving be made on behalf

of all men; for kings and rulers in positions of responsibility, so that our lives may be lived in peace and quiet with a proper sense of God and of our responsibility to Him (2:1-2).

Continue to remind the brethren of the things I have told you, and you will be a faithful minister of Jesus Christ. Take time and trouble to keep yourself spiritually fit. Bodily fitness has a certain value, but spiritual fitness is essential, both for this present life, and for the life to come.

Don't let people despise you because you are young. See that you are an example to them in speech and behaviour. Concentrate on your reading and your preaching and teaching. Never forget that you received the gift of proclaiming God's word when the elders laid their hands upon you (4:6-8, 12-14).

I charge you in the sight of God who give us life, and Jesus Christ who fearlessly witnessed to the truth before Pontius Pilate, to keep your commission clean and above reproach until the coming of Christ (6:13-14).

ON TO TROAS, EPHESUS, AND MILETUS

In his letter Paul indicated the hope that he could soon visit Timothy again. That hope was fulfilled, for Paul left Macedonia and visited Troas, where he conferred with the leaders in the church which met in the home of Carpus; then he pushed on to the south and to Ephesus.

In fact, Paul was in such haste that he abandoned his precious books and rolls of writing material, intending to pick them up, with his cloak, before the winter.

After a satisfying visit with Timothy, with tears in his eyes he said farewell and took the highway that led to Miletus, some thirty miles down the coast.

The day had come when every city had its Christian church. In Paul's lifetime the picture had changed greatly. A few years ago there were few Christians, but now the gospel had been heralded so fearlessly that everywhere believers had their place of worship, and this seaport was no exception.

PAUL AND TITUS IN CRETE

After visiting the brethren in Miletus for several weeks and comforting them and establishing them in their faith, Paul took Titus, his trusted young fellow worker, and sailed for Crete. There the church was poorly organized. There were many believers, but for the effectiveness of their own testimony they needed to be brought together with the elders and bishops in charge of their meetings, caring for their souls, and cultivating their spiritual lives.

Titus was a Greek, one of Paul's converts. He had accompanied the great apostle to Jerusalem, to the conference concerning the admission of Gentiles into the church, and Paul trusted him completely. He determined to leave him in Crete and put him in charge of organization in every city of the island. This was a colossal task, but with the Lord's help, Titus was equal to it.

IN CORINTH

While Titus settled down to his new responsibility, Paul left for Corinth, and entered into a brief ministry to that great church. He was glad to see that the evils in Corinth about which he had written a few years before had been corrected, and his meeting with the disciples there was cordial and profitable. Christians from all over the city came to hear and meet Paul, and the aged servant of the Lord seemed never to tire of exalting Christ and confirming the faith of His followers.

THE EPISTLE TO TITUS

He thought, too, of Titus in Crete and wrote him a letter similar to the one sent to Timothy outlining the qualifications of church officers and the proper conduct of church members. As in the case of Ephesus and Crete, he left a worthy representative at Corinth and hastened on to Nicopolis on the west coast of Greece. Erastus, his faithful co-worker, remained in Corinth to help the believers there.

PAUL'S ARREST IN NICOPOLIS

Paul surely felt that his life was hastening to its close, and everywhere he was making arrangements to locate trusted workmen in strategic places. The time was short, and he must hasten from place to place. Nicopolis was an important center for missionary work and Paul planned to spend an entire winter there. It was a town which he had never visited before, and the prospect of an early start in a new work was enticing. Accompanied by five coworkers, he entered the city and began to preach.

But his hopes were short lived. It was now A.D. 67; three years earlier a great fire had burned the city of Rome and made thousands homeless. No one knew how the fire originated. There were people who said that Nero himself had set the city on fire in a drunken stupor, hoping in his madness that a new and better Rome would rise as a monument to his reign.

But another cry went out—that the Christians had set fire to the city. In a moment the hatred of the populace arose higher than the flames, and the most cruel persecutions broke out that the church had ever faced. Christians were thrown to the lions in the Coliseum, beaten to death, and dipped in pitch and set on fire in Nero's gardens to serve as torches to illuminate the night.

All who could get away from Rome fled. Aquila and Priscilla escaped to Ephesus. The church went into hiding, and throughout the whole empire, Christians were arrested and persecuted unmercifully. Horrible tales of torture came to Paul and his five helpers. They themselves had many narrow escapes, but now a cloud of gloom settled over them and a fear of inevitable arrest. Nero and his men seemed bent on ending their testimony for Christ.

In the midst of the crisis, Demas grew frightened and deserted Paul, leaving for Thessalonica. It was a denial of the faith, and it hurt the apostle deeply. But Demas was not the only one who left. Crescens fled to Galatia, and even Titus, the one whom Paul trusted with so great a task, under the pressure of persecution fled into the hills of Dalmatia, hoping to hide until the storm was over.

Only Luke and Tychicus remained with Paul, and the latter was sent to Ephesus to stand with Timothy and strengthen his hand. And then the blow fell. A Roman officer, recognizing Paul as the leader of the Christian forces, arrested him while he was preaching the gospel of Christ in the public square. And because he believed it would please Nero to have the leader of the church in his power, he sent him to Rome.

THE DAY OF THE FIRST HEARING

This time Paul was not treated with such respect and leniency. He was a celebrated prisoner and any friendship shown him only served to mark a man as a follower of those accused of burning their city. Few people came to visit Paul; but faithful Luke, the beloved physician, came each day.

Paul was kept in the dungeon beneath the street. There was no outlet except a narrow manhole in the pavement. The walls were cold and damp, and the winter chill was in the air. The loneliness of the dungeon depressed his spirits, but the loneliness of being abandoned was even harder to bear.

Onesiphorus the Ephesian was one who tried to help him. He had been unlike so many friends from Asia. They had all forsaken the aged apostle, but Onesiphorus was not ashamed of Paul's chain. After a long search, he found out where the prisoner was kept and visited him frequently, bringing cheer and the few comforts which he needed. But one day his visits ceased, and Paul heard that he had been arrested and quickly put to death. He had paid for his fidelity with his life.

Then came the day of Paul's hearing. According to Roman custom, everyone had to be given a fair hearing. Before the court he stood alone. The room was crowded, but in all the sea of faces not one was friendly to him. Not a voice was raised in his behalf. The old man conducted his own defense with a vigor that sprang from his certainty that the Lord was standing by his side. Christ was as real that day as He had been on the Damascus road so many years earlier.

Paul was eloquent in his address. All the old fire was there. All the logic and power of the gospel were at his command. His sentences began slowly, but as he warmed to the defense and told the gospel story to the crowded courtroom, his words came faster. The flash of conviction was in his eye. He was preaching for a verdict, and his argument fell in heavy blows upon the hearts of his listeners. This was his last sermon on earth.

Alexander the coppersmith was the chief witness against him. He arose and identified him as the leader of the Christian church and the center of much controversy. He testified that wherever Paul went, he raised up a brotherhood of Christians whose allegiance was given to Jesus of Nazareth and whose loyalty to the Emperor was always questionable. But despite the testimony of Alexander, the court was impressed by the burning words of the great apostle and the case was adjourned for a further hearing at some later day.

He had been delivered from the teeth of the lion but sent back to his dismal prison to await the slow turning of the wheels of Roman justice. It was a temporary victory, but Paul could see the end appearing. He hoped that his trial would come quickly. He had only one last wish, and that was to see Timothy before the ax of the executioner fell.

THE SECOND EPISTLE TO TIMOTHY

He looked at the days ahead with their enforced idleness, and he dreaded them beyond words. He thought of the cloak he had left at Troas with the books and parchments. If only he had them now! He made a request for pen and ink and a scroll, and permission was granted him to write a letter to his friend Timothy in Ephesus:

Timothy, stir up the gift of God which came to you when I ordained you. Don't be ashamed of the testimony of our Lord nor of me, His prisoner, but accept all the hardships that must come with the preaching of the gospel. As for me, I am not ashamed, for I know whom I have believed and am persuaded that He is able to keep the work which I am doing safely in His hands until that day (2 Ti 1:6, 8, 12).

So, my son, be strong in the grace that is in Christ Jesus. Endure hardships like a good soldier of Jesus Christ. Study to show yourself approved of God, being a workman with nothing to be ashamed of, who knows how to use the word of truth to the best advantage (2:1, 15).

I need you here, for Demas has forsaken me, having loved this present world, and he has left for Thessalonica. Crescens is in Galatia and Titus is now in Dalmatia. Only Luke is with me. Find Mark and bring him with you when you come, for his ministry could be profitable here. Beware of Alexander, the coppersmith. He has done me much harm. Watch out for him!

At my first hearing nobody stood with me. I was absolutely alone. But despite all of this enmity, the Lord delivered me out of the hands of Nero and stood with me through all this experience and I am persuaded that He will deliver me from every trap of the enemy, and bring me at last to His heavenly kingdom (4:9-11, 14-18).

Dear Timothy, remember to bring the cloak which I left at Carpus' home in Troas. Bring also the books, because I cannot bear to be idle; and especially the parchments so I can go on writing. Try to get here before winter (vv. 13, 21).

He warned the young preacher of the wickedness of evil men and the danger of false doctrine, and he gave him a solemn charge that he should preach the Word of God and never lose his sense of urgency:

For the time will come when they will not listen to sound teaching but will want something to tickle their ears and will wander off into man-made fictions. So, Timothy, stand fast by the commission God gave you, meeting whatever suffering that it may involve.

As for me, I am now ready to go. I feel that the last drops of my life are being poured out for God. I have fought a good fight; I have finished my course; I have kept the faith. I look into the future and can clearly see the crown of righteousness which God, my true Judge, will give me at that day; and not to me only, but to all who love His appearing (4:3-8).

It was his last letter, and before there was time for a reply and before Timothy could summon Mark or pick up the cloak and scrolls at Troas, the fateful message came. It was passed by word of mouth from church to church. Paul, the great apostle, was dead.

The Second Trial

His second trial had followed swiftly upon his first hearing. There was no one to defend him and no man to stand by him. He was accused of being the leader of the Christians, against whom public feeling ran so high. Alexander the coppersmith and the others who accused him had their way. Under the listless eyes of Nero the vote was taken. It was a vote for death. And because Paul was a Roman citizen, he was not to be crucified but beheaded.

And so with his face pale but his head erect, he was led outside the city wall to a great pyramid on the road to the sea. There, amid a hostile crowd intent upon the spectacle of an execution, the aged missionary of the cross lifted his eyes in prayer. This was the moment from which the Lord had delivered him many a time. But others had faced it, and the grace of God would be sufficient for him too. His Lord Jesus had suffered a shameful death outside the gate of another city; but by His victory, He made it a glorious thing to die, for every Christian. As Paul thought of the resurrection, a smile of triumph danced in his eyes and played at the corners of his mouth. His face was radiant with the light of another world.

IN THE ARMS OF JESUS

The captain of the guard ordered the halt. The block was cold with the winter air as the aged Paul knelt beside it. "I have fought a good fight, I have finished my course, I have kept the faith: henceforth there is laid up for me the crown—." There was a flash of a sword in the sunlight, and it was over. He closed his eyes on the howling mob and when he opened them again, it was in the presence of Jesus of Nazareth, where there is fullness of joy and at whose right hand there are pleasures forevermore (Ps 16:11).